2025年度版

岩手県の
英語科

過 去 問

協同教育研究会 編

協同出版

本書には，岩手県の教員採用試験の過去問題を
収録しています。各問題ごとに，以下のように5段
階表記で，難易度，頻出度を示しています。

難 易 度

非常に難しい　☆☆☆☆☆
やや難しい　　☆☆☆☆
普通の難易度　☆☆☆
やや易しい　　☆☆
非常に易しい　☆

頻 出 度

◎　　ほとんど出題されない
◎◎　　あまり出題されない
◎◎◎　普通の頻出度
◎◎◎◎　よく出題される
◎◎◎◎◎　非常によく出題される

※**本書の過去問題における資料，法令文等の取り扱いについて**
　本書の過去問題で使用されている資料や法令文の表記や基準は，出題さ
れた当時の内容に準拠しているため，解答・解説も当時のものを使用して
います。ご了承ください。

はじめに～「過去問」シリーズ利用に際して～

　教育を取り巻く環境は変化しつつあり，日本の公教育そのものも，教員免許更新制の廃止やGIGAスクール構想の実現などの改革が進められています。また，現行の学習指導要領では「主体的・対話的で深い学び」を実現するため，指導方法や指導体制の工夫改善により，「個に応じた指導」の充実を図るとともに，コンピュータや情報通信ネットワーク等の情報手段を活用するために必要な環境を整えることが示されています。

　一方で，いじめや体罰，不登校，暴力行為など，教育現場の問題もあいかわらず取り沙汰されており，教員に求められるスキルは，今後さらに高いものになっていくことが予想されます。

　本書の基本構成としては，出題傾向と対策，過去5年間の出題傾向分析表，過去問題，解答および解説を掲載しています。各自治体や教科によって掲載年数をはじめ，「チェックテスト」や「問題演習」を掲載するなど，内容が異なります。

　また原則的には一般受験を対象としております。特別選考等については対応していない場合があります。なお，実際に配布された問題の順番や構成を，編集の都合上，変更している場合があります。あらかじめご了承ください。

　最後に，この「過去問」シリーズは，「参考書」シリーズとの併用を前提に編集されております。参考書で要点整理を行い，過去問で実力試しを行う，セットでの活用をおすすめいたします。

　みなさまが，この書籍を徹底的に活用し，教員採用試験の合格を勝ち取って，教壇に立っていただければ，それはわたくしたちにとって最上の喜びです。

協同教育研究会

CONTENTS

第1部 岩手県の英語科
　　　出題傾向分析 ･･････････････3

第2部 岩手県の
　　　教員採用試験実施問題 ･･････････9

▼2024年度教員採用試験実施問題 ･････････････････････10

▼2023年度教員採用試験実施問題 ･････････････････････52

▼2022年度教員採用試験実施問題 ･････････････････････89

▼2021年度教員採用試験実施問題 ･････････････････････124

▼2020年度教員採用試験実施問題 ･････････････････････166

▼2019年度教員採用試験実施問題 ･････････････････････209

▼2018年度教員採用試験実施問題 ･････････････････････246

▼2017年度教員採用試験実施問題 ･････････････････････283

▼2016年度教員採用試験実施問題 ･････････････････････322

第１部

岩手県の
英語科
出題傾向分析

岩手県の英語科　傾向と対策

◆中高共通

　リスニング問題は中高共通として，2024年度も2023年度と同様に，英文と質問を聞いて，その答えとして適切なものを選ぶ形式で3題出題された。すべて1度ずつしか読まれないため，はじめにまとまった英文を聞いたときに内容をよく把握し，解答の際はひとつひとつ考え込まずに一問ずつ頭を切り替えて，解答のタイミングを外さないようにすることが必要である。中級英会話の教材や各種検定試験のリスニング教材などで，英文を一度聞いて内容を把握する学習をしておきたい。学習方法としては，ある程度の範囲に区切った英文を一度聞き，覚えている限りの要素を自分で書いてみる方法が有効であり，いろいろな英文をできるだけ多く聞き，集中して聞く学習を繰り返すことが大切である。この形式の他に，まず英文を聞き，それについての文が途中まで読み上げられ，選択肢から後半の文を選んでその文を完成させる，という問題も過去に出題されたことがあるが，対策としては同じと考えてよいだろう。

◆中学校

　近年出題されているのは，リスニング問題，文法・語法問題，会話文問題，読解問題，英作文問題，学習指導要領に関する問題である。

　文法・語法問題は，空所補充・正誤判断の形式で出題されている。語彙問題に関しては，英検準1級の単語・語彙を習得しておくことが望ましい。2024年度についても，文法問題の難易度は標準レベルなので，大学入試レベルの文法問題集を1冊仕上げておけば十分に対処できるだろう。

　会話文問題は空所補充の形式で出題されており，セリフの一部を選択肢から選んで補充する形式である。難易度は低いので満点を目指したい問題である。

　読解問題は，長文問題が3題出題されている。それぞれの問題文はさほど長くなく，設問内容も大学入試レベルだが，全体的に問題量がかなり多い。問題の内容は，いくつかの空所補充問題の他は，ほとんどが問題

文と一致する内容を選択する問題であり，文法知識等よりは内容把握の力が問われているといえよう。なお，2024年度は1問だけ英問英答の問題が出題されたが，本文中から語句を抜き出すような問題なので，英語を書く力までは求められていない。過去問題を解くほか，大学入試レベルの長文問題集を利用して，英文を読むスピードをつけておくとともに，一読して大体の内容をつかめるよう，語彙力もつけておくことが重要である。

英作文問題は自由英作文の形式で出題されている。具体的には，学習指導要領の一部を参考にして，具体的な英語の指導方法を英語で書くという形式である。2023年度も同様の形式であった。80語程度の語数制限を踏まえ短く的確にまとめる必要がある。英語指導に関するいろいろなテーマで実際に書き，語数(文の長さ)の感覚をしっかり身につけておくとともに，まとまった内容にすることが重要である。

学習指導要領に関する問題は，学習指導要領の内容の空所補充や内容について記述する問題，さらに具体的な指導場面を踏まえて生徒へのコメントなどを記述するが出題されている。学習指導要領の問題については，上記の英作文問題にも関連するが，日本語版・英語版の学習指導要領や解説をしっかり読んで内容を把握し，学習指導要領の意図や，それについての自分の考え，そして自分なりの授業計画を日本語・英語どちらでも表現できるようにしておくことが必要である。また，具体的な指導場面を踏まえた問題については，教育現場の状況を踏まえて様々な生徒をイメージしながら，生徒が主体的に学習に取り組めるような手立てなどを考えるようにしたい。教育実習などの経験を具体的に説明できるようにしておくのもよいだろう。

◆高等学校

近年は，リスニング問題，文法・語法問題，読解問題，英作文問題，学習指導要領に関する問題が出題されている。

文法・語法問題は，2024年度は2023年度と同様に誤文訂正問題であった。さほど難解なものではなく，特別な対策は必要ないと思われるが，年度により問題数の増減も考えられるので，過去問題を解いてみて気に

5

なるようなら文法中心の問題集を仕上げておくとよいだろう。

　読解問題は，長めの長文読解問題が3題出題されていて，設問は内容に関する選択肢問題のほか，空所補充問題，英問英答で内容を説明する問題，本文のテーマに沿った英作文問題など，これまでにいろいろな形式で出題されている。本文中から抜き出す問題だけではなく，2024年度は本文中に書かれていない例を英語で書く問題が出題されているため，自分の考えを短く英語で書く練習も必要である。基本的に内容把握に重点が置かれている。難易度は大学入試レベルだが，英文が長いので読むスピードが要求される。過去問題を解くほか，大学入試レベルの長文問題集や英字新聞などを利用して，速読力をつけておく必要がある。

　英作文は自由英作文が1題出題されている。2023年度は機械翻訳の発達の中で英語学習の必要性をどのように生徒に説いていくかという設問で，2024年度は英語教師になるべき理由を友人に説くエッセイを書くという設問であった。教育関係の時事問題に対応できるように，新聞記事等をチェックして，自分なりの意見をもっておきたい。英作文については，英語エッセイのパターンを守り，簡潔にまとめる学習を積んでおくことが必要である。できれば毎日ひとつを目安に100〜150語程度でいろいろなテーマについてまとめる学習が効果的である。整序英作文は2017年度から姿を消しているが，過去に出題された経緯があるので，過去問題でチェックするとよい。基本的には高等学校英語レベルの文法事項をしっかり押さえていれば特に苦労せず解ける問題である。

　学習指導要領に関する問題に対する対策は，中学校向けの対策と同様であるが，余裕があれば，高校の学習指導要領だけでなく，小学校および中学校の学習指導要領にも目を通しておくとよい。

過去5年間の出題傾向分析

中学＝●　高校＝▲　中高共通＝◎

分類	設問形式	2020年度	2021年度	2022年度	2023年度	2024年度
リスニング	内容把握	◎	◎	◎	◎	◎
発音・アクセント	発音					
	アクセント					
	文強勢					
文法・語法	空所補充	●▲	●	●	●	●
	正誤判断	●	●▲	●▲	●▲	●▲
	一致語句					
	連立完成					
	その他					
会話文	短文会話	●	●	●	●	●
	長文会話	●				
文章読解	空所補充	●▲	●▲	●▲	●▲	●▲
	内容一致文	●▲	●▲	●▲	●▲	●▲
	内容一致語句					●▲
	内容記述	▲	▲	▲	▲	
	英文和訳					
	英問英答	▲	▲	▲	▲	●▲
	その他					
英作文	整序					
	和文英訳					
	自由英作	●▲	●▲	●▲	●▲	●▲
	その他					
学習指導要領		●▲	●▲	●▲	●▲	●▲

第2部

岩手県の
教員採用試験
実施問題

2024年度　実施問題

【中高共通】

【1】これから，会話と質問が4つ放送されます。質問に対する答えとして最も適切なものをア〜エの中から一つずつ選び，その記号を書きなさい。なお，会話と質問は一度だけ放送されます。

1
ア　Get another candle holder.
イ　Look around other shops.
ウ　Purchase the candle holder.
エ　Sell the little candle holder.

2
ア　Adam's address.
イ　A stranger's address.
ウ　George's address.
エ　Kate's address.

3
ア　They did not communicate well.
イ　They forgot about the meeting.
ウ　The man did not upload the right file.
エ　The man was busy with another report.

4
ア　Because he practices English hard.
イ　Because he pretends to be an interviewer.
ウ　Because he said something rude to her.
エ　Because he unintentionally said something funny.

(☆☆☆◎◎◎◎)

【2】 これから，まとまりのある英文が放送されます。その内容について
の次の質問に対する答えとして最も適切なものをア〜エの中から一つ
ずつ選び，その記号を書きなさい。なお，英文は一度だけ放送されま
す。

1 What does EU law currently require the citizens to do in October?
　ア　Move their clocks an hour backward on the first Sunday.
　イ　Move their clocks an hour backward on the last Sunday.
　ウ　Move their clocks an hour forward on the first Sunday.
　エ　Move their clocks an hour forward on the last Sunday.

2 Why did people first start "daylight saving"?
　ア　To go home earlier.
　イ　To improve their health.
　ウ　To receive additional daylight.
　エ　To reduce traffic accidents.

3 What have critics said about the negative effects of adjusting the clocks
twice a year?
　ア　The time change can allow people less time for sleeping.
　イ　The time change can give people health problems.
　ウ　The time change can lead to fewer employees in factories.
　エ　The time change can result in more traffic accidents.

4 What should EU member countries do to avoid damaging Europe's
economy?
　ア　Adjust their policies on the time change.
　イ　Make quick decisions on the time change.
　ウ　Keep switching between summer and winter time.
　エ　Stop switching between summer and winter time.

(☆☆☆◎◎◎◎)

【3】 これから，まとまりのある英文が放送されます。その内容について
の次の質問に対する答えとして最も適切なものをア〜エの中から一つ

11

ずつ選び，その記号を書きなさい。なお，英文は一度だけ放送されます。

1　What did Ms. James hope to become when she moved to France?

　ア　A communications director.

　イ　A judge for the Michelin Guide.

　ウ　A translator.

　エ　A restaurant chef.

2　How old is Ms. James now?

　ア　21　　イ　33　　ウ　44　　エ　45

3　What does Ms. James want?

　ア　To be considered "a la mode" for being a black chef.

　イ　To only be judged for the food she serves.

　ウ　To open a new restaurant in her home country.

　エ　To win another Michelin star next year.

4　Which of the following is true of Ms. James?

　ア　Her restaurant was awarded a star by the Michelin Guide.

　イ　Her restaurant is located in Benin.

　ウ　She was the only self-taught chef to receive a Michelin star.

　エ　She was the only woman to win a Michelin star.

(☆☆☆◎◎◎)

【中学校】

【 1 】 To complete each item, choose the best word or phrase from among the four choices.

1　Betty's job involved mostly (　　) work such as making copies and entering data.

　ア　parental　　イ　clerical　　ウ　nutritional　　エ　radical

2　The mayor presented the man with a Good Citizen Award as a (　　) to his efforts to help the homeless in his area.

　ア　testament　　イ　foundation　　ウ　bureau　　エ　deficiency

3 Mr. Grieg went to a school that ( ) good manners and self-discipline.

　ア　harvested　　イ　cultivated　　ウ　blossomed　　エ　planted

4 A major accident caused serious ( ) on the highway, as two lanes of traffic were closed for over two hours.

　ア　testimony　　イ　visibility　　ウ　congestion　　エ　drainage

5 Many students complained the book was too difficult to understand in places, so the teacher tried to ( ) those sections using simpler language.

　ア　paraphrase　　イ　contradict　　ウ　obstruct　　エ　scorn

6 A fire broke out on Bloor Street last night. It took firefighters almost eight hours, but they eventually managed to get the ( ) under control.

　ア　clamp　　イ　drizzle　　ウ　comet　　エ　blaze

7 Richard is extremely busy with his job, but he always makes sure to ( ) time for his children in the evening.

　ア　roll up　　イ　stay off　　ウ　miss out　　エ　set aside

8 Glen realized his long years of service to the company did not ( ) anything when he was suddenly fired as part of a cost-cutting measure.

　ア　count for　　イ　go back on　　ウ　sell out　　エ　do away with

(☆☆☆○○○○○)

【2】For each conversation, choose the answer that best fills in the blank.

1 *A:* I have no idea where we can have a farewell party for Bob.

　B: You always ask me for help, Ken.

　A: ( )

　B: It's OK. Leave it to me. I'll find a nice restaurant.

　　ア　Who else can I depend on?

　　イ　Where can I find out?

　　ウ　How can I take off?

　　エ　When can I talk with you?

2 *A:* Have you lived here long?

　B: About five years. Come in. ( )

13

A: Wow! You have a great view from up here.

B: Yes. It's amazing, isn't it?

　ア　I've just checked in.

　イ　I'm not allowed to have guests.

　ウ　I made a reservation for you.

　エ　I'll show you around.

3　*A:* I did some volunteer work over the summer break. It was such an invaluable experience.

B: (　　　)

A: Sure. Why don't we have a seat and chat?

　ア　Why did you do that? That's expensive.

　イ　I see. What's next?

　ウ　That's great! Tell me more, about it!

　エ　I'm sorry to hear that. You should have done something else.

4　*A:* When is the assignment due?

B: Next Monday. (　　　)

A: Yes, I am really overworked now.

B: OK. How about Wednesday? I look forward to receiving it.

　ア　Can you get it in on time?

　イ　Have you already turned it in?

　ウ　Do you need an extension?

　エ　Have you already finished?

5　*A:* Emily, do you want to go to the new movie theater this weekend?

B: Sorry, but I can't. I have to work all weekend to get ready for a big presentation on Monday.

It's really important.

A: That's too bad. Do you have time for dinner Sunday evening?

B: (　　　) Sorry.

　ア　I'll finish working as soon as possible.

　イ　I may not be working late on Sunday.

ウ I'll be there.

エ I may not be finished by then.

(☆☆○○○○)

【3】 For each question, choose the one underlined, word or phrase that should be corrected or rewritten.

1 I'm still in the middle _アof lunch right now, _イbut I will be ready _ウto leave _エten minutes later.

2 _アWhile I _イdrive to Sendai, _ウI was stopped by a policeman for _エgoing over the speed limit.

3 If he _アhad stopped _イto read the instruction manual before _ウturning on the machine, I'm sure this _エdidn't happen.

4 Her telephone _アwasn't functioning because her cat _イhad knocked _ウa receiver off the hook without _エher noticing it.

5 I could _アrise public awareness about _イanimal abuse in America and many other countries _ウas a result of your _エwonderful research.

(☆☆☆○○○)

【4】 Read the following passage and answer the questions below.

In our own childhoods, we were not taught how to deal with anger as a fact of life. We were made to feel guilty for experiencing anger and sinful for expressing it. We were led to believe that to be angry is to be bad. Anger was not merely a misdemeanor; it was a felony. With our own children, we try to be patient; in fact, so patient that sooner or later we must explode. We are afraid that our anger may be harmful to children, so we hold it in, as a skin diver holds his breath. In both instances, however, the capacity for holding in is rather limited.

Anger, ① , is a recurrent problem. We may not like it, but we cannot ignore it. We may know it intimately, but we cannot prevent its appearance. Anger arises in predictable sequences and situations, yet it always seems

15

sudden and unexpected. And, though, it may not last long, anger seems eternal for the moment.

When we lose our temper, we act as though we have lost our sanity. We say and do things to our children that we would hesitate to inflict on an enemy. We yell, insult, and attack. When the fanfare is over, we feel guilty and we solemnly resolve never to render a repeat performance. But anger inevitably strikes again, undoing our good intentions. Once more we lash out at (あ)those to whose welfare we have dedicated our life and fortune.

Resolutions about not becoming angry are worse than futile. They only add fuel to fire. Anger, ②, is a fact of life to be acknowledged and prepared for. The peaceful home, ③, does not depend on a sudden benevolent change in human nature. It does depend on deliberate procedures that methodically reduce tensions before they lead to explosions.

Emotionally healthy parents are not saints. They're aware of their anger and respect it. They use their anger as a source of information, an indication of their caring. Their words are congruent with their feelings. They do not hide their feelings. (い)The following episode illustrates how a mother encouraged cooperation by venting her anger without insulting or humiliating her daughter.

Jane, age eleven, came home screaming: "I can't play baseball. I don't have a shirt!" The mother could have given her daughter an acceptable solution: "Wear your blouse." Or, wanting to be helpful, she could have helped Jane look for the shirt. Instead, she decided to express her true feelings: "I'm angry, I'm mad. I've bought you six baseball shirts and they're either mislaid or lost. Your shirts belong in your dresser. Then, when you need them, you'll know where to find them."

Jane's mother expressed her anger without insulting her daughter, as she commented later: "Not once did I bring up past grievances or reopen old wounds. Nor did I call my daughter names. I did not tell her she's a scatterbrain and irresponsible. I just described how I felt and what needed to be done in the future to avoid unpleasantness."

Her mother's words helped Jane herself come up with a solution. She hurried off to search for the mislaid shirts at her friend's house and in the locker room in the gym.

There is a place for parental anger in child education. In fact, failure to get angry at certain moments would only convey to the child indifference, not goodness. Those who care cannot altogether shun anger. This does not mean that children can withstand floods of fury and violence; it means only that they can stand and understand anger that says, "There are limits to my tolerance."

For parents, anger is a costly emotion: To be worth its price, it should not be employed without profit. Anger should not be used so that it increases with expression. The medication must not be worse than the disease.

1   In paragraph 3, what does the underlined part (あ) refer to? Answer in English.

2   Which is the best phrase to fill in the each blank from ① to ③ ? Choose the correct order.

ア   like a hurricane
イ   like the common cold
ウ   like the hoped-for peaceful world

A   ① ア   ② ウ   ③ イ
B   ① イ   ② ア   ③ ウ
C   ① ウ   ② ア   ③ イ
D   ① イ   ② ウ   ③ ア

3   In paragraph 5, what does the underlined (い) refer to?

ア   Finally, Jane's mother helped Jane look for the shirt.
イ   Jane's mother instructed Jane to wear a blouse when Jane came home screaming.
ウ   Jane's mother didn't say anything when Jane said that she couldn't play baseball.

エ　Jane's mother expressed her anger without insulting Jane.

4　Choose the answer that best completes the sentence below.

According to the passage, if parents never get angry at their child, the child _____.

ア　will learn there are limits to their tolerance

イ　will not think that they are interested in him/her

ウ　will think that they are emotionally healthy

エ　will never get angry with other people

(☆☆☆○○○○○)

【5】Read the following passage and answer the questions below.

When I was in seventh and eighth grades, one of my teachers was in her first and second year of teaching. I have to admit that we gave her a pretty rough time during that first year. It was not malicious by any means, but my classmates and I were perhaps a bit more rambunctious than a first-year teacher was ready to face. No doubt she often said to herself, "(あ)They didn't tell me about this in college!"

My particular story, however, is about an incident on one of the last days in her class during my eighth-grade year. I was in my typical seat — last row, last column, over by the window — as Miss Serena was returning our term papers. She commented that if we wanted to read a very well-written paper, one that was mechanically sound, we should read Nick's. That sounded familiar. But she then went on to say that if we wanted to read "a really interesting paper, a paper that had something to say," we should read ... Olivia's. There was an audible gasp in the room. Most audible of the gasps was mine. At that moment the paper arrived at my desk. There was a large A emblazoned on the cover page. My classmates turned and looked at me in disbelief as I stared at the graded paper. In my mine's eye I can still see that page.

I was not a terrible student but certainly not an outstanding one. As far as I

18

was concerned, school was simply the place where kids had to be during the day. I was just there. A major part of my ambivalence toward school was that I disliked writing papers that were returned to me with only a grade and no response from the teacher other than the marking of grammar and punctuation errors. This time, and it was the first time that I can recall, a teacher had valued my thinking.

It would be difficult for me to express how much of an effect that one act has had on my life. No, it's not the reason that I became a teacher, but when Miss Serena recognized the ideas in that paper she empowered me as a thinker. (い)What I had to say had merit. I often refer to that event when telling students of education that they need to empower the children of any age in their classrooms. A sure way to cultivate student thinking is to find merit in their ideas. Finding that merit, however obscure it may be, is what makes a teacher a professional.

Miss Serena never knew that on that last day of her second year of teaching she had touched someone for a lifetime. Unfortunately, that's part of the territory that goes along with teaching. She probably taught for a number of years, got married, maybe raised a family. Perhaps she enjoyed a long and rewarding career as an educator. What is important now, however, is that teachers have a similar effect on some child. Some child is waiting to be empowered by a teacher.

1 Which answer best describes the underlined part (あ)?

   ア   My classmates didn't tell me that they were interested in college.

   イ   My professors didn't teach me how to promote students' health.

   ウ   In college I wasn't told about students' bad behavior.

   エ   My teachers didn't tell me how to teach college students.

2 Which answer best describes the underlined part (い)?

   ア   My essay received a high grade since there were few mistakes.

   イ   My paper took advantage of others' thought.

   ウ   My paper was admired for its interesting ideas.

エ　The teacher praised my spelling.

3　Which statement best describes the content of the text?

ア　A teacher needs to train students to write correctly.

イ　A teacher should work diligently to improve students' attitudes.

ウ　A teacher's role is to maintain a good relationship with students.

エ　A teacher's task is to recognize and value students' ideas.

(☆☆☆○○○○○)

【6】Read the following passage and answer the questions below.

How the Internet is Changing Our Lives

(1)　One morning, Mike and his family were getting ready to visit Mike's grandmother in Springport, a town about a hundred kilometers away. Mike and his father were eating breakfast and watching a live European tennis match on TV. Mike's mother was rushing to prepare for their trip. "I forgot to check the weather report," she said to Mike's father. "Could you get on the Internet and see what the weather will be like in Springport for the next week? Also, check the local web cameras there to see the road conditions. I hope there isn't too much snow." Mike knew that he could use the Internet to check the weather, but he didn't know about the traffic camera. The Internet was a part of his daily life, but he realized that it was even more useful than he had thought.

(2)　Year after year, as the amount of information available on the Internet increases, the number of people using the Internet worldwide also rises. Because we are able to obtain all kinds of information via the Internet, people feel less restricted by time when getting information online. In other words, our concept of "business hours" has completely changed. The Internet Community is open 24 hours a day, all over the world. This is true not only for obtaining information such as news, weather and traffic conditions, but also for buying merchandise and making financial transactions.

(3)　Many people today say that when they want to buy or learn about a product, the first place they turn is the Internet. Getting online is much faster than making a phone call or going to a store, and the shopper can find, compare, and buy all kinds of goods at any time he or she likes. Furthermore, shoppers can now accomplish these and other tasks not only with their PCs, but also with their mobile phones. For example, if a person is traveling on business and suddenly has to change her plans, she can use her mobile phone to establish communication with her coworkers and her family. Then— even if it is the middle of the night—she can go to her airline's mobile website to cancel her existing flight reservation and make a new one, and even make hotel reservations for the following night.

(4)　The Internet has changed human behavior in other ways. Say a person suddenly feels a desire to eat a certain kind of food, but does not know how to prepare the dish with the ingredients he has. Ten or twenty years ago, if the person had no cookbooks in his house — and there were no bookstores nearby — he probably would have eaten something else. However, now he can enter the information into a search engine and find dozens, or perhaps hundreds, of websites that offer simple and clear instructions on how to make the dish, possibly even with photographs and ideas for substitute ingredients. Therefore, the Internet is giving people the courage and inspiration to try new things they may not have tried before.

(5)　Mike had never thought so carefully about the Internet before. He has been using the Internet for several years, but now he knows that there are even more possibilities and opportunities than he had imagined.

1　Our lifestyles have changed in recent years due to [　　].

　　ア　the ability to watch overseas sports live on TV

　　イ　the amount and types of information easily accessed via the Internet

　　ウ　the decrease in frequency of weather forecasts and traffic information on TV

　　エ　the reduced value of information because of the amount that is available on the Internet

2　The statement "our concept of 'business hours' has completely changed" implies that [　　].

　　ア　businesspeople are feeling that they need to work longer hours to be successful

　　イ　people buy fewer things on the Internet when regular shops are open

　　ウ　people can buy the things they want online at any time that is convenient for them

　　エ　shops are changing the times of the day in which they are open

3　In the example described in paragraph (3), the person first used her mobile phone to [　　].

　　ア　contact people, and then cancel unnecessary things using the Internet

　　イ　contact people, and then purchase necessary things using the Internet

　　ウ　contact people, then cancel unnecessary things, and finally purchase necessary things using the Internet

　　エ　contact people, then purchase necessary things and finally cancel unnecessary things using the Internet

4　According to paragraph (4), the Internet [　　].

　　ア　has become more popular than books because of the use of photographs on websites

　　イ　has increased the need for recipes when cooking

　　ウ　has not reduced the cost of obtaining necessary information

　　エ　has reduced the restrictions more people feel on their activities

（☆☆☆○○○○○）

【7】次の文は，中学校学習指導要領(平成29年3月)第2章「第9節　外国語」における「第2　各言語の目標及び内容等」の「3　指導計画の作成と内容の取扱い」の一部を抜粋したものです。文中の(　1　)～(　4　)にあてはまる語句を，以下のア～エから一つずつ選び，その記号を書きなさい。

> エ　文法事項の指導に当たっては，次の事項に留意すること
>
> 　(ア)　英語の特質を理解させるために，関連のある文法事項は
> 　　　　(　1　)など，効果的な指導ができるように工夫すること。
>
> 　(イ)　文法はコミュニケーションを支えるものであることを踏
> 　　　　まえ，コミュニケーションの目的を達成する上での(　2　)
> 　　　　や有用性を実感させた上でその知識を活用させたり，繰り
> 　　　　返し使用することで当該文法事項の(　3　)や構造などにつ
> 　　　　いて気付きを促したりするなど，言語活動と効果的に関連
> 　　　　付けて指導すること。
>
> 　(ウ)　用語や用法の区別などの指導が中心とならないよう配慮
> 　　　　し，実際に活用できるようにするとともに，(　4　)や修飾
> 　　　　関係などにおける日本語との違いに留意して指導すること。

1　ア　明示的に示す　　　　イ　積極的に活用する
　　ウ　意味を重視する　　　エ　まとめて整理する
2　ア　楽しさ　　　　　　　イ　必要性
　　ウ　利便性　　　　　　　エ　必然性
3　ア　規則性　　　　　　　イ　時制
　　ウ　意味　　　　　　　　エ　使用場面
4　ア　熟語　　　　　　　　イ　目的
　　ウ　語順　　　　　　　　エ　音声

(☆☆☆☆◎◎◎◎)

【8】次の文は，中学校学習指導要領(平成29年3月)第2章「第9節　外国語」における「第2　各言語の目標及び内容等」の「1　目標」の一部

23

です。

　次の事項において，下線部のような学習の充実を図るためには，どのような指導が考えられるか，あなたの考えを80語以上の英語で書きなさい。

　なお，最後に語数を記入すること。語数については，同じ語を2回使用した場合，2語と数えること(のべ数)とします。

---

(2)　読むこと

　イ　日常的な話題について，簡単な語句や文で書かれた短い文章の概要を捉えることができるようにする。

(☆☆☆☆◎◎◎◎)

【9】あとの英作文は，「中学校の思い出を英語で残し，仲間とこれまでの歩みを振り返ろう」という単元の途中で生徒が書いたものです。次の問いに答えなさい。

1　この英作文を書いた生徒が，英作文をよりよくするためにアドバイスをしてほしいと言っています。あなたなら，どのように誤りを修正しますか。英作文に書き込む形で生徒に伝えなさい。

単元のゴール

　中学校の思い出について，事実や自分の考え，気持ちなどを整理し，これまでに学んだ表現を用いてまとまりのある英文を書くことができる。

Chorus Contest

The chorus contest was my fovorite memory.

We practiced every day for a month.

It was difficult for us to singing the different parts.

We could sings well at the end.

I remember will our beautiful harmony and our victory!

Aya

2　単元のゴールに向けて，生徒がさらに意欲的に取り組んでいける
　　ように，あなたならどのようにコメント欄に記入して返却しますか。
　　50語程度の英語で書きなさい。

3　あなたは，生徒に単元のゴールを達成させるために，英作文を返
　　却後に全体に対してどのような指導を行いますか。具体的な指導場
　　面を2つ日本語で書きなさい。

(☆☆☆☆◎◎◎)

【10】次の問いに答えなさい。
　　中学校学習指導要領(平成29年3月)の外国語科の目標は「外国語によ
　るコミュニケーションにおける見方・考え方を働かせ，外国語による
　聞くこと，読むこと，話すこと，書くことの言語活動を通して，簡単
　な情報や考えなどを理解したり表現したり伝え合ったりするコミュニ
　ケーションを図る資質・能力を次の通り育成することを目指す。」で
　ある。小学校学習指導要領(平成29年3月)，高等学校学習指導要領(平
　成30年3月)においても，下線部が共通して明記され，小学校，中学校，
　高等学校を通じて，外国語によるコミュニケーションにおける見方・
　考え方を働かせた言語活動の充実が求められている。中学校指導にお
　いて，言語活動の充実を図る上で，特に必要なことについて「小学校
　における指導」と「高等学校への橋渡し」の二つの観点を踏まえ，日
　本語で書きなさい。

(☆☆☆☆◎◎◎)

【高等学校】

【1】次の英文1～5にはそれぞれ誤りや不適切なところがある。修正が必要な箇所を(ア)～(ウ)からそれぞれ一つずつ選び，適切な形に直しなさい。

1　Sam would (ア)appreciate very much (イ)if you (ウ)could show him how to cook your special paella.

2　For (ア)those of you who don't (イ)exercise regularly, it will probably be extremely difficult to (ウ)enjoy to run until you get used to it.

3　Anyone who has tried to study for an exam, (ア)write a report or read a book (イ)know how hard it is to concentrate (ウ)for significant chunks of time.

4　A record 10.3% of new graduate nurses in Japan (ア)quit from their jobs (イ)within a year of employment in fiscal 2021, (ウ)which ended in March last year, a survey by the Japanese Nursing Association showed.

5　"(ア)Compared to 20 years ago, there are fewer students in our school. Although a little sad about that, our homeroom teacher always says that we can realize our dreams if every one of us (イ)are determined to never give up. So we should look forward to the school life that is about (ウ)to begin."

(☆☆☆◎◎◎◎)

【2】次の空所[　(1)　]～[　(5)　]に入る最も適切な文を，ア～キより一つずつ選び，その記号を書きなさい。ただし，同じ記号を複数回用いてはならない。

As artificial intelligence systems play a bigger role in everyday life, they're changing the world of education, too. OpenAI's ChatGPT, Microsoft's Bing and Google's Bard all come with both risks and opportunities. I am a literacy educator and researcher, and here are four ways I believe these kinds of systems can be used to help students learn.

Teachers are taught to identify the learning goals of all students in a class and adapt instruction for the specific needs of individual students. But with 20

26

or more students in a classroom, fully customized lessons aren't always realistic. Everyone learns differently. An AI system can observe how a student proceeds through an assigned task, how much time they take and whether they are successful. [　(1)　] This type of real-time feedback is often difficult for an educator or school to do for a single student, let alone an entire class or campus. AI adaptive learning tools have been shown to quickly and dynamically make changes to the learning environment, content, and tasks to help individuals learn more and quickly improve. For instance, researchers at the Human-Computer Interaction Institute at Carnegie Mellon University taught a system how to solve a math problem. The system can follow instructions from a human supervisor to understand mathematical rules and adapt its approach to problems it has never seen before. The system can also identify areas where it had to make multiple attempts before arriving at the correct answer, flag those for teachers as places human students may get confused, and highlight methods the system used to more efficiently arrive at the right answer.

Researchers at Stanford have been developing and testing a prototype of what's called an "intelligent textbook," titled "Inquire." [　(2)　] The interactive text includes definitions of key words accessible by touch or click and allows students to highlight and annotate while reading. The textbook can also suggest questions about the content and areas for future inquiry that are customized for each individual. It can change the reading level of the text and also include supplemental photos, videos and materials to help students understand what they're studying.

Educational assessment focuses on how an educator knows whether a student is learning what is being taught. Traditional assessments — essays, multiple-choice tests, short-answer questions — are little changed from a century ago. Artificial intelligence has the potential to change that by identifying patterns in learning that may not be apparent to individual teachers or administrators. [　(3)　] The tests start with a series of standard questions, but based on how the student does with those, the system will select harder or easier questions to more quickly identify a student's exact abilities and weaknesses. Another assessment project, Reach Every Reader, staffed by the Harvard Graduate School of Education, MIT and Florida State University, creates educational games for parents to play with their children while teaching them to read. Some of the games have adults and children role-play as characters based on real-life scenarios. [(4)]

Personalized learning occurs when the students' interests and goals guide learning. The teacher is more of a facilitator, while the what, why and how of learning are mostly dictated by the student. Artificial intelligence systems can provide individualized instruction tailored to each student's individual interests. AI adaptive learning systems can quickly identify when a student is struggling and then provide more or different support to help them succeed. As the student shows that they have mastered the content or skill, the AI tool provides more difficult tasks and materials to further challenge the learner. Chatbots have been used to respond to typed or spoken input. Many individuals interact with a chatbot when they ask Alexa or Siri a question. In education, chatbots with artificial intelligence systems can guide students with personalized, just-in-time feedback or assistance. These chatbots can answer questions about course content or structure. [(5)]

Much like an automated playlist of musical or video recommendations, an AI-powered recommender system can generate tailored assessment questions, detect misunderstandings and suggest new areas for a learner to explore. These AI technologies have the potential to help learners today and in the future.

＜選択肢＞

ア　This software would create more opportunities for both teachers and students to cooperate and interact with each other.

イ　For instance, the language-learning company Duolingo uses AI and machine learning to create and score tests of English proficiency for universities, companies and government agencies.

ウ　If students use these books, they will read at a level, which is appropriate for their grade.

エ　If the student is struggling, the system can offer help; if the student is succeeding, the system can present more difficult tasks to keep the activity challenging.

オ　It is an iPad app that monitors students' focus and attention while they read by paying attention to how students interact with the app.

カ　These games can help parents and teachers efficiently determine whether children are reading at their appropriate grade level and get them on track if they are not.

キ　This helps students keep track of their own learning while keeping them motivated and engaged.

(☆☆☆○○○○○)

【3】次の英文を読んで，1～5の問いに対する答えとして最も適切なものをア～エの中から一つずつ選び，その記号を書きなさい。

In 2009, Lady Gaga sang about being caught in a bad romance, and people the world over were, almost instantly, able to sing along. Even now, seven years later, the odds are pretty good that her love woes are already playing on loop in your mind, based solely on the fact that you just read something about it. "Rah-rah ah-ah-ah." Just in case you weren't there yet.

"Bad Romance" and many songs like it are well-known to musical experts as "earworms," due to their ability to stick inside your brain, on repeat, long after you've heard them. But a new study, published in the journal Psychology of Aesthetics, Creativity and the Arts, now has some insight into why this happens. "We were interested because it's such a common phenomenon. People say certain songs are more catchy than others, but there wasn't a lot of scientific evidence on this topic," said Kelly Jakubowski, a music psychologist at Durham University in the UK who herself gets earworms all the time.

It's estimated that 90% of us experience an earworm at least once a week, with some having them even more frequently than others. Jakubowski's team identified three main reasons why they occur, and it comes down to pace, the shape of the melody and a few unique intervals that make a song stand out. "These three factors stood out above the rest ... the songs need to be not too simple and not too complex," Jakubowski said. "None of these have been revealed in previous research."

As for pace, the earworms highlighted in the study were faster and more upbeat in tempo and generally had a rhythm that people could move to. "We have a propensity to move to earworms," Jakubowski said, citing songs that people may use to pace themselves during a run.

Next on the list was musical shape or contour, with earworms generally being simple in structure, but with a rhythmic pattern. Sounds may rise in pitch, go back down low and then rise again as a pattern, such as "Twinkle, Twinkle, Little Star." Many nursery rhymes fit this pattern to help children remember them — so their creators knew what they were doing. "The quite simple melodic contour might help the brain to recall these things," said Jakubowski.

Last was the need for some unusual intervals within the song, just enough to add some catchy surprises while maintaining a simple, uniform pattern overall. "Although the overall melody has a simple shape, you'll find some unique intervals," Jakubowski said. "So it's simple but different."

To find out what makes certain song catchier than others, the researchers used an online survey to ask 3,000 people, mostly from the UK, between 2010 and 2013 to name their most frequent earworms. The songs most commonly listed as earworms were compared against other songs by the same artists that had ranked similarly on the UK music chart to look for differences in their musical structure. Lady Gaga's "Bad Romance" was at the very top with Jakubowski saying she hears it in her head every time she looks at the

The team believes that in addition to simply understanding how and why this common phenomenon happens, understanding how earworms affect our brains could add insight into how we process memories and moods, as earworms are also known to be linked to memories and to perk people up. Memories can trigger an earworm, even if you haven't heard it recently, if you are with a person or in a place that you associate with a certain song. "It's memory association," Jakubowski said.

According to the researchers, two-thirds of earworm episodes are considered to be either neutral or positive by the people experiencing them. "Some people find them helpful ... for various reasons, such as getting things done," she said. "There are so many cues in our environment," she said.

Though (A) of us may not find earworms offensive, the reality is that at some point, a song may become annoying, and you'll want it to wiggle out of your head. To enable this, the study has three options: Engage fully with the song by listening to it through to the end, distract yourself with a different song — though this could just leave you with another to get rid of — or simply let it run its course and don't think about it, which is easier said than done. "A lot of the time, people get the song stuck because they don't remember how it ends," Jakubowski said, explaining why it could work to listen to a song through to the end.

Once a tune becomes stuck in our heads, how can you get rid of it? In a separate study, Dr Jakubowski and her colleagues discovered that the most common method is the "let it be" strategy, which involves trying to ignore it until it fades away on its own. However, others preferred to engage with the earworm song. "Those who chose to engage with the earworm song itself often found that doing something like listening to the whole song all the way through to break the loop or identify some unknown element, such as lyrics or song title, helped to get rid of the earworm." Other research efforts have noted that chewing gum can decrease the occurrence of earworms. This is likely to be because chewing gum interferes with the articulatory muscles that are need to mentally 'sing' a piece of music.

Yet another strategy is filling your mind with a different song. Jakubowski asked the trial participants to name other songs they use to get rid of an earworm. The most common answer was "God Save the Queen," the national anthem of the UK. Before you reach for the medication, perhaps try the other options first and, if you can remember how it goes, try praising the Queen of England in musical form.

1　The phenomenon in the passage is called "earworms" because

　ア　it has the ability to repeat itself in the brain long after it has been heard.

　イ　it has the power to make songs catchy for many people.

　ウ　it is a common symptom among music experts.

　エ　it is caused by insects entering the brain through the ears.

2　Choose the correct feature of a song that is most likely to cause earworms.

　ア　Songs made with simple and featureless melodies.

　イ　Songs with a slow tempo that are just right for exercise.

　ウ　Songs with a specific pattern of rising and falling pitch.

　エ　Songs you wrote by yourself when you were a child.

3　Choose the correct one about the 2010-2013 survey in this passage.

　ア　It was the survey asking what features made a song catchy.

　イ　Jakubowski and her colleagues asked 3,000 people living in the UK.

　ウ　The songs listed were compared to other songs by the same artists.

　エ　The survey was carried out for a decade.

4　Which is the most suitable to put into (　A　)?

　ア　few　　イ　half　　ウ　one-third　　エ　two-thirds

5　Which of the following is NOT mentioned as an effective means of getting rid of earworms?

　ア　Chewing gum white singing the song.

　イ　Filling your mind with another song.

ウ　Listening to the entire earworm song.

エ　Waiting until it disappears with time.

(☆☆☆○○○○)

【4】次の英文を読んで，1〜6の問いに答えなさい。

Joseph Ferrari, a professor of psychology at DePaul University in Chicago, has found that about 20 percent of adults are chronic procrastinators. "That's higher than depression, higher than phobia, higher than panic attacks and alcoholism. And yet all of those are considered legitimate," he said. "We try to trivialize this tendency, but it's not a funny topic."

Ferrari was speaking while on a road trip with his wife, who chimed in to say that she's a procrastinator. Her tendencies helped spur her husband's research interests. He doesn't procrastinate — he has a 107-page résumé, he said, because he gets things done — but he's built a career around understanding those who do.

Among his findings: Chronic procrastination doesn't discriminate based on gender, race or age; we're all susceptible. As he put it: "Everybody procrastinates, but not everyone is a procrastinator." And contrary to popular belief, procrastinating has little to do with laziness. It's far more complicated, he said, than simply being a matter of time management.

To understand what causes procrastination (outside of conditions such as attention-deficit/hyperactivity disorder where executive functioning issues might interfere with task completion), it's important to be clear about what it is — and isn't. Procrastination is different from delaying a task because you need to talk to someone who isn't available, or not getting around. Fuschia Sirois, a professor of psychology at the University of Sheffield in England, defines procrastination this way: "The voluntary, unnecessary delay of an important task, despite knowing you'll be worse off for doing so."

On its surface, procrastination is an irrational behavior, Sirois said: "Why would somebody put something off to the last minute, and then they're stressed out of their mind, and they end up doing a poor job or less than optimal job on it? And then they feel bad about it afterward, and it may even have implications for other people." Whatever type of procrastinator you are, pushing off tasks over and over again is a risk factor for poor mental and physical health, experts say. Chronic procrastinators have higher levels of stress and a greater number of acute health problems than other people, Sirois has found. The mental health implications include experiencing general psychological distress and low life satisfaction (particularly in regard to work and income), as well as symptoms of depression and anxiety.

Those who procrastinate are also more likely to experience headaches, insomnia and digestive issues, and they're more susceptible to the flu and colds. The association with health problems is best explained by stress, but another factor is that procrastinators often delay preventive treatment, such as regular checkups. Research suggests that procrastination is associated with sleep problems, such as shorter sleep duration and an increased risk of insomnia symptoms and daytime sleepiness. Lots of people engage in "revenge bedtime procrastination," which describes a tendency to push off sleep to make time for personal activities.

Procrastinating is also linked to heart problems. Sirois led a 2015 study in the Journal of Behavioral Medicine that found that people with heart disease were more likely than healthy people to self-identify as procrastinators. According to the study, procrastinators with hypertension and heart disease were less likely to take action to cope with their illness, such as changing their diet or exercising.

By overcoming your tendency to stall, you can improve your mental and physical well-being. Here are experts' suggestions. Procrastinators are often hard on themselves. They might feel guilt about letting others down or be appalled by their own slowness. Sirois's research indicates a connection between procrastinating and low levels of self-compassion. To counter that, treat yourself with kindness and understanding. "Just sort of recognizing that, yeah, maybe I screwed up and maybe I could have gotten started earlier, but I don't need to beat myself up," she said. Tell yourself: "I'm not the first person to procrastinate, and I won't be the last." Sirois notes that self-compassion doesn't make people lazy. On the contrary, "research has shown that it actually increases people's motivation to improve themselves," she said.

One of the best ways to stop procrastinating, Sirois said, is to find meaning in the task in question. Write down why it's important to you: It could be because getting it done on time is helpful to other people, or because it will help you avoid negative repercussions, such as a late fee or bad grade. Think about how completing it will be valuable to your personal growth or happiness. Doing so will help you feel more connected to the task and less likely to procrastinate, Sirois said.

Ferrari likes to reference the expression, "Cannot see the forest for the trees." The problem of procrastinators is the opposite: All they can see is forest. And they become so overwhelmed by the size of the forest (or project) that they're paralyzed into inactivity. "I tell them to cut down one tree at a time," he said. "You can't do one tree? Give me three branches." Once you've gotten started, and made even a small bit of progress on your task, there's a good chance you'll keep going, he said. This can be particularly helpful to indecisive procrastinators, or "procs," as Ferrari calls them. These people, who are often perfectionists, do best when they split up a task into manageable parts, rather than feeling pressure to perform perfectly on a big, daunting project.

It is also important to situate yourself in a spot that's interruption-free. This is particularly important for demanding tasks, Gretchen Rubin, an author whose books include "Better Than Before," said. We get interrupted constantly: by our phones, our families, howling dogs, the TV. But once you're interrupted, she said, it's much harder to resume the task you finally started.

Finally, reward yourself. Many teachers and parents use the Premack

35

principle, which essentially stipulates that "something somebody wants to do becomes the reward for something they don't want to do," Ferrari said. If you have 12 dirty dishes in your sink and your favorite TV show comes on in a half-hour, make a deal with yourself: You can only watch it if you do the dishes first. The idea can be applied to almost anything that you're pushing off, he said.

1　According to the passage, what is the definition of procrastination? Answer in English.

2　According to Fuschia Sirois, which is a feature of procrastinators?

　ア　They always catch the flu and colds because they never take medical checkups.

　イ　They are likely to self-identify as such when they have heart disease.

　ウ　They are prone to have higher levels of stress and end up being on a low income.

　エ　They tend to have insomnia symptoms that keep them awake during the day.

3　According to the research indicated in the passage, how should procrastinators motivate themselves? Answer in English.

4　Who is NOT described by the idea, "Cannot see the forest for the trees." in this passage?

　ア　A person who desires his or her growth and happiness.

　イ　A person who has a habit of being lazy.

　ウ　A person who takes a long time to start a project.

　エ　A person who wants to be helpful to others.

5　According to the passage, why is an interruption-free situation important? Answer in English.

6　Give an example of procrastination which is NOT mentioned in this passage. Answer in English.

(☆☆☆☆○○○○)

【5】 次の英文を読んで，以下の問いに120語程度の英語で答えなさい。

　　　Imagine this situation. Your friend is trying to decide whether to become an English teacher or do something else for their career. You must encourage them to become an English teacher. Write a persuasive essay in which you explain to your friend the most important reason why they should become an English teacher, including supporting details, as well as specific examples.

(☆☆☆☆◎◎◎)

【6】 次の1，2の問いに日本語で答えなさい。

1　 次の文章は，「高等学校学習指導要領(平成30年告示)」からの抜粋である。空所(A)〜(E)に適する語句を書きなさい。

> 第1款　目標
>
> 　外国語によるコミュニケーションにおける(A)を働かせ，外国語による聞くこと，読むこと，話すこと，書くことの言語活動及びこれらを結び付けた統合的な言語活動を通して，情報や考えなどを的確に理解したり適切に表現したり伝え合ったりするコミュニケーションを図る資質・能力を次のとおり育成することを目指す。
>
> (1)　外国語の音声や語彙，表現，文法，言語の働きなどの理解を深めるとともに，これらの知識を，聞くこと，読むこと，話すこと，書くことによる実際のコミュニケーションにおいて，目的や場面，状況などに応じて適切に活用できる(B)を身に付けるようにする。
>
> (2)　コミュニケーションを行う目的や場面，状況などに応じて，日常的な話題や(C)について，外国語で情報や考えなどの概要や要点，詳細，話し手や書き手の意図などを的確に理解したり，これらを活用して適切に表現したり伝え合ったりすることができる力を養う。
>
> (3)　外国語の背景にある文化に対する理解を深め，聞き手，

37

読み手，話し手，書き手に（　D　）しながら，（　E　），自律的に外国語を用いてコミュニケーションを図ろうとする態度を養う。

2　「高等学校学習指導要領(平成30年告示)解説　外国語編　英語編」には，「授業を実際のコミュニケーションの場面とする」と示されているが，「授業を実際のコミュニケーションの場面とする」目的とそれを達成するために教師がすべきことや工夫しなければならないことについて書きなさい。

(☆☆☆☆◎◎◎◎)

解答・解説

【中高共通】

【1】1　ウ　　2　ア　　3　ア　　4　エ
〈解説〉スクリプトは非公開である。短めの会話とそれに関する質問が放送され，それに対する答えとなる選択肢を選ぶ問題である。会話と質問は1回しか放送されないため，前もって選択肢に目を通しておき，会話の大まかなトピックなどを予想しておくとよいだろう。

【2】1　イ　　2　ウ　　3　イ　　4　ア
〈解説〉スクリプトは非公開である。長めのパッセージが放送され，それに関する質問に対する答えとなる選択肢を選ぶ問題である。英文は1回しか放送されないが，この設問では質問も事前に与えられているため，聞き取るポイントを事前に決めておくとよいだろう。質問から判断すると，パッセージの内容はEUにおけるサマータイムのデメリットについてであると思われる。

38

【3】1 ウ 　2 エ 　3 イ 　4 ア

〈解説〉スクリプトは非公開である。問題形式は設問【2】と全く同じであるが，設問【2】に比べて配点が高くなっているため，パッセージがより難しい，または長いものと推測される。質問から判断すると，ジェームズ氏がシェフとして成功するまでの過程が述べられていると思われる。

【中学校】

【1】1 イ 　2 ア 　3 イ 　4 ウ 　5 ア 　6 エ 　7 エ 　8 ア

〈解説〉1 「ベティの仕事はコピーやデータ入力などの事務的な仕事がほとんどであった」。clericalは「事務的な」の意味である。　2 「市長は，その地区のホームレスの支援に尽力してきた証として，その男性を善良な市民賞で表彰した」。testamentは「証」の意味である。　3 「グリーグは作法と自制心を養う学校に通っている」。cultivateは「養う，育てる」の意味である。　4 「その大事故によって，2車線が2時間以上も封鎖となり，その高速道路に深刻な渋滞が引き起こされた」。congestionは「渋滞」の意味である。　5 「多くの生徒が，その本はところどころ難しすぎて理解できないところがあると苦情を言ったので，教師はより易しい言葉を使って該当箇所を言い換えるようにした」。paraphraseは「言い換える」の意味である。　6 「ブロア通りで昨晩火事が起き，約8時間かかったが，最終的に，消防隊はなんとか鎮火することができた」。blazeは「炎」の意味である。　7 「リチャードは仕事で非常に忙しいが，夕方に子どもたちとの時間を確保するようにしている」。set asideは「確保する，取っておく」の意味である。8 「グレンは，コストカットの一環として突然解雇された時，会社に対する自分の長年の貢献が何にもならなかったと気がついた」。count forは「価値がある，ものを言う」。

【2】1　ア　　2　エ　　3　ウ　　4　ウ　　5　エ

〈解説〉1　空欄の前後のBの発話に着目する。空欄の前では「ケン，いつも僕に助けを求めるよね」と言っており，空欄の後では「わかったよ。まかせて。素敵なレストランを探すよ」と言っている。「他のだれを頼ればいいの」を意味するアが正解。　2　空欄の前後のAとBの発話に着目する。空欄の前でBは「どうぞ入って」と言っており，空欄の後でAは「わぁ。ここからすごく良い景色が見えるね」と言っている。「案内するよ」を意味するエが正解。　3　空欄の前後のAの発話に着目する。空欄の前では「夏休みのボランティアはかけがえのない経験だったよ」と言っており，空欄の後では「いいとも。座って話をしよう」と言っている。「それはすごいね。もっと教えてよ」を意味するウが正解。　4　空欄の前後のAとBの発話に着目する。空欄の前でBは「次の月曜だよ」と言っており，空欄の後でAは「うん。いま本当にオーバーワークなんだ」と言っている。「延期が必要かな」を意味するウが正解。　5　空欄の前後のAとBの発話に着目する。空欄の前でAは「日曜に夕食を食べる時間はあるかな」と聞いており，空欄の後でBは「ごめん」と言っている。「その時までに準備が終わっていないかもしれない」を意味するエが正解

【3】1　エ　　2　イ　　3　エ　　4　ウ　　5　ア

〈解説〉1　該当箇所はten minutes laterではなくin ten minutesが正しい。未来のことを表現する際，具体的な時間を示すときにlaterは使用しない。2　「車を運転しているとき，警察に止められた」の意。接続詞whileが「〜する間に」という「同時性」を表しているので，while I was drivingとなる。主節と主語が一致しているので，通常はwhile drivingと表せるが，本問では，Iが下線部に含まれていないので不可。　3　仮定法過去完了の文章。「もし機械の電源を入れる前に立ち止まって取扱説明書を読んでいたら，こんなことは起こらなかったに違いない」なので，wouldn't have happenedとなる。　4　該当箇所はa receiverではなくthe receiverが正しい。彼女の電話の受話器であることが特定されている。

5　rise public awarenessではなくraise public awareness「人々の意識を高める」が正しい。riseは主語が「上がる」を意味する自動詞である。

【4】1　our children　　2　B　　3　エ　　4　イ
〈解説〉1　下線部を含んだ文は「私たちは再び，私たちが人生と財産を捧げてきた人たちを激しく批判する」の意である。この文を含んだ第3パラグラフの2文目にあるように，怒りをぶつける対象は子どもたちである。　2　まず，空欄①は，その空欄前後に着目すると，「怒りは再発する問題である。私たちはそれを好まないかもしれないが，それを無視することはできない」とある。従って，「普通の風邪のような」を意味するイが適切である。次に，空欄②は，その前後に着目すると，「怒りは人生の事実であって，それを認めて備えておくべきである」とある。従って，「台風のような」を意味するアが正解である。この時点で正答選択肢は選べるが，最後に，空欄③は，その前後に着目すると，「平和な家庭は，人間の本性が突然慈悲深く変化することに依拠しているわけではない」とある。従って，「望まれる平和な世界のように」を意味するウが正解である。　3　下線部は，「下記のエピソード」の意味であり，下線部の直後に着目すればよい。「どのように母がジェーンを侮辱したり辱めたりすることをせずに怒りをぶつけつつ，協力を促したか」の意であり，この内容をまとめているのはエである。　4　与えられた文の空欄の前までは「文章によると，親が子どもに対して全く怒らないと，子どもは」の意である。第9パラグラフの2文目に対応する記述がある。

【5】1　ウ　　2　ウ　　3　エ
〈解説〉1　下線部は，「彼らは大学でこのことを教えてくれなかった」の意である。この文のTheyとthisが指す内容を考えればよい。第1パラグラフの主に2〜3文目にあるように，経験の浅い教師に対して著者を含む生徒たちが手荒いことをしたと述べられていることを踏まえると，「大学時代に生徒たちの素行不良について聞かされなかった」の意で

あるウが正解。　2　下線部は,「私が言わなければいけなかったことに価値があった」の意である。下線の直前の文の後半に着目すると,「セレナ先生はレポートにあるアイデアを認め,考える人としての自信を与えてくれた」とある。従って,「私のレポートは興味深いアイデアであると賞賛された」を意味するウが正解。　3　第4パラグラフの5〜6文目に対応する記述がある。2の解説で述べたところと重複するが,教師は生徒のアイデアを認め賞賛することが重要であると述べられている。

【6】1　イ　　2　ウ　　3　ウ　　4　エ
〈解説〉1　第1パラグラフの最後の文と第2パラグラフの1文目に対応する記述がある。インターネットは生活の一部になっており,インターネットを通じて様々な情報が入手できるようになっている。　2　設問文にある記述は第2パラグラフの3文目にある。対応する記述はその後の4文目と5文目の後半にある。商品の購入や金融取引が24時間できるようになっていると述べられている。　3　第3パラグラフの4〜5文目に対応する記述がある。まず,家族や同僚に連絡をして,飛行機の予約をキャンセルし,新しい飛行機などの予約をすると述べられている。　4　第4パラグラフの最後の文に対応する記述がある。インターネットは,今までであれば挑戦しなかったかもしれない新しいことに挑戦するよう,促してくれると述べられている。

【7】1　エ　　2　イ　　3　ア　　4　ウ
〈解説〉現行の学習指導要領では,コミュニケーション能力の育成が一層強調され,文法事項については,実際のコミュニケーションの場で活用できるような指導をすることが求められている。　(1)「関連のある文法事項」に着目するとよい。1つ1つ文法事項を独立して扱うのではなく,既習の文法事項などを関連づけた効果的な指導が求められている。　(2)「コミュニケーションの目的を達成する上で」に着目するとよい。文法事項を独立して扱うのではなく,コミュニケーションを行

う上で当該文法事項の必要性や有用性に気づかせる必要がある。

(3)「繰り返し使用することで当該文法事項の」に着目するとよい。言語活動を通じて，文法事項の学習を促していくことが求められているため，ここには文法事項の特徴に関する語が入ることがわかる。

(4)「日本語との違いに留意して」に着目するとよい。英語と日本語の類似性および相違性を踏まえ，また「修飾関係」と並列関係にあるものを考えればよい。

【8】 Before reading passages, teachers can casually introduce the topics and key information to students and ask them what they know about them. It is necessary to give students lots of chances to read stories from beginning to the end, but they don't have to translate all the vocabulary words one by one. Also, it is important to focus on conjunctions and finding key words to get the information that they need. Then, students can exchange information by doing pair-work or group-work. This helps students understand stories more deeply. In addition, arranging pictures is a very effective task to help students understand a story's timeline. (104 words)

〈解説〉「概要を捉える」というのは，まとまりのある文章を一通り読み，一語一語や一文一文などの局所的な理解に固執するのではなく，文章全体の大まかな内容を捉えることである。この点は解答例の2文目後半にも記述されているように，できれば内容に含められるとよいだろう。また，具体的な指導方法についても考えを書くことが求められているため，解答例にあるような背景知識の確認，ペアワークやグループワークの導入，または視覚情報による補助に加え，英文を読んで「概要を捉える」必要感のある目的設定なども考えられるだろう。あまり多くの方法を思いつかなかったとしても，生徒に「概要を捉える」ための手立てを述べられるようにしたい。

【9】1

2　Great job with your details! Practicing every day is hard, but I can see this contest was a very good memory. Try using words like "and" and "but" to connect sentences. I also want to know how you chose the song which that you sang. I'm looking forward to reading more of your work. (54 words)

3　・生徒と直接的な対話によって書きたい内容を引き出しながら，書く活動への抵抗感を減らしたり少しずつでもその内容を表現できるように支援していく。　　・それぞれの英作文をグループ内で読み合うことで得られる気付きを自分の英作文の中に活かせるように支援していく。

〈解説〉「書くこと」について，具体的な指導場面を踏まえて生徒へのフィードバックの方法を説明することが求められている。　1　英作文の誤りを修正することが求められているため，生徒の英作文のスペリングや文法的なミスについて指摘をすればよい。その際，解答例にもあるように，生徒が前向きに捉えられるような形で指摘をしたい。2　指定されている単元のゴールを踏まえて，生徒へのコメントを英語で書くことが求められている。単元のゴールにある「事実や自分の考え，気持などを整理し，これまでに学んだ表現を用いてまとまりのある英文を書く」が達成できるようなコメントを書くとよいだろう。特に，「自分の考え，気持などを整理」と「まとまりのある英文」という点に課題があるので，どこを修正すればよいのかが具体的にわか

るように書きたい。本問も1と同様に，生徒が前向きに捉えられるようにするため，書かれている内容や，既に達成されている点については褒めるなどの工夫をしたい。なお，公式解答の4文目のthe song which that you sangには，関係代名詞が重複している。the song that you sangの誤りと思われる。　3　英作文の返却後にクラス全体に対して行う具体的な指導について，日本語で書くことが求められている。1および2で記入した修正やコメントを踏まえて考えていくとやりやすいかもしれない。そもそもトピックが中学校の思い出であることから，中学校3年生であることが想定される。しかし，生徒によっては基本的なスペルや文法的なミスがあり，また，「まとまりのある英文」を書くことに課題がある生徒がいる可能性が示されているため，スモールステップで少しずつでも英作文を改善していけるような働きかけを書けばよいだろう。

【10】中学校は小学校と高校をつなぐ校種であることから，次のようなことに留意することでより一層の活動の充実が図られると考える。まず，小学校での学びを把握し，音声を中心とした言語活動からスタートさせることである。その上で，音声から文字，そして読む活動，書く活動へとつなげていく。次に高校では統合的な言語活動が求められているため，聞いて理解するだけで終わらせず，聞いた内容について話したり，書いたりする活動へつなげていくことが大切である。

〈解説〉見方・考え方を働かせる必要のある言語活動をキーワードとして，小学校および高校と連携できるような中学校の指導について説明することが求められている。小学校の外国語活動および外国語科は「聞くこと」および「話すこと」による音声中心の学習であり，「読むこと」および「書くこと」の文字指導については慣れ親しみに留まっていることを踏まえ，音声言語から文字言語への円滑な接続を支援することが重要である。また，高校においては，高等学校学習指導要領に「五つの領域別の言語活動及び複数の領域を結び付けた統合的な言語活動を通して」とあるように，複数領域を統合した活動が求められ

ている。従って，中学校の後半においては，「聞くこと」または「読むこと」を通して理解したことについて，「話すこと[やり取り]」，「話すこと[発表]」または「書くこと」で自分の考えなどを表現する言語活動も必要になる。

【高等学校】

【1】1　記号…(ア)　修正…appreciate it　　2　記号…(ウ)　修正…enjoy running　　3　記号…(イ)　修正…knows　　4　記号…(ア)　修正…quit　5　記号…(イ)　修正…is

〈解説〉1　appreciateは「(～を)感謝する，正しく評価する」の意味の他動詞である。appreciate it if～で「～してもらえるとありがたい」の意になる。　2　enjoyの目的語となる動詞は動名詞のみである。　3　文の構造がやや複雑であるが，whoから始まる関係代名詞節がwho has tried to study for an exam, write a report or read a bookまでであり，study for an exam, write a report or read a bookがtriedの目的語のto不定詞であることがわかれば，この文の動詞となるknowは主語がAnyoneであるために三単現のsが必要になることがわかる。　4　「(仕事など)を辞める」場合，quitは他動詞として目的語を取る形で使うことができる。そのためfromは不要である。　5　「every one of us」は「私たち1人1人」の意であり単数であることから，動詞はisにする必要がある。

【2】(1)　エ　　(2)　オ　　(3)　イ　　(4)　カ　　(5)　キ

〈解説〉(1)　空欄の前後に着目する。空欄前では，与えられた課題について生徒がどのように，どのくらい時間をかけ，そしてできているかをAIは観察することができると述べられている。また，空欄後では，このようなリアルタイムなフィードバックは難しいと述べられていることから，「もし生徒が苦戦していればシステムが助けることができ，一方で，生徒がうまくいっていれば，システムがもっと難しい課題を課すことで，挑戦的な活動を続けさせることができる」を意味するエが正解。　(2)　空欄の前後に着目する。空欄前では，スタンフォード

大学の研究者が，Inquireと名付けたいわゆるインテリジェント・テキストブック(学習者の質問に答える機能を備えたデジタル教科書)の原型を開発し，テストを行っていることが述べられている。また，空欄後では，その双方向的なテキストはタッチやクリックでキーワードの意味が表示され，生徒は読解の間にマーカーを引いたり注記を書いたりできると述べられている。従って，「それ(Inquire)は，生徒がどのように双方向的にやりとりしているかに注意することで，生徒の読解中の集中や注意を観察することができるiPad用のアプリである」を意味するオが正解である。　(3)　空欄の直後に着目すると，そのテストは一連の標準的な問題から開始されるが，生徒がどのように問題に解答したかに基づいて，生徒の正確な能力や弱みをすぐに特定し，より難しい問題や簡単な問題を選択すると述べられており，あるテストの具体的な内容について述べられている。従って，「例えば，Duolingoという言語学習の会社は，AIと機械学習を用いて，大学，企業そして政府機関向けの英語熟達度テストの作成と採点を行っている」を意味するイが正解。　(4)　空欄の直前に着目すると，ゲームの中には，大人と子どもが現実のシナリオに基づいたキャラクターとしてロールプレイをするものもあると述べられており，このゲームについての説明として，「これらのゲームは，子どもたちが適切な学年のレベルで読解ができるかどうかを効率的に判断し，できていない場合は，親や教師がそれを改善させるのを支援する」を意味するカが正解である。

(5)　空欄の直前に着目すると，これらのチャットボットは科目の内容や構成に関する質問に答えることができると述べられており，このチャットボットについての説明が続くことが予想できる。従って，「このことは，学生たちがモチベーションや意欲を維持したまま，自身の学習状況を把握することに役立つ」を意味するキが正解である

【3】1　ア　　2　ウ　　3　ウ　　4　エ　　5　ア
〈解説〉1　対応する記述は第2パラグラフの1文目にある。ある曲が頭の中で繰り返し再生されるような現象がearwormと呼ばれる理由を求め

られているので，due to以下に着目すればよい。　2　対応する記述は第5パラグラフの2文目にある。earwormを引き起こすような曲の特徴として正しいものを選ぶことが求められている。直接的な記述はないが，第3パラグラフの2文目にもearwormが生じる要因が述べられている。　3　第7パラグラフの2文目に対応する記述がある。　4　第9パラグラフの1文目に着目すると，earwormを経験した3分の2の人はearwormを中立的または肯定的に捉えていると述べられている。空欄の前後はこの部分の言い換えになっており，「私たちの3分の2はearwormを不快に思っていないかもしれないが」という意味になる。5　第11パラグラフの最後から1〜2文目に着目すると，アはwhile singing the songが不適切であることがわかる。なお，イは第12パラグラフの1文目，ウは第11パラグラフの3〜4文目に，そしてエは同パラグラフ2文目に対応する記述がある。

【4】1　The voluntary, unnecessary delay of an important task, despite knowing you'll be worse off for doing so.　2　イ　3　They should have self-compassion.　4　ウ　5　Because once you are interrupted, it is much harder to resume the task you finally started.　6　Some teachers procrastinate until midnight. For example, they make handouts or mark tests late at night.

〈解説〉1　第4パラグラフの最後の文に対応する記述があるので，それを抜き出せばよい。後半部分のdefines procrastination this wayに着目する。2　第7パラグラフの2文目に対応する記述がある。それ以外の選択肢についても類似した記述はあるが，例えば，アのbecause they never take medical checkupsなどのように部分的に誤りがある。　3　第8パラグラフの3〜5文目に着目すると，先延ばしをする人は自分自身に厳しく，先延ばしとself-compassionの低さには関連性があるため，優しさと理解をもって自分自身に接する必要があると述べられている。ここを踏まえて書けばよい。　4　第10パラグラフの1〜3文目に着目する。「木を見て森を見ず」の人は先延ばしをする人とは逆であると述べら

れていることを踏まえ，先延ばしをしてしまう人の特徴を選べばよい。
なお，イがやや紛らわしいが，先延ばしと怠け癖とは異なるというこ
とが，第3パラグラフの3文目に述べられている。　5　第11パラグラ
フの4文目に対応する記述があるので，そこを抜き出して書けばよい。
6　本文の内容を踏まえて，先延ばしの例を英語で答える問題である。
設問1および設問4と関連している問題である。先延ばしは単なる怠け
癖とは異なり，先延ばしにすることで状況が悪くなることはわかって
いながらも，重要な仕事を遅れさせてしまうことである。そして，仕
事の大きさに圧倒されて動けなくなってしまうと述べられている。こ
れらの点を踏まえて具体例を考えればよい。

【5】 The most important reason you should become an English teacher is that
you can change students' lives, making them into global citizens. Firstly, as an
English teacher, by creating appropriate classroom settings, you can give
students opportunities to develop their communication skills and learn to
respect different ideas. Specifically, you can give them opportunities for
opinion exchange and other interaction, both inside and outside the classroom.
Also, you can help them cultivate a willingness to communicate proactively
and autonomously, deepening their understanding of the underlying culture of
English. Consequently, students may choose to study or work abroad, or
engage in international affairs while working in Japan. Their way of living
and thinking will be transformed and globalized, thanks to you. (120 Words)

〈解説〉友人に対し，英語の教員になるように勧めるという状況設定であ
　　る。具体的な根拠や例を含めて，英語の教員を勧める最大の理由を
　　120語程度で説明する。基本的なパラグラフ構造として，勧める理由
　　をトピックセンテンスとして書き，その根拠を具体的な例を挙げて書
　　き，最後に結論を書くといった構成が書きやすいと思われる。トピッ
　　クセンテンスとなる理由さえ決まれば，その理由について具体例を挙
　　げつつ丁寧に説明すればよい。

【6】1　A　見方・考え方　　B　技能　　C　社会的な話題
D　配慮　　E　主体的　　2「授業を実際のコミュニケーションの場
面とする」目的は，生徒が英語でコミュニケーションを行う目的や場
面，状況などを設定した言語活動を授業に取り入れ，生徒のコミュニ
ケーションを図る資質・能力を育成することである。そのために，教
師は，授業を英語で行い，生徒が英語に触れる機会を増やし，英語に
よる言語活動を行うことを授業の中心にしなければならない。実際の
授業においては，単に英語と日本語を置き換えるような指導とならな
いよう，生徒が意味のある文脈でのコミュニケーションを通して，学
習する言語材料に繰り返し触れることができるようにしなければなら
ない。工夫点としては，実際の言語の使用場面や言語の働きに配慮し
た題材を取り上げること，また，言語活動の目的に応じて，ペア・ワ
ークやグループワークなどの様々な学習形態を活用していくことであ
る。

〈解説〉1　まず，空欄Aは全体の目標について書かれており，B〜Eは
「知識及び技能」，「思考力，判断力，表現力等」そして「学びに向か
う力，人間性等」のそれぞれに対応する目標が書かれていることに着
目する。Aは小学校および中学校とも共通するところであり，「見方・
考え方」が正解である。次に，Bは「知識及び技能」に関する目標で
あることから，「技能」が正解である。また，Cは「思考力，判断力，
表現力等」に関する目標であるが，小学校で「身近な話題」と「日常
的な話題」，中学校で「日常的な話題や社会的な話題」を扱ったこと
を踏まえ，高校でも中学校に引き続き「日常的な話題や社会的な話題」
を扱うことが求められている。なお，扱う話題は中学校と同じでも，
高校ではより多面的または多角的に扱うことが求められている。最後
に，DとEは「学びに向かう力，人間性等」に関わる目標であり，これ
らはどちらも小学校および中学校と共通するところである。なお，E
の後にある「自律的」は高校になって新たに加わるものであることも
押さえておくとよいだろう。　2　高等学校学習指導要領解説外国語
編・英語編の「指導計画作成上の配慮事項」において，「生徒が英語

に触れる機会を充実させるとともに，授業を実際のコミュニケーショ
ンの場面とするため，授業は英語で行うことを基本とする。その際，
生徒の理解の程度に応じた英語を用いるようにすること」と示されて
いる。このことを踏まえ，生徒が英語でコミュニケーションをする機
会を増やし，それを授業の中心とすること，生徒の理解状況を踏まえ
る必要があること，より実際のコミュニケーションに近い場面を作る
ための工夫などを書くとよいだろう。

2023年度　　実施問題

【中高共通】

【1】これから，会話と質問が4つ放送されます。質問に対する答えとして最も適切なものをア～エの中から一つずつ選び，その記号を書きなさい。なお，会話と質問は一度だけ放送されます。

1

ア　March 3rd.
イ　March 10th.
ウ　April 3rd.
エ　April 10th.

2

ア　She said the price was increasing.
イ　She said the product was sold out.
ウ　She said the product was supposed to be released.
エ　She said there was already an official announcement.

3

ア　The baby looks after his father.
イ　The baby stops crying to eat.
ウ　The father is a babysitting expert.
エ　The mother is on childcare leave.

4

ア　Enter the museum.
イ　Join a big meeting.
ウ　See a famous painting.
エ　Take a photograph.

(☆☆☆◎◎◎)

【2】これから，まとまりのある英文が放送されます。その内容についての次の質問に対する答えとして最も適切なものをア～エの中から一つずつ選び，その記号を書きなさい。なお，英文は一度だけ放送されます。

1　What was a significant cause of the low national English test scores at the age of 11?

　　ア　Family background.

　　イ　Poor language skills in early childhood.

　　ウ　Struggling with mathematics.

　　エ　The quality of nursery workers.

2　What is most likely to happen later for young children who have low language abilities?

　　ア　They will be able to do math well.

　　イ　They will express their feelings easily.

　　ウ　They will need to go to secondary school again.

　　エ　They will need to take the national test again.

3　What is important to improve this situation?

　　ア　To employ a quality teacher at each nursery.

　　イ　To estimate children's abilities more accurately.

　　ウ　To give experiences by communicating with adults.

　　エ　To reset the expected standards in national tests.

4　What is this passage mainly about?

　　ア　Effects of early language skills on academic success.

　　イ　Effects of mathematics competency on English ability.

　　ウ　Poor early language skills as the cause of poverty.

　　エ　The necessity to reform national tests in English.

(☆☆☆◎◎◎)

【3】これから，まとまりのある英文が放送されます。その内容についての次の質問に対する答えとして最も適切なものをア〜エの中から一つずつ選び，その記号を書きなさい。なお，英文は一度だけ放送されます。

1　Why are interpreters important even in sports?

　　ア　Because audiences are from various countries.

　　イ　Because coaches should be invited from abroad.

　　ウ　Because players need to communicate by themselves.

　　エ　Because teams are made up of many nationalities.

2　When did Mr. Sakai decide to be an interpreter?

　　ア　When he failed to be a professional player.

　　イ　When he graduated from university.

　　ウ　When he joined Avispa Fukuoka.

　　エ　When he started playing soccer.

3　What has Mr. Sakai learned from his career?

　　ア　The older interpreters become, the harder it is for them to learn language.

　　イ　The older players become, the better they play a certain sport.

　　ウ　The more experience interpreters have, the more useful they become.

　　エ　The more experience players have, the better they can communicate.

4　What does Mr. Sakai think of sports interpreters?

　　ア　They need a cooperative attitude with people around them.

　　イ　They need a license from an international authority.

　　ウ　They need detailed knowledge of multiple languages.

　　エ　They need fulfilling experiences as professional athletes.

(☆☆☆◎◎◎)

54

【中学校】

【1】次の1〜8の英文の(　　)にあてはまる最も適切な英語を、それぞれ
ア〜エから一つずつ選び、その記号を書きなさい。

1　Ken's parents often told him that he could (　　) whatever he wanted
through hard work.

　　ア　offend　　イ　appeal　　ウ　accomplish　　エ　indicate

2　A bear suddenly ran into the middle of the road. The driver of the truck
(　　) to avoid it and as a result crashed into a tree. Luckily, the driver was
not hurt.

　　ア　grazed　　イ　scanned　　ウ　lodged　　エ　swerved

3　After finishing high school, Peter plans to go to college in order to get a
(　　) in economics.

　　ア　territory　　イ　committee　　ウ　degree　　エ　condition

4　The company places a great emphasis on (　　). Even if employees were
only a minute late, they would still have to meet the chief and explain why.

　　ア　complexity　　イ　extremity　　ウ　immortality
　　エ　punctuality

5　The politician solved the (　　) problem in a short time.

　　ア　intricate　　イ　introvert　　ウ　frisky　　エ　sedate

6　The police officer made Barry pay a (　　) for driving twenty kilometers
over the speed limit.

　　ア　tax　　イ　fine　　ウ　fee　　エ　fare

7　Richard could not remember what size envelope his wife wanted, so he
bought a box of (　　) ones to be on the safe side.

　　ア　assorted　　イ　scripted　　ウ　dedicated　　エ　crooked

8　The only (　　) to the proposal for a new library is that it would be
expensive to implement.

　　ア　withdrawal　　イ　backlash　　ウ　downtrend　　エ　drawback

(☆☆☆◎◎◎)

【2】次の1〜5の会話文中の(　　)にあてはまる最も適切な英語を，それ
ぞれア〜エから一つずつ選び，その記号を書きなさい。

1　*A:*　Hi, Bob. How are you?

　　B:　Not so well, I'm afraid.

　　A:　Really? (　　)

　　B:　I've got a slight cold.

　　　ア　How long have you been suffering?

　　　イ　Where did you catch it?

　　　ウ　What's the matter?

　　　エ　Why are you afraid?

2　*A:*　Have you cleaned our living room yet?

　　B:　Sorry, the TV is too loud. (　　)

　　A:　Did you clean up our living room?

　　　ア　No, I haven't.

　　　イ　Now, what did you say?

　　　ウ　Now, what do you mean?

　　　エ　Yes, an hour ago.

3　*A:*　How do you like my collection of toy cars?

　　B:　Very much. But I didn't know you collected toy cars.

　　A:　Sure, I've been collecting them since I was in junior high school.

　　B:　(　　)

　　　ア　Why don't you start to collect toy cars again?

　　　イ　Oh, I see. You've stopped collecting them now.

　　　ウ　You should have collected them earlier, when you were in high
　　　　　school.

　　　エ　Oh, for several years! What made you start?

4　*A:*　Do you have all your suitcases with you?

　　B:　No, I have some more.

　　A:　(　　)

　　B:　I left the other three at the baggage room.

ア　Why do you still have them with you?

イ　Where are the rest?

ウ　Can I help you find the baggage room?

エ　You should leave this one, too, shouldn't you?

5　*A:*　My wife was ill last Tuesday, so I took a day off to look after her.

　　B:　(　　)

　　A:　Well, I never knew cooking was so difficult!

ア　I'm sorry to hear that. And how did you manage?

イ　Well, how did she become ill?

ウ　Really? Did you go to see her in the hospital?

エ　That's too bad. Did you have to do any shopping?

(☆☆☆○○○)

【3】次の1～5の各文にある下線部ア～エには，英語の文法上または表現上適切ではない語句があります。適切ではない語句をそれぞれア～エから一つずつ選び，その記号を書きなさい。

1　I ｱwould like to work for a company ｲwhich ｳthe use of French ｴis necessary.

2　ｱThe injured student ｲwas left ｳthe hospital ｴafter five days.

3　I was ｱdeep in conversation with my friend, but ｲkeeping an eye on my son, ｳwho I noticed was so ｴeagerly to play on a swing.

4　Teachers' approaches to ｱteach are ｲvery different in spite of their ｳshared opinions in a great variety of ｴissues.

5　I ｱreturned home and carefully ｲexplained my father what I had done, and tried to ｳmake an excuse for causing him to have ｴsuch a shock.

(☆☆☆☆○○○○)

【4】次の英文を読んで，空欄　A　〜　E　に入る発言として最も
適切なものを，それぞれ以下の選択肢より選び，その記号を書きなさ
い。ただし，同じ記号を二度以上用いてはならない。

> 【John Smith is an elementary school student. His mother is called to
> school by his homeroom teacher, Mrs. Williams because of John's bad
> behavior.】
>
> John stood at the front door and yelled, "　A　! Don't
> believe anything she tells you."
>
> John's mother got into the car, and drove to school. She was afraid of
> what Mrs. Williams would tell her.
>
> She wanted to believe John when he told her he was getting all A's or
> was elected class president. Though, she knew it couldn't be true. She
> knew her son. And she knew Mrs. Williams wouldn't call her on the
> phone if everything were really as wonderful as John said it was. Still,
> she hoped.
>
> She opened the door to John's classroom. No one was there. "Hello?"
> she called out timidly.
>
> She looked around. There was a bulletin board covered with A
> papers. She looked from one paper to another and hoped that she'd see
> one with John's name on it. She didn't.
>
> In the back corner of the room she saw a chart that listed the name of
> every student in the class. Next to each name was a row of gold stars.
> Next to "John Smith," there were no stars.
>
> "Mrs. Smith?"
>
> Surprised, she turned around to see Mrs. Williams.
>
> "　B　," she said, then smiled.
>
> Mrs. Williams didn't smile.
>
> Mrs. Smith sat at a chair next to the teacher's desk and bravely
> listened as Mrs. Williams told her about John. There was nothing Mrs.

Williams said that she didn't already know. Still, it hurt to hear it.

"Deep down, he really is a good boy," she tried to tell John's teacher.

" [C] ," said Mrs. Williams. "However, I have twenty-eight other children in my class, and I can't spend all my time trying to help John. He has to decide whether he wants to be a part of the class or not. And if he doesn't want to be a part of the class, then he shouldn't be here."

"What can I do?" asked John's mother.

"The school has just hired a counselor," said Mrs. Williams. "I'd like your permission for John to begin seeing her once a week. John has a very serious behavior problem. If he doesn't show improvement soon, more serious measures will have to be taken."

" [D] ," said John's mother.

"Well, let's go meet the counselor," said Mrs. Williams. She led John's mother down the halls to the counselor's office. The door was open, but no one was there.

John's mother stepped into the room. Boxes were everywhere. There was hardly room for John's mother and teacher to stand.

"She's just moving in," Mrs. Williams explained. "I'm sure she'll have it cleaned up by tomorrow."

Suddenly there was a loud grunt and a young woman entered the room. "Oh, hello," she said.

She was a lot younger than either Mrs. Williams or Mrs. Smith.

"I'm Carla Davis," she said, and smiled.

"She needs to sign the form so that you can start seeing her son," said Mrs. Williams.

Miss Davis looked hopelessly around her office.

"They're around here somewhere... Found them!" said the counselor, holding up the forms.

John's mother looked around the messy office, then at the young woman. She shrugged her shoulders and signed her name.

Miss Davis took the form from her. "Oh! You're John Smith's mother!"

Mrs. Smith nodded.

"You would not believe all the horror stories I've heard about John Smith," said the new counselor.

"Deep down, he really is..." John's mother started to say.

"   E   ," the counselor interrupted. "He sounds charming, just delightful."

ア　Oh, you scared me

イ　I can't wait to meet him

ウ　Mrs. Williams is a liar

エ　I'm afraid I won't

オ　Deep down, he really is a good boy

カ　I'm sure he has a lot of good qualities

(☆☆☆◎◎◎)

【5】次の英文は，ある海外留学誌の記事です。これを読んで，以下の1～3の（　）に入れるのに最も適切なものを，それぞれ一つずつ選び，その記号を書きなさい。

Flowers and Their Hidden Meanings

Giving flowers is definitely a nice thing to do. However, when you are in a foreign country, you should be aware of cultural differences.

Emma, who was at our school in Japan for four-week language program, was nervous at first because there were no students from Australia, her home country. But she soon made many friends and was having a great time inside and outside the classroom. One day she heard that her Japanese teacher, Mr. Chida, was in the hospital after falling down some stairs at the station. She was really surprised and upset, and wanted to see him as soon as possible. Emma decided to go to the hospital with her classmates and brought a red begonia in a flower pot to make her teacher happy. When they entered the hospital room, he welcomed them with a big smile. However, his expression suddenly changed when Emma gave the red flower to him. Emma was a little puzzled, but she didn't ask the reason because she didn't want to trouble him.

Later, in her elementary Japanese and with the help of a dictionary, Emma told me about her visit to the hospital, and how her teacher's expression changed when she gave him the begonia. Emma said, "It's my favorite flower because red is the color of passion. I thought my teacher, who was always passionate about teaching, would surely love it, too."

Unfortunately, flowers growing in a pot are something we shouldn't take to a hospital in Japan. This is because a plant in a pot has roots, and so it cannot be moved easily. In Japanese culture some people associate these facts with remaining in the hospital. Soon after Emma heard the hidden meaning of the potted begonia, she visited Mr. Chida again to apologize.

1 According to the story, Emma's feelings changed in the following order: (   ).

ア nervous → confused → happy   → shocked   → sorry
イ nervous → happy   → shocked → confused → sorry
ウ nervous → happy   → sorry   → shocked   → confused
エ nervous → shocked → happy   → sorry   → confused

2 The gift Emma chose was not appropriate in Japan because it may imply (   ).

ア a long stay
イ congratulations
ウ growing anger
エ passion for living

3 From this story, you learned that Emma (   ).

ア chose a begonia for her teacher because she learned the meanings of several flowers in her class

イ　not only practiced her Japanese but also learned about Japanese culture because of a begonia

ウ　visited the hospital with her teaching assistant to see her teacher and enjoyed chatting

エ　was given an explanation about the begonia by Mr. Chida and learned its hidden meaning

(☆☆☆◎◎)

【6】次の英文を読んで，以下の1～4の空欄の内容として最も適切なものを，一つずつ選び，その記号を書きなさい。

1　Wildfires, fires that spread quickly on mountains, sometimes extend to regions where humans live. There are typically two causes of wildfires. One is natural phenomena including lightning strikes or volcanic activity. Wildfires also occur when dry leaves rub against each other on extremely windy days. In addition, periods of intense heat called heat waves can heat up dead leaves, causing them to catch fire and lead to a wildfire. The other cause is human activity, and the incidence rate in this case is actually higher than the first source of wildfires. Along with fires set on purpose, wildfires can be caused by sparks from electric cables, grass cutters, or through carelessness with campfires or burning trash. However, whatever their cause, wildfires tend to spread in very warm and dry climates.

2　It is said that in a wildfire that happened in Australia in February, 2009, the damage greatly increased because many common causes of wildfires occurred at the same time. Among these causes were a record-breaking shortage of rainfall, a heat wave, unusual dryness, and strong winds. Furthermore, eucalyptus, a famous plant in Australia, burns extremely well, so it is also known as the "gasoline tree." If a fire spreads to the trees' bark, the fire is hard to put out. The big wildfire that happened in California in November, 2018, is also said to have occurred in conditions that made it easy for the fire to spread. In October, in that area, it is often rainy, but there was less rain than usual that year. The fire grew terribly quickly because a strong wind was blowing in spots where plants were dried out.

3 It is said that the damage from wildfires is increasing due to the effects of global warming. A national nonprofit organization of scientists in the USA insists that wildfires are increasing because of global warming, and the U.S. Forest Service has said that shortages of rainfall and dryness caused by global warming are a key problem. In fact, lots of wildfires have been reported around the world in recent years. The occurrence of extensive wildfires causes considerable increases in CO_2 and leads to a negative cycle. That is a problem, too.

4 While firefighting on the front lines, some regions have started to use drones. Even flying fire trucks may be used in the future. If that happens, it will be possible to safely send firefighters to the central area of a fire and transport fire victims from burning buildings to hospitals. Therefore, rescue teams around the world have been paying attention to this development.

5 Although it is said that there are not any preventive measures for wildfires that are very effective, in California, they spend a large amount of money to cut down trees in dangerous areas to prevent fires. They also have a campaign called "One Less Spark." They promote the following things; first, do not use electrical tools when fires can easily occur, second, extinguish campfires completely, third, do not park near high, dry grass, and so on.

6 Occasionally, wildfires destroy entire towns and kill lots of people. Once a fire occurs, it usually takes a long time to put it out. You should know wildfires are one of the most frightening disasters imaginable, even if you live in areas where wildfires don't usually occur.

1　In the article, it is started that one of the reasons wildfires occur is that
[　　]
ア　heat is produced when dry leaves rub against each other.

イ　heat waves can heat up the dead bodies of wild animals.

ウ　people collect dead leaves for campfires and put out the fire when they are done.

エ　people deliberately start fires using drones.

2　According to the article, the spread of wildfires in Australia and the USA was [　　]

ア　affected by high humidity and global warming.

イ　caused by several negative factors occurring at the same time.

ウ　predicted by local organizations, but the predictions were ignored.

エ　prevented because gasoline trees do not burn well.

3　In Paragraph ④ , the author most likely mentions a flying fire truck in order to give an example of [　　]

ア　how an advanced technology will be used at the sites of fires.

イ　how difficult putting out fires at their source is.

ウ　how many people were saved by firefighters from wildfires.

エ　how technology will provide a safer life.

4　Which of the following statements best summarizes the article? [　　]

ア　As California stated in "One Less Spark," you have to pay attention when making a fire in a dry area.

イ　There are various reasons wildfires happen and effective preventive measures for them and you should know them.

ウ　Wildfires have a variety of causes and are hard to prevent but everyone should take the issues seriously.

エ　You should know the best way to avoid wildfires is moving as far away from forests as possible.

(☆☆☆◎◎)

【7】 次の文は，中学校学習指導要領(平成29年3月)第2章「第9節　外国語」における「第2　各言語の目標及び内容等」の「1　目標」を一部抜粋したものです。

　アの事項において，下線部のような学習の充実を図るためには，どのような指導が考えられるか，あなたの考えを80語以上の英語で書きなさい。

　なお，最後に語数を記入すること。語数については，同じ語を2回使用した場合，2語と数えること(のべ数)とします。

> (3)　話すこと[やり取り]
> 　ア　関心のある事柄について，<u>簡単な語句や文を用いて即興で伝え合うことができるようにする。</u>

(☆☆☆☆◎◎◎)

【8】 次の表は，中学校学習指導要領(平成29年3月)第2章「第9節　外国語」における「第2　各言語の目標及び内容等」の「1　目標　(2)読むこと」の目標の実現を目指した第2学年の単元指導計画です。単元の目標に向けて，どのような工夫がされているか，工夫されている点を3つ挙げ，その理由を書きなさい。

　単元の目標

　ホームステイについての英文を読んで概要，要点を捉えるとともに，その内容を基に自分の意見や考えを伝え合ったり，意見文を書いたりすることができる。

時間	ねらい（■）・主な言語活動等（丸数字）	知	思	態	備考
1 2	■教科書本文から必要な情報を読み取り、読み取った内容を伝え合う。 ①教科書本文を読む際の一般的な読み方の学習として、以下のことを学習する。 　・本文を読む前に質問を読み（聞き）、予想する。 　・予想が合っているかどうか本文を読んで確認する。 ②本文の中で、比較表現がどのように使われているかを確認し、比較表現を使って本文を要約して話す。 ③自己目標を設定する。（第1時）				・第2時から第6時の学習の振り返りは適宜行わせる。 ・第1～5時までは記録に残す評価は行わな

3	■教科書本文の要点を捉え、書き手の最も伝えたいことを伝え合う。 ①教科書本文（第１、２時の続き）を読んで、書き手の最も伝えたいこと（要点）を捉える。 ・本文のタイトルから要点を予想する。 ・本文を読んで予想が合っていたかを確認する。また、要点だと判断した根拠となる英文を選ぶ。 ②第１〜２時の②と同じ活動に繰り返し取り組む。			い。ただし、ねらいに即して生徒の活動の状況を確実に見届けて指導に生かすことは毎時間必ず行う。活動させているだけにならないよう十分留意する。
4	■教科書本文の概要や要点を捉え、伝え合う。 ①教科書本文（第３時の続き）を読み、要点や概要を捉える。 ・概要を捉えるために、本文内容を表にまとめたり、マッピングを作成したりする。 ・要点を捉えるために、タイトルから予想したり、各段落にタイトルを付けて比較したりする。 ②内容を整理した表を使い、本文内容とその内容に対する自分の考えなどをペアで伝え合う。			
5	■教科書本文全体のテーマについて自分の考えなどを伝え合う。 ①教科書本文で比較表現がどのように使われているかを再度確認した上で、教科書本文全体のテーマに対する自分の考えを、本文に書いていることを引用しながら、複数のペアと伝え合う。 ②伝え合ったことを踏まえ、自分の考えを再構築し、その内容を書く。			
6	■意見文を読んで、概要や要点を捉え、自分の感想や考えを伝え合う。 ①教科書本文のテーマについて教師が書いた意見文を、第３、４時に学習した読み方で読み、概要や要点を捉える（ワークシート） ②書き手（教師）が一番伝えたいことに対する自分の考えなどを、引用しながら複数のペアと伝え合う。 ③自己目標の達成状況を振り返り、次の課題を明確にする。	○	○	

（☆☆☆○○○○○）

【9】次の文は，中学校学習指導要領(平成29年3月)第2章「第9節　外国語」における「第2　各言語の目標及び内容等」の「2　内容　〔思考力，判断力，表現力等〕　(3)言語活動及び言語の働きに関する事項①言語活動に関する事項」に示されている言語活動例の一部です。文中の(　　)にあてはまる語句として，最も適切なものを，それぞれ以下のア〜エから一つずつ選び，その記号を書きなさい。

(1)　「聞くこと」

[　日常的な話題について，(　　)口調で話される英語を聞いて，話し手の意向を正確に把握する活動。　]

ア　はっきりとした　　イ　流暢な　　ウ　自然な

エ　ゆっくりとした

(2)　「読むこと」

[　書かれた内容や文章の(　　)を考えながら黙読したり，その内容を表現するよう音読したりする活動。　]

ア　構成　　イ　概要　　ウ　要旨　　エ　量

(3)　「話すこと[発表]」

　関心のある事柄について，(　　)考えを整理して口頭で説明する活動。

ア　事前に　　イ　その場で　　ウ　慎重に　　エ　段階的に

(4)　「書くこと」

(　　)話題に関して聞いたり読んだりしたことから把握した内容に基づき，自分の考えや気持ち，その理由などを書く活動。

ア　文化的な　　イ　伝統的な　　ウ　身近な　　エ　社会的な

(☆☆☆◎◎◎)

【10】次の問に答えなさい。

　中学校学習指導要領(平成29年告示)では，実際に英語を使用して互いの考えや気持ちを伝え合うなどの言語活動を行う際，「小学校第3学年から第6学年までに扱った簡単な語句や基本的な表現などの学習内容を繰り返し指導し定着を図ること」としている。このことに関して，中学校第1学年の指導において，特に必要なことは何か。「小学校における指導」と「言語活動の充実を図ること」の二つの観点に触れながら，日本語で書きなさい。

(☆☆☆◎◎◎◎)

【高等学校】

【１】次の英文1〜5にはそれぞれ誤りや不適切なところがあります。修正が必要な箇所を(a)〜(c)から1つずつ選び，適切な形に直しなさい。

1　Amid (a)rapid accelerating depopulation, many municipalities are facing the problem (b)of how to stop the flight of the young generation (c)in order to sustain their community.

2　As overseas workers (a)have become more and more important, municipalities are coming up with ideas to (b)welcome to them as members of communities while (c)trying to stop young people from leaving their hometowns.

3　A local newspaper (a)visited some cities and towns that continue to seek (b)coexistent with foreign residents (c)even under the coronavirus pandemic.

4　Many youngsters (a)leave for their hometown entirely after they finish high school there, (b)leaving the mainstay fishing and seafood (c)processing industries chronically understaffed.

5　A local processor says no one (a)takes up the jobs as young people tend to avoid (b)to deal with the cold water in seafood processing; this is (c)where foreign technical trainees come in.

(☆☆☆☆◎◎◎◎)

【２】次の英文中の空所（　1　）〜（　5　）に入れるのに最も適切な文を，以下の＜選択肢＞(a)〜(g)から一つずつ選び，その記号を書きなさい。ただし，同じ記号を複数回用いてはならない。

"Many people simply don't know that creativity is a trainable skill," says Professor Gerard Puccio, who chairs the Department for Creativity and Change Leadership at SUNY Buffalo state College, US. And this assumption — that creativity is innate, rather than learnt — can be very off-putting whenever we are tasked with original thinking. （　1　）. Their evidence shows that, with practice, we can all learn to think more originally in our day-to-day lives, building greater innovation — and fulfilment — into whatever we choose to do.

Of the many creativity-training programmes out there, Puccio's Thinking Skills Model offers one of the best-tested attempts to teach workplace creativity. The program emphasizes the need to balance two types of thinking: convergent and divergent. Divergent thinking is the kind of free-wheeling idea generation that we often associate with the stereotypically scatty inventor; with novel — if sometimes hairbrained — solutions to problems. Convergent thinking, in contrast, concerns the selection and development of the best ideas to make sure that they have potential use. Both are essential. (2).

Martin Meinel recently tested a creativity-training program at Germany's Friedrich-Alexander Universität in Erlangen-Nürnberg, with very similar conclusions. "You can think of creativity as a muscle," he says — it needs constant practice to grow and to remain strong. With a little work, you may be surprised by your progress, says Meinel — even if you have never shown any great feats of creativity previously. "(3)".

This is all true, provided you start out with the right mindset. Ella Miron-Spektor, an associate professor of organizational behavior at the INSEAD business school in Fontainebleau, France, has shown that people's beliefs and attitudes to work will have a big impact on their creative development. Some people, she says, are "performance-oriented" : they are very concerned about how they compare to others. In general, they see their talents as fixed, and so prefer to stick to tasks that will consistently result in a success. A failure, for someone who is performance-oriented, would be deeply discouraging. "They tend to take feedback more personally," says Miron-Spektor. "They think that if you are unable to perform well, it's because of a lack of capability — and it's not something you can develop." (4). They are also more resilient in the face of failure, since they analyse what went wrong and use those lessons as an opportunity for growth.

To see whether these mindsets could influence people's creativity over time, Miron-Spektor examined the employees of a large electro-optical manufacturer in Israel. The management had introduced an innovation program, asking employees to submit any ideas that might improve processes or products. Each idea was evaluated by an expert panel, who rated the potential of the proposal and gave feedback to the original inventor.

Looking at seven years of data from the scheme, Miron-Spektor was able to plot each employee's "creativity trajectory" and compare them to the results of questionnaires measuring people's learning or performance orientations. Overall, she found that the learning-oriented employees showed greater improvement in the number and quality of ideas they contributed to the scheme. "(　5　)," says Miron-Spektor.

＜選択肢＞

(a)　In a world where business and society are both focused on innovation and change, creativity is the leading skill that people will need in order to adapt and succeed

(b)　It's not just that the people with the learning orientation are more creative, on average; we saw that they learned faster, so they were able to improve their creativity over time

(c)　Now, we have a common language around creativity that's user-friendly and practical and can be easily taught

(d)　Others are "learning-oriented" : they tend to be more focused on the opportunity to increase their skills and broaden their knowledge

(e)　The ones who were least creative at the beginning, they made the biggest gains

(f)　With a steady stream of research, however, psychologists like Puccio have identified the best ways to kickstart the learning process

(g)　Without the former, your ideas will be too mundane and boring; without the latter, they may be impractical

(☆☆☆◎◎)

【3】次の英文を読んで，1〜5の問いに対する答えとして最も適切なもの
をア〜エの中から1つずつ選び，その記号を書きなさい。

Identical twins may not be quite as identical as we thought; researchers in
Iceland have discovered genetic differences that begin at the early stages of
human embryo development. An embryo is an unborn human or animal in the
earliest stages of growth when its basic structures are being formed.

Scientists have long used the study of identical twins to examine the effects
of nature versus nurture, as the accepted view has been that, because they
share the same genes, any physical or behavioral differences between such
siblings must be determined by outside influences. However, this may not be
the case, suggested the new research, published Thursday in the journal
Nature Genetics.

Identical twins come from a single fertilized egg, or zygote, which is
formed when a female egg and a male sperm are joined. In any embryo, cell
division can lead to mutations, but this type of genetic difference had not
previously been measured between identical twins. Over the course of a four-
year study, a team of Icelandic researchers at DeCode Genetics, a Reykjavík
biopharmaceutical company, found that monozygotic, or identical, twins have
genetic differences that begin in the early stages of embryonic development.
The scientists sequenced the genomes of 387 pairs of identical twins and their
parents, spouses and children to track the number of mutations in their genes.
The authors found that twins differed by 5.2 early developmental mutations,
on average. In approximately 15% of twin pairs, one sibling carried a high
number of these mutations that the other twin did not have.

A genetic mutation is an error or a change in DNA. A mutation occurs
when the sequence of the genetic code breaks or changes in some way. While
most mutations are harmless, some can be serious and can lead to illnesses
such as cancer. Mutations can also affect physical attributes like hair color.

This is not the first study to suggest differences between so-called identical
twins. A paper published in The American Journal of Human Genetics in

2008 revealed some genetic differences between the siblings. However, the new research goes a step beyond that by including the DNA of the extended family.

Some of the research subjects revealed startling differences, study co-author Kari Stefansson told CNN.

"We found a pair of identical twins where a mutation was found in all cells in the body of one of them but was not present in the other twin at all. Then we found twins where a mutation was found in all cells in the body in one twin, but in only 20% of the cells of the other," said Stefansson, the founder and CEO of DeCode Genetics, which is a subsidiary of the US pharmaceutical company Amgen.

The implications of this are significant, according to Stefansson, as the research led the team to conclude that "the role of genetic factors" in shaping the differences observed between monozygotic twins "has been underestimated." He acknowledged that both science and wider society are fascinated by identical twins, adding, "There's something magical about the connection between identical twins."

His team's research, however, is more about what makes the twins different than what they have in common. For example, if identical twins are reared apart and one of them develops an illness, the classic interpretation is that it is determined by environmental factors. Stefansson's team's research shows that before you conclude that it's caused by the environment, you have to sequence the genome of the twins to know what could account for any illnesses.

The "mutation divergence," Stefansson told CNN, could account for a range of "devastating childhood illnesses" such as severe epilepsy and a range of metabolic disorders. "It's absolutely amazing how large a percentage of such horrific syndromes of very early childhood are down to genome mutations," he said.

"This is an extraordinary, exciting and insightful effort to pinpoint early cellular mechanisms that explain genetic differences between MZ (monozygotic) twins," said Nancy Segal, an author and professor of psychology who studies twins at California State University, Fullerton, and was not involved in the research.

"It is well known that MZ co-twins do not show perfect resemblance and that some dissimilarities may reflect genetic differences. The present study offers new information as to the source of MZ co-twin differences," said Segal, who is also director of CSU's Twin Studies Center.

The research did "not negate environmental factors in early and later development," she added, but showed that "some twin models underestimate genetic effects and require revision."

The study, according to Segal, has made researchers wonder how the findings should be applied, such as whether to intervene before babies are born to correct certain genetic disorders. "(A) this extraordinary study," she said.

Effectively, the study concluded that it's not nature or nurture; it's a complex interaction between our genes, our environment, and our non-genetic markers that shape who we are and what illnesses happen to us. And researchers will have to take this into account moving forward when using twins in future studies.

Monozygotic twins may at first glance appear identical, but under the surface very complex dynamics are at work. Though there is no telepathy at work despite what many have thought, the very real dynamics between genes, the things that regulate them, and the environment are much more complex and much more fascinating than we previously thought.

1 Which of the following numbers does NOT refer to the degree of mutation discovered in researching twins?

ア 15
イ 20
ウ 387
エ 5.2

2　According to the passage, what is unique about this research compared with previous research on identical twins?

　ア　It supports the idea that any differences in twins are determined by environment.

　イ　It revealed that there are some genetic differences between twin siblings.

　ウ　It expands the research to include the DNA of members of the extended family.

　エ　It discovered that some mutations in DNA can lead to serious illnesses.

3　According to Stefansson's research, what should we do before concluding environmental factors as the cause of a childhood illness in a twin?

　ア　We should assume it is a serious illness such as cancer.

　イ　We should check if the other twin was raised separately.

　ウ　We should consider what the twins have in common.

　エ　We should do a sequence of the twins' genome.

4　Which of the following words would be most suitable for (　A　)?

　ア　Many genetic disorders will be fixed through

　イ　Scientists can create true identical twins using

　ウ　There are many interesting questions raised by

　エ　We have already solved many problems thanks to

5　Which of the following best summarizes this passage?

　ア　Monozygotic twins are more likely to develop serious illnesses.

　イ　Monozygotic twins can communicate with each other through telepathy.

　ウ　Monozygotic twins' cells never have genetic mutations.

　エ　Monozygotic twins' differences are not only due to the environment.

(☆☆☆○○○○)

【4】次の英文を読んで，1〜6の問いに答えなさい。

People often call eyes the windows to the soul. But what exactly do we see when we gaze into the eyes of another person? In fact, the eyes do provide lots of information about another person's emotional state.

When people are sad or worried, they furrow their brow, which makes the eyes look smaller. Yet when people are cheerful, we correctly call them "bright-eyed." That's because people raise their eyebrows when they're happy, making the eyes look bigger and brighter.

We can tell a true (or Duchenne) smile from a fake by looking at a person's eyes. The mouth shape of a smile is easy to fake — we do it all the time out of politeness. But the eyes are the giveaway: When we're truly happy, we not only smile but also crinkle the corners of our eyes in a "crow's feet" pattern. But when people fake a smile, they usually forget about their eyes.

If the eye is the window into the soul, the pupil is — quite literally — an opening into the eye. The pupil acts like the aperture on a camera, dilating — getting bigger — or contracting — getting smaller — to regulate the amount of light coming into the eye. We all know that our pupils get smaller in the light and bigger in the dark. This is the pupillary light response.

The pupillary light response isn't just a mechanical reaction to ambient light. Rather, as we shift our gaze from one spot to another, our pupils adjust their size in advance to the amount of light we expect to encounter at the new location.

Consider working at a computer: Most of the time, our gaze is fixed on the bright screen, so our pupils are contracted. But every now and then, we glance down at the keyboard, as when we need to reposition our fingers. The authors of the article claim that the pupils begin to dilate even before the downward eye movement begins. Because the pupillary light response is relatively slow — about a quarter of a second — anticipating the amount of light at the new location improves vision once our gaze gets there. (All of this, of course, operates below the level of consciousness.)

The pupillary light response is only one reason why the pupils change size. They also dilate when we're aroused. The body has an alarm network called the autonomic nervous system that prepares us to take action whenever we detect a threat — or an opportunity — in our environment.

Encounter a bear while walking through the woods, and your autonomic nervous system goes on alert. The autonomic nervous system prepares your body to take action against the threat — perhaps scampering up the nearest tree. We also need to take action when we encounter opportunities. Meet an attractive person at a party, and what happens to your body? Your heart and breathing rates increase, you begin to sweat — and your pupils dilate.

Psychologists consider pupil dilation to be an honest cue to sexual or social interest. That's because pupil size isn't under your voluntary control. Let's say you're trying to fake interest as your coworker recounts every play in his weekend golf game. You can force a smile. You might even remember to crinkle the corners of your eyes, to make that smile look real. But your tiny pupils will reveal your lack of interest.

Arousal increases pupil size irrespective of the amount of ambient light present because optimal pupil size involves a trade-off between two factors. The first is visual acuity, or how well you can see the details of whatever you're looking at. In this case, you need "Goldilocks" pupils — not too bright and not too dark, with just the right amount of light coming in. Thus, the pupillary light response is important for visual acuity.

The second factor is visual sensitivity, or how well you can detect something that's in the environment. If you want to really see what's out there, you need to have your eyes — especially your pupils — wide open. This is where the connection between arousal and pupil dilation comes in.

Psychologists consider pupil size in terms of the two functions of vision — exploration and exploitation. When we're exploring our environments, we're on the lookout for threats and opportunities, so we're in a heightened state of arousal. Visual sensitivity is most important in exploration, so our pupils are wide open, taking in as much visual information as possible.

Once we've identified an object of interest and have it under our control, we shift to exploitation mode: We need to examine the item carefully to find all the ways we can use it, to understand it as fully as possible. Now, visual acuity is most important, and our pupils dilate or contract so that just the right amount of light comes in.

1 According to the passage, in what case do we have a "crow's feet" pattern in the corners of our eyes? Answer in English.

2 What happens to our pupils when we change our focus from what we are seeing now to what we will see next? Answer in English.

3 What happens to the pupils when you are exploring the environment? Answer in English.

4 Choose the most appropriate sentence about the passage.

   (a) After we identify an object of interest from our surroundings, our pupils always widen.

   (b) When students have negative feelings like sadness, they tend to keep their eyes wide open.

   (c) When you find an attractive dress at the mall, your pupils become smaller to have good visual acuity.

   (d) The pupillary light response is only a physiological phenomenon for the right quantity of light.

5 Choose the sentence that least matches the content of the story.

   (a) Your eyes really are the window to your soul.

   (b) Your eyes don't act exactly like cameras.

   (c) You can change your pupil size to show a true smile.

   (d) You can tell the state of mind by looking into one's eyes.

6 Give an original example of a situation where visual sensitivity is important. Answer in English.

(☆☆☆◎◎◎)

【5】次の英文を読んで，以下の問いに120語程度の英語で答えなさい。

　　In recent years some students in Japan influenced by recent technology say they no longer need to study English thanks to the development of machine translation software such as Google Translate or DeepL. Thanks to such software, students can simply input what they want to communicate by typing or speaking into their smartphone or computer in Japanese and the software will automatically output the English translation. Students may rely on this software not only for translating sentences and documents, but also when communicating with people in and outside of Japan.

Question:　As a high school English teacher in Japan, how would you persuade your students that studying English is still necessary? Write a persuasive essay in English and support your opinion with reasons and examples.

(☆☆☆◎◎◎◎)

【6】次の1と2の問いに日本語で答えなさい。

1　次の文章は，「高等学校学習指導要領(平成30年告示)解説　外国語編　英語編」からの抜粋である。空所（　A　）～（　E　）に適する語句を書きなさい。

> 　　「外国語によるコミュニケーションにおける見方・考え方」とは，外国語によるコミュニケーションの中で，どのような視点で物事を捉え，どのような考え方で思考していくのかという，物事を捉える視点や考え方であり，「外国語で表現し伝え合うため，外国語やその背景にある文化を，社会や世界，他者との関わりに着目して捉え，コミュニケーションを行う目的や場面，状況等に応じて，情報を整理しながら考えなどを形成し，（　A　）すること」であると考えられる。
> 　　このうち，外国語やその背景にある文化を，社会や世界，他者との関わりに着目して捉えるとは，外国語で他者とコミ

ュニケーションを行うには，社会や世界との関わりの中で事象を捉えたり，外国語やその背景にある文化を理解するなどして相手に十分（　B　）したりすることが重要であることを示している。また，コミュニケーションを行う目的や場面，状況等に応じて，情報を整理しながら考えなどを形成し，（　A　）することとは，多様な人々との対話の中で，目的や場面，状況などに応じて，既習のものも含めて習得した概念(知識)を相互に関連付けてより深く理解したり，情報を精査して考えを形成したり，課題を見いだして解決策を考えたり，身に付けた思考力を発揮させたりすることであり，「外国語で表現し伝え合う」ためには，適切な言語材料を活用し，（　C　）して情報を整理するとともに，自分の考えなどを形成し，（　A　）することが重要であることを示している。

　外国語によるコミュニケーションの一連の過程を通してこのような「見方・考え方」を働かせながら，自分の思いや考えなどを表現することを通して，生徒の（　D　）に応じて「見方・考え方」を豊かにすることが重要である。この「見方・考え方」を確かで豊かなものとすることで，学ぶことの意味と自分の生活，人生や社会，世界の在り方を主体的に結び付ける学びが実現され，学校で学ぶ内容が生きて働く力として育まれることになる。さらに，こうした学びの過程を実現することが，外国語教育における（　E　）の実現に向けた授業改善につながる。その鍵となるものが，教科等の特質に応じた「見方・考え方」である。

2　ICTの具体的な活用法について，ある50分の英語の授業を想定し，その授業のどの場面で，どんなICT機器をどのように活用するのか，活用の目的あるいは効果にも触れながら書きなさい。

（☆☆☆◎◎◎◎）

解答・解説

【中高共通】

【1】1　ウ　　2　ウ　　3　エ　　4　ウ

〈解説〉スクリプトは公開されていない。会話と質問を聞き，質問に対する答えを問題冊子に印刷された選択肢から選ぶ問題。会話と質問は1回しか放送されないため，放送前に選択肢に目を通し，聞き取るべきポイントをあらかじめ押さえておくこと。例えば，選択肢の主語を確認することで，誰の発言や行動に注意して聞き取るべきか判断できる。

【2】1　イ　　2　エ　　3　ア　　4　ア

〈解説〉本問は，1つのパッセージとその内容に関する4つの質問から成る。質問文と選択肢は問題冊子に印刷されている。パッセージは1回しか放送されないため，放送前に，選択肢内のキーワード(本問ではlanguage skillsなど)を確認しておきたい。パッセージのトピックは，幼い子どもと言語習得の関係についてであろうと推測できる。

【3】1　エ　　2　ア　　3　ウ　　4　ア

〈解説〉本問も，設問【2】と同様の形式である。選択肢より，トピックはスポーツ通訳者のサカイ氏についてだとわかる。選択肢の英文量が多いので，放送前に最低限質問文だけには目を通しておきたい。質問文中の疑問詞why，when，whatから，何が問われているかがわかる。

【中学校】

【1】1　ウ　　2　エ　　3　ウ　　4　エ　　5　ア　　6　イ　　7　ア
8　エ

〈解説〉1　accomplishは「達成する」の意。　2　swerveは「(進行方向から急に)それる」の意。　3　degreeはここでは「学位」の意で用いられている。　4　空所の次の文を表すのはpunctuality「時間厳守」とな

る。　5　intricateは「複雑な」の意。　6　fineは「罰金」の意。

7　assortedは「様々に取りそろえた，詰め合わせの」の意。

8　drawbackは「障害，欠点」の意。

【2】1　ウ　2　イ　3　エ　4　イ　5　ア

〈解説〉1　Bの2回目の発話で「ちょっと風邪をひいた」と説明していることから，ウ「何があったの」が適切。　2　Aの2回目の発話で1回目と同じことをBに聞いていることから，Bはテレビの音が大きくて聞き取れず，聞き返していることがわかる。よってイが適切。

3　Aの2回目の発話「中学生の時から集めている」に続くのはエ「まあ，何年もの間集めているのですね。どうして集めようと思ったのですか」が適切。　4　Bの2回目の発話「他の3つは荷物預かり所に置いてきました」より，イ「残りはどこですか」が適切。　5　Aの2回目の発話「料理がこんなに難しいなんて知らなかった」より適切なのはア「それはお気の毒に。どうやってやりくりしたのですか」となる。

【3】1　イ　2　イ　3　エ　4　ア　5　イ

〈解説〉1　companyの後にS＋Vが続くことから関係副詞whereを用いなければならない。　2　他動詞leave「出発する，去る」の過去形leftとする。　3　be eager to Vで「熱心に〜したがる」の意。　4　approach to 〜のここでのtoは前置詞で「〜に対するアプローチ」の意。よってtoの目的語には名詞teachingが来る。　5　explainは目的語を2つ取る第4文型を取ることができず，explain (to 人) Oという構造にする。

【4】A　ウ　B　ア　C　カ　D　オ　E　イ

〈解説〉A　直後の文Don't believe anything she tells you.「彼女が言うことは一切信じないで」からMrs. Williamsを信用していないウが適切。

B　直後の文のshe smiledから冗談めかして言った発言のアが適切。

C　直後の文「しかしながら，クラスには他に28人の子どもがいて，ジョン君を助けるためにすべての時間を費やすことはできません」と

逆接のHoweverを用いて好ましくない内容が続いている。よって空所はジョンについての良い内容と考えられ，カが適切。　**D**　残った選択肢を検討すると，Johnの母親は現実を受け入れられず上の空になっていて空所Cの前文で言いかけたことを繰り返しているオが入ると考えられる。　**E**　直後にHe sounds charming, just delightful.とカウンセラーがジョンの母親を遮って褒めていることから，イ「彼に会うのが待ちきれないです」が適切。

【5】1　イ　　2　ア　　3　イ

〈解説〉1　第2段落でオーストラリアからの生徒が他にいなくて緊張していた(nervous)→実際には友達が多くできて幸せを感じ(happy)→先生が階段から落ちて入院したことにショックを受け(shocked)→お見舞いとして鉢植えの花を病院に持参したら先生に喜んでもらえず困惑した(confused)，というEmmaの心情の変化が述べられている。そして第4段落でなぜ先生に喜んでもらえなかったかを知り，申し訳ない気持ちになっている(sorry)。　2　第4段落2目文に，鉢植えの花は病院に長くとどまることを連想させると述べられており，アが適切。　3　先生のお見舞いを通してEmmaは日本の文化を学んだことが本文全体から読み取れるためイが適切。

【6】1　ア　　2　イ　　3　ア　　4　ウ

〈解説〉1　山火事の原因の一つとして，第1段落3文目に落雷や噴火，同4文目に強風下での乾燥した木の葉の摩擦による発火が挙げられており，アが4文目の内容と一致する。　2　第2段落全体を通して，オーストラリアとアメリカの山火事の原因が複数あり組み合わさって大きな被害となったことが述べられているためイが適切。　3　ドローンや飛行する消防車という技術で山火事に対処することが第4段落では述べられているので，アが適切。　4　本文全体の結論として述べられている最終の第6段落の内容に合致するのはウとなる。

【7】 It is important to expand the range of students' ability gradually to improvise and express what they want to say by selecting familiar topics. It is also important to provide specific feedback on language use during the activity, and to give students opportunities to reflect on their own use of English after the activity and confirm appropriate ways of expression for the situation. It is necessary to emphasize the importance of communicating with each other, and to value the students' motivation to communicate. (83 words)

〈解説〉中学校学習指導要領解説外国語編では，本問の下線部「簡単な語句や文を用いて」とは，「小学校での学習やこれまでの経験の中で触れてきた語彙や表現を含め，中学校で扱う語句や文を用いることである」と説明している。また，「即興で伝え合う」とは，「話すための原稿を事前に用意してその内容を覚えたり，話せるように練習したりするなどの準備時間を取ることなく，不適切な間を置かずに相手と事実や意見，気持ちなどを伝え合うことである」と説明している。解答例では上記の内容に加えて生徒へのフィードバックや話すことに対するモチベーションの維持にも触れている。5領域における指導法の具体例については，日頃から80～100語を目安に自分の意見をまとめる練習をしておくとよいだろう。

【8】 ・単元を通して，目標である「読んだことを基に自分の意見や考えを伝え合ったり，意見文を書いたりする」ことに向かって繰り返し言語活動に取り組めるよう計画している。実際のコミュニケーションにおいて活用する学習の充実を図っている。　　・「読むこと」の言語活動において，コミュニケーションを行う目的や場面，状況等に応じて，情報を整理しながら考え等を形成し，再構築している。　　・「概要を捉える」ために，本文内容を表にまとめたり，マッピングを作成したりしている。表やマッピングにまとめることで，一語一語や一文一文の意味にのみとらわれたりすることなく，全体のあらすじなど，大まかな内容を捉える言語活動を設定している。

〈解説〉解答例では，「読むこと」，「概要を捉える」における工夫と理由

について述べているが，「読むこと」だけでなく，読み取ったことについて自分の考えを伝えるペアワーク等の導入により，「話すこと」の力を併せて伸ばすようにも配慮されている。

【9】(1)　ウ　　(2)　ア　　(3)　イ　　(4)　エ
〈解説〉中学校学習指導要領解説外国語編の巻末には，「外国語活動・外国語の言語活動の例」の学校段階別一覧表が収められている。本資料は，「小学校第3・4学年」，「小学校第5・6学年」，「中学校」別に，それぞれの5領域における言語活動をまとめたもので，段階別にどのように発展していくのか大変わかりやすい。ぜひ活用されたい。また，本問には出題されていないが，「話すこと[やり取り]」領域の言語活動についても確認しておきたい。

【10】小学校外国語活動・外国語科の内容を踏まえて，中学校での指導を行うことが大切である。第3・4学年での「書くこと」，「話すこと」の目標に，第5・6学年で「読むこと」「書くこと」が加わり，実際にどのような言語活動を行うのか，学習指導要領や小学校で使用する教科書，教材等を通じて理解することができる。小学校段階での「好きなこと・好きなもの」，「道案内」，「買い物」などの内容は，中学校での学習との重複も見られ，生徒の興味・関心等を踏まえた上で，言語活動の充実につなげることができる。また，生徒が在籍していた小学校において，どのような時間割編成や指導体制によって授業が行われているかを把握することも大切である。小学校での言語の使用場面を意識した授業の進め方や，活動内容，さらには活動をとおして作成した具体物を把握するなどしたことを，中学校1年生での指導に活かし，円滑な接続を図ることで，小学校での学習内容を単に繰り返すのではなく，生徒の主体的な学びへとつなげることができる。
〈解説〉学習指導要領の記述が具体的に何を示しているのかは，同解説外国語編に詳述されている。必ず参照して学びを深めてほしい。中学1年への指導ということから小学校外国語活動・外国語科の内容や目標

についても理解を深めて解答に反映させる必要がある。

【高等学校】

【1】 1 記号…(a)　　修正…rapidly　　2 記号…(b)　　修正…welcome
3 記号…(b)　　修正…coexistence　　4 記号…(a)　　修正…leave
5 記号…(b)　　修正…dealing

〈解説〉1　直後の形容詞acceleratingを修飾するのは副詞rapidlyとなる。
2　welcome「歓迎する」は他動詞のため直後に目的語を取りtoは不要。
3　seek「探し求める」の目的語とするためには名詞coexistenceとする。
4　「出発する，去る」という意味のleaveは他動詞のため直後に目的語
を取りforは不要。　5　avoidは動名詞を目的語に取るためdealingとす
る。

【2】 1 (f)　　2 (g)　　3 (e)　　4 (d)　　5 (b)

〈解説〉1　直後のTheir evidence shows thatに着目。証拠を出して物事を主
張するのは科学者・研究者の類であり，選択肢では(f)が適切と判断で
きる。Theirはpsychologistsを指している。　2　空所のある第2段落で
はconvergent thinkingとdivergent thinkingという2つの説明がされている。
空所直前のBothはこの2つを指し，空所にはそれぞれの説明をしてい
る(g)が適切と判断できる。　3　空所のある第3段落では創造性が筋肉
と同じように成長させることができるものだという説明がされてい
る。それを踏まえると空所には最初は創造的でなくともその後に創造
性を身に着けて大きな利益を得られるという(e)が適切。　4　空所の
前ではperformance-orientedの特性が述べられている。それに対し，空
所の後では全く別の特性について述べられている。よって空所のある
第4段落では2つの特性を対比しているということが読み取れる。選択
肢を検討するとlearning-orientedの説明がされている(d)が適切と判断で
きる。　5　空所直前ではlearning-oriented employeesのほうがよりアイ
デアの量も質も勝っていることが述べられている。空所ではこの事実
と関連する内容が入ると読み取れ，その理由が述べられている(b)が適

切と判断できる。

【3】1　ウ　　2　ウ　　3　エ　　4　ウ　　5　エ
〈解説〉1　第3段落4文目で，387組の一卵性双生児らのゲノム解読は，遺
伝子の突然変異数を追跡するためと述べられており，突然変異の程度
を表す数字ではないためウが適切と判断できる。　2　第5段落3文目
の内容がウに一致する。　3　第9段落3文目の内容がエに一致する。
4　空所直前の文で，この研究によって発見されたことをどのように
適用するか，研究者たちに考えさせたと述べられている。つまり，研
究者たちの研究意欲の向上を示しており，それに対応するのはウと判
断できる。　5　第2段落および最終段落で，双子の違いは環境による
ものだと従来考えられていたがそうではないという研究について述べ
られており，この内容が本文全体の要旨であるためエが適切。

【4】1　When we're truly happy, we have the pattern.　2　They adjust their
size in advance to the amount of light we expect to encounter at the new
location.　3　They are wide open.　4　(c)　5　(c)　6　We use
visual sensitivity when we need to find someone in a crowd.
〈解説〉1　第3段落3文目が該当するので余分な箇所を省いて英文を組み
立てる。　2　第5段落2文目の後半部分が該当する。our pupilsを代名
詞theyと置き換え，それ以外はそのまま用いるとよい。　3　第12段落
の3文目が該当する。設問2と同じくthe pupilsはtheyで置き換える。
4　第8段落4文目及び5文目と合致するのは(c)となる。　5　(c)が第9段
落の内容と一致しない。この段落では，笑顔は本物のように見せるこ
とはできるが瞳孔は本心を偽ることができないということが述べられ
ている。　6　第12段落3文目にvisual sensitivityは探索に重要であるこ
とが述べられている。これを踏まえて解答例では雑踏の中で人を探す
という具体例を示している。

【5】 I believe despite the availability of translation software, studying English is still necessary. Firstly, by studying a foreign language like English, we will learn about the background of the language, including aspects such as the culture, society or world-view of that language. For example, by studying English we can learn about various customs and manners in other countries. Secondly, we can learn new ways of thinking as we process information by communicating in various situations. For example, we may learn how to debate in English or how to improve our countries' ideas with the ideas of others. Such things make it possible for us to understand not only others but also ourselves, which shows the great importance of studying English. (120 words)

〈解説〉機械翻訳が発達する中での英語学習の必要性という，比較的書きやすいテーマと言える。教育的な観点から，解答例では言語学習を通した他国の文化を学べること，外国語を通して様々な人とコミュニケーションが取れることなどを必要性として述べている。

【6】1 A 再構築　B 配慮　C 思考・判断　D 発達の段階　E 主体的・対話的で深い学び　2 リーディング教材を使用した内容理解の授業において，内容理解をした後に，本文で述べられていた内容についての個々の考えや感想を書いて表現する場面で，ICT機器を活用する。生徒は，キーボードを使って自分の考えや感想を英語で入力する。入力後，それぞれの英文をオンライン上のフォルダに提出する。教師は，提出された英文を黒板にプロジェクターを使って投影し，英文をクラス全体で共有する。教師は，英文の添削も行う。生徒は，授業の終わりに，自分の英文を修正し，再度フォルダに保存して教師に提出する。このような場面でICT機器を活用することで，生徒全員の多様な考えや感想を瞬時に共有することができる。これは，生徒がより多くの考えに触れ，自分の考えを深めることにつながる。また，教師が生徒の英文に共通した間違いをその場で指導することから，英語の表現力の向上が期待できるとともに，生徒はお互いの英文から

　様々な英語表現を見つけ，刺激を受けることで，学習意欲の向上につなげることができる。

〈解説〉空所補充問題は記述式問題ではあるが，外国語科の目標および英語科の目標を理解していれば，対処可能な問題であろう。ICT機器の活用はいろいろなことが考えられるが，解答例では生徒の解答の瞬時の共有を挙げている。問題文の指示に沿って効果や効果にも必ず触れる必要がある。

2022年度　実施問題

【中高共通】

【1】これから，会話と質問が4つ放送されます。質問に対する答えとして最も適切なものをア～エの中から一つずつ選び，その記号を書きなさい。なお，会話と質問は一度だけ放送されます。

1
ア　2:00
イ　8:00
ウ　9:00
エ　10:00

2
ア　Monday
イ　Tuesday
ウ　Wednesday
エ　Thursday

3
ア　In the bedroom
イ　In the dining room
ウ　In the living room
エ　In the study room

4
ア　She can't use water because she drained all water out of the pipe.
イ　She can't use water because the faucet is broken.
ウ　She can't use water because the water bill hasn't been paid.
エ　She can't use water because the water became frozen.

(☆☆☆○○○)

【2】これから，まとまりのある英文が放送されます。英文の後に，その内容について質問が4つ出されます。その質問に対する答えとして最も適切なものをア～エの中から一つずつ選び，その記号を書きなさい。なお，英文と質問は一度だけ放送されます。

1

ア　Cacao products sold well in Jamaica.

イ　How to produce tasty cacao fruit.

ウ　How to utilize every part of the cacao fruit.

エ　The efficient way cacao products are distributed.

2

ア　Cacao water is used to make liquor or juice.

イ　Local farmers are obliged to work hard.

ウ　Most of the cacao fruit is thrown away.

エ　We waste a great amount of water.

3

ア　All parts of the cacao plant are nutritious for our body and mind.

イ　Cacao is made up of 4 components.

ウ　70％ of cacao is processed into other food.

エ　The price of cacao has increased recently.

4

ア　Because cacao water can be digested slowly in our body.

イ　Because cacao water can prevent disease and is easily digested.

ウ　Because it can play an important role in causing sugar spikes.

エ　Because it can play an important role in stopping heart attacks.

(☆☆☆◎◎◎)

【3】これから，まとまりのある英文が放送されます。その内容についての次の質問に対する答えとして最も適切なものをア～エの中から一つずつ選び，その記号を書きなさい。なお，英文は一度だけ放送されます。

1　Which of the following is an advantage of using a pen and paper when taking down notes?

　ア　It allows students to move around the page easily while adding new notes.

　イ　It gives students an opportunity to write verbatim statements.

　ウ　It helps students make use of cognitive offloading.

　エ　It takes less time and effort to make notes.

2　Why did the pen and paper group do better than the laptop group after being allowed to revise their notes?

　ア　It was easier for them to refer back to their notes if they needed to remember something.

　イ　Their notes were more complete and provided more information.

　ウ　The pen and paper method allowed them to examine the material more deeply.

　エ　The pen and paper method helped them learn small and simple facts.

3　What is cognitive offloading?

　ア　Freeing up the mind from extra tasks so one can concentrate more effectively.

　イ　Lessening the information given so that the mind can remember more.

　ウ　Making the concepts simpler so that they are not too hard to understand.

　エ　Taking care of the students' mental health so they can focus more.

4　Which statement summarizes the article most accurately?

　ア　Pen and paper note taking is a faster form of cognitive processing.

　イ　Recording lectures is better than using laptops to take down notes.

　ウ　The younger generation can use new technologies to help them take notes more effectively.

　エ　Using pen and paper when taking notes allows for better understanding of the material.

(☆☆☆○○○)

【中学校】

【１】次の1～8の英文の(　　)にあてはまる最も適切な英語を，それぞれ
ア～エから一つずつ選び，その記号を書きなさい。

1　(　　) being a famous writer, he is a professor, teaching Japanese
literature to foreign students.
　　ア　Over　　イ　Beyond　　ウ　Above　　エ　Besides

2　At the press conference, he said he had been thinking about retirement for
more than a year. He had (　　) his basketball life to the Washington
Wizards for fifteen years.
　　ア　dedicated　　イ　donated　　ウ　alleviated　　エ　abandoned

3　Haruka often reads books about how people lived in ancient (　　). She
likes to learn about the way that societies developed.
　　ア　proportion　　イ　appointments　　ウ　civilizations
　　エ　supplements

4　After Jeremy entered an (　　) password three times, his account was
locked.
　　ア　invalid　　イ　incessant　　ウ　unstable　　エ　offensive

5　The computer program has already beaten a number of professional shogi
players. Defeating it in a match would be an impressive (　　).
　　ア　lunge　　イ　duct　　ウ　feat　　エ　balm

6　Mr. Brown studied judo for many years and (　　) became the judo
teacher at his local sports center.
　　ア　eventually　　イ　slightly　　ウ　mildly　　エ　heavily

7　Many of the buildings that were not designed to (　　) earthquakes
collapsed when the magnitude 7.2 earthquake hit the area.
　　ア　reconstruct　　イ　dodge　　ウ　withstand　　エ　withhold

8　The soccer team's bus broke down, so they weren't able to get to the
tournament before it started, and they were forced to (　　) their match.
　　ア　cuddle　　イ　forfeit　　ウ　shear　　エ　ascend

(☆☆☆◎◎◎)

【2】 次の1～5の会話文中の(　　)にあてはまる最も適切な英語を，それ
ぞれア～エから一つずつ選び，その記号を書きなさい。

1　*A*:　I grew up in a very small town.

　B:　(　　)

　A:　It wasn't at all. You can't imagine the fun we had.

　　ア　I'd like to live in a small town.

　　イ　That must have been boring.

　　ウ　That sounds like a lot of fun.

　　エ　You must have spent a happy boyhood there.

2　*A*:　Do you have all your suitcases with you?

　B:　No, I have some more.

　A:　(　　)

　B:　I left the other three at the baggage room.

　　ア　Where are the rest?

　　イ　Why do you still have them with you?

　　ウ　Can I help you find the baggage room?

　　エ　You should leave this one, too, shouldn't you?

3　*A*:　How much will a ticket for the evening performance cost?

　B:　(　　)

　A:　Do I have to pay right now?

　B:　If you like.

　　ア　Sorry, there are no more tickets.

　　イ　The same as for the afternoon performance.

　　ウ　There is no tomorrow performance.

　　エ　You can buy a ticket now.

4　A:　Dr. Anderson's office. Can I help you?

　B:　Yes, I have an awful toothache. Can I see the doctor some time
today?

　A:　I'm afraid he's very busy today, (　　).

　B:　I don't think I can wait that long. I'll try another dentist. Thanks, anyway.

　ア　but he can see you at 10:00 tomorrow morning

　イ　but we can give you some medicine to ease the pain

　ウ　but we can recommend another dentist if it is urgent

　エ　but you can come and wait in our office if you like

5　*A*:　I'll meet you under the clock at 3:15 the day after tomorrow.

　B:　Which clock do you mean?

　A:　The one at Central Station, where we always meet.

　B:　Oh, of course! (　　)

　ア　I'll do my best to get there on time.

　イ　OK. I'll see you at a quarter to four.

　ウ　Till tomorrow, then.

　エ　You know where I mean, don't you?

(☆☆☆◎◎◎)

【３】次の1～5の各文にある下線部ア～エには，英語の文法上または表現上適切ではない語句があります。適切ではない語句をそれぞれア～エから一つずつ選び，その記号を書きなさい。

1　ァThere is little doubt that ィworking with someone ゥin great ability is more than ェsatisfying.

2　She thought that the time ァhas come ィto produce new ゥevidence ェsupporting her claim.

3　ァThe quizzes were not ィtoo difficult, so ゥeveryone was really fun ェto guess the answers.

4　ァGiven a choice between ィfinishing college and getting a job, he ゥchooses ェto work.

5　ァHad there been another option, I ィwill have ゥmade reservations for the ェnight flight to Milano.

(☆☆☆☆◎◎◎◎)

【4】 グラフをもとに，次の1〜3の各問いに対する答えとして最も適切な
ものをア〜エから一つ選び，その記号を書きなさい。

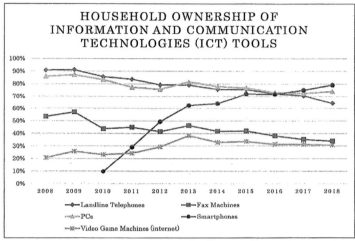

(Source：総務省「令和元年度情報通信白書」をもとに作成)

1 According to the graph, which of the following is true about landline
telephones?

ア Homes without a landline phone are gradually increasing.

イ The number of landline phones in 2016 compared to 2009 has risen
substantially.

ウ Households have completely stopped using landline phones since
2015.

エ Landline phones are at the bottom of the graph as the least purchased
tool.

2 According to the graph, which of the following is true about smartphones?

ア The number of smartphones being used has decreased dramatically
since 2010.

イ Smartphones were more popular in 2014 than using a landline phone
at home.

ウ More smartphones were owned than video game machines in 2010.

エ　Smartphones are the fastest growing ICT tool that people own in the last decade.

3　According to the graph, which of the following is true for the year 2011?

ア　Video game machines were the least common item owned by households.

イ　The ownership of fax machines dropped compared to 2010.

ウ　The number of computers owned was the lowest compared to other ICT items.

エ　The second most owned ICT tool was the landline telephone.

(☆☆☆◎◎◎)

【5】次の英文は，中学生の恵美(Emi)が英語の授業で書いた作文です。これを読んで，以下の質問に答えなさい。

I'm a member of the volunteer club. We do volunteer work after school. For example, we clean our town and sing some songs with elderly people living in our town. We also write articles for our club newspaper about our volunteer work. I'm especially interested in helping people in developing countries. I've never visited any one of these countries, but I want to help people living in them. We collect things like clothes and shoes. We also collect money in front of the station and at our school. There are many children who don't have enough food in those countries. Most of them can't go to school. The money and things we collect are used for such children.

Last week, a woman called Ms. Oka came to our school. She told her story to the members of the volunteer club. She's a member of a group helping people in developing countries. Her group sends the money and things we collect to them. She said, "It's important to send money and things to help people in developing countries. It's also important to talk with people who need help." Ms. Oka worked with members of her group in one of the developing countries for three years. Each member had expert knowledge of their jobs. When she met people there, she heard from them that the money

96

and things sent from Japan helped them. She felt happy to hear that and wanted to find good ways to make their lives better.

One day, when Ms. Oka went to a field in a village, she met a boy who lived near the field. He couldn't go to school because he had to help his family. For example, he had to grow vegetables for his family. Ms. Oka wanted to help the boy and said to him, "You need to grow vegetables, right? I want to find a good way to do that with you. What can I do for you?" However, he didn't try to talk with her because he didn't believe her. She wanted him to know more about her and spent a lot of time with him. Then they began to talk to each other. She found something that he wanted to do. He wanted to grow vegetables that he could keep for a long time. He didn't know how to do that because he couldn't get any information about it. He asked her about the ways to grow such vegetables well.

First, Ms. Oka tried to find the things which she could do for the boy. She read some books and learned what vegetables he could grow in his field, but the books didn't say how to grow them. Then she went to see a man who was a member of her group. He had expert knowledge about growing those kinds of vegetables. She learned how to do that from him and taught it to the boy. She and the boy grew the vegetables that he wanted together. He learned how to grow them well and grew a lot of them. Sometimes he could get many vegetables and sell some of them. His life became better than before.

Ms. Oka said to the members of our volunteer club, "The boy looked happy when he was able to grow the vegetables that he wanted. I'll never forget his smile. At first, I couldn't really understand his problem, but I understood it by talking with him. I was able to tell the boy and his family how to grow the vegetables well, and it made their life better. Like this, I talked with other people in his village and found the things they needed. Now, I want to give children like him a chance to go to school."

I learned there are things we cannot understand just by sending money and things. It's important for us to understand what people in developing countries are thinking. Ms. Oka talked with people who lived in the village. She understood what they were thinking and found what to do for them. I'm going to write an article for our club newspaper about the things I learned from my experience. I want many students to know about them and to join us. I think I have to understand how people in developing countries live. To do that, I want to go to such countries in the future and talk with people there like Ms. Oka.

次の英文は，この作文を読んだ中学生のハナ(Hana)と留学生のメアリー(Mary)の会話の一部です。これを読んで，以下の1〜3の問いに答えなさい。

Hana: All the money and things I gave to the volunteer club helped people in developing countries. I was very happy to learn about that. I didn't understand the importance of the volunteer work ☐ i ☐ learning it from Emi.

Mary: Yes. We can help many people by doing volunteer work.

Hana: Ms. Oka understood what was ☐ ii ☐ to the boy and told him how to grow vegetables.

It was good for him to learn how to do it.

Mary: Yes. Ms. Oka thinks it is important to send money and things to developing countries and she also thinks it is important to ☐ iii ☐.

Hana: Right. We many also find the things we can do for other people by doing like Ms. Oka.

1　本文の内容から考えて，☐ i ☐ に入る最も適切な語を，次のア〜エから一つ選び，その記号を書きなさい。
　　ア　till　　イ　before　　ウ　from　　エ　through

2　本文の内容から考えて，☐ ii ☐ に入る最も適切な語を，次のア〜エから一つ選び，その記号を書きなさい。
　　ア　needed　　イ　famous　　ウ　necessary　　エ　traditional

3　本文の内容から考えて，　iii　に入る表現として最も適切なものを，次のア〜エから一つ選び，その記号を書きなさい。

ア　write some books to give new information about such countries

イ　tell the members of the volunteer club how to grow vegetables

ウ　go there to learn about growing vegetables

エ　talk with people there to know about them

(☆☆☆○○○)

【6】次の英文は，ケイコが交換留学生としてアメリカにいた時に書いた日記です。これを読んで，以下の1〜3の空欄の内容として最も適切なものを，それぞれ一つずつ選び，その記号を書きなさい。

July 23rd

I've been sad recently because I haven't made many friends at school. On Monday, a girl named Sandra invited me to join her at the county fair. I wasn't expecting her to invite me, so it seemed very sudden.

The county fair is a kind of festival in the United States. There're rides and games. Farmers show their animals and products there, too. I'd never been to one, but it sounded like fun, and I was looking forward to it. I took a bus and got off at Central Bus Station. I didn't know the way from there, but I thought I heard a group of boys say that they were going to the fair, so I decided to follow them. They walked for about three kilometers and then started to enter a building. I knew it wasn't the fair so I got a little worried. I didn't want to be late and miss my meeting with Sandra, so I asked the boys where the fair was. They looked surprised. One of them said, "The fair is on the other side of the station." Then he asked, "Why have you been following us?" I explained that I thought they were going to the fair. He smiled and gave me some directions.

I walked as fast as I could, but I got to the fair thirty minutes late. Sandra wasn't waiting for me. I didn't know what to do, and I started crying. Just

99

then, a ticket seller walked up to me. She asked if I was Keiko. When I told her I was, she said that Sandra had called the ticket office and asked her to tell me that she was sick and could not come. Of course, I hoped Sandra was OK, and I was thankful to the ticket seller for finding me, but most of all, I was happy that my friendship with Sandra hadn't been hurt.

1 According to the story, Keiko's feelings changed in the following order:
   ⬚ 1

　ア　lonely → anxious → excited → surprised → glad
　イ　lonely → excited → surprised → glad → anxious
　ウ　lonely → glad → anxious → surprised → excited
　エ　lonely → glad → surprised → anxious → excited
　オ　lonely → surprised → excited → anxious → glad
　カ　lonely → surprised → glad → anxious → excited

2 The ticket seller ⬚ 2 .
　ア　didn't think Keiko had enough money
　イ　had been contacted by Sandra
　ウ　had seen Sandra enter the fair
　エ　wondered why Keiko was crying

3 From this story, you learned that Keiko ⬚ 3 .
　ア　got off the bus at the wrong stop on her way to the fair
　イ　had not understood what some boys were planning to do
　ウ　kept Sandra waiting for too long and failed to make a friend
　エ　was unpopular because she did not know about American culture

(☆☆☆◎◎◎)

【7】次の文は,「中学校学習指導要領(平成29年3月)第2章「第9節　外国語」における「第2　各言語の目標及び内容等」の「1　目標」を一部抜粋したものです。
　　イの事項において,下線部のような学習の充実を図るためには,ど

のような指導が考えられるか，あなたの考えを80語以上の英語で書きなさい。

　なお，最後に語数を記入すること。語数については，同じ語を2回使用した場合，2語と数えること(のべ数)とします。

> (4)　話すこと[発表]
>
> 　イ　日常的な話題について，<u>事実や自分の考え，気持ちなどを整理し，簡単な語句や文を用いてまとまりのある内容を話すことができるようにする。</u>

(☆☆☆☆◎◎◎◎)

【8】次の文は，中学校学習指導要領(平成29年3月)第2章「第9節　外国語」における「第2　各言語の目標及び内容等」の「2　内容〔思考力，判断力，表現力等〕」を一部抜粋したものです。文中の(　①　)〜(　③　)にあてはまる語句として，最も適切なものを，以下のa〜iから一つずつ選び，その記号を書きなさい。

> (2)　情報を整理しながら考えなどを形成し，英語で表現したり，伝え合ったりすることに関する事項
>
> 　　具体的な課題等を設定し，コミュニケーションを行う目的や場面，状況などに応じて，情報を整理しながら考えなどを形成し，これらを(　①　)ことを通して，次の事項を身に付けることができるよう指導する。
>
> 　ア　(　②　)について，英語を聞いたり読んだりして必要な情報や考えなどを捉えること。
>
> 　イ　(　②　)について，英語を聞いたり読んだりして得られた情報や表現を，選択したり抽出したりするなどして活用し，話したり書いたりして(　③　)などを表現すること。
>
> 　ウ　(　②　)について，伝える内容を整理し，英語で話したり書いたりして互いに(　③　)などを伝え合うこと。

101

a　論理的に表現する　　　　　b　主体的に表現する
c　簡潔に表現する　　　　　　d　身近で簡単な事柄
e　自分のことや身近で簡単な事柄　f　日常的な話題や社会的な話題
g　事実や自分の考え，気持ち　h　自分の考え，気持ち
i　事実や自分の考え

(☆☆☆○○○○○)

【9】次の文は，中学校学習指導要領(平成29年3月)第2章「第9節　外国
語」における「第2　各言語の目標及び内容等」の「3　指導計画の作
成と内容の取扱い」を一部抜粋したものです。文中の(　①　)〜
(　④　)にあてはまる適切な語句を書きなさい。

> (1)　指導計画の作成に当たっては，小学校や高等学校における
> 指導との接続に留意しながら，次の事項に配慮するものとす
> る。
> ア　単元など内容や時間の(　①　)を見通して，その中で育む
> 資質・能力の育成に向けて，生徒の主体的・対話的で深い
> 学びの実現を図るようにすること。その際，(　②　)な課
> 題等を設定し，生徒が外国語によるコミュニケーションに
> おける見方・考え方を働かせながら，コミュニケーション
> の目的や場面，状況などを意識して活動を行い，英語の音
> 声や語彙，表現，文法の知識を(　③　)の領域における実
> 際のコミュニケーションにおいて(　④　)学習の充実を図
> ること。

(☆☆☆○○○○○)

【10】次の1と2は中学校学習指導要領解説　外国語編(平成29年7月)第2章
「外国語科の目標及び内容」における「第2節　英語」の「1　目標」
を一部抜粋したものです。
1　次の目標で示されたことができるようにするために，関心のある

事柄について例を取り上げながら，具体的にどのような指導が考えられるか日本語で書きなさい。

> (3) 話すこと〔やり取り〕
>   ア　関心のある事柄について，簡単な語句や文を用いて即興で伝え合うことができるようにする。

2　次の目標で示されたことができるようにするために，卒業を控えた中学校3年生段階で指導する際に，社会的な話題について例を取り上げながら，具体的にどのような指導が考えられるか日本語で書きなさい。

> (5) 書くこと
>   ウ　社会的な話題に関して聞いたり読んだりしたことについて，考えたことや感じたこと，その理由などを，簡単な語句や文を用いて書くことができるようにする。

(☆☆☆○○○○○)

【高等学校】

【1】次の英文1～5にはそれぞれ誤りや不適切なところがある。修正が必要な箇所を(a)～(c)から一つずつ選び，適切な形に直しなさい。

1　I need to tell our boss (a)that 3 months (b)is too short (c)time to carry out the plan.

2　(a)For the past sixty years, Thompson Corp. (b)having held the number one position (c)in the New Zealand frozen food market.

3　(a)As of January 13 of last year, more than 150 applicants (b)on the new role of the lead actor (c)had been submitted.

4　Adam was the applicant (a)whom I thought (b)was (c)thoroughly competent.

5　John P. Company (a)plans to change its board members before the next (b)annually product launch (c)held on August 28.

(☆☆☆☆○○○○)

103

【２】次の空所(1)～(5)に入れるのに最も適切な段落を，(a)～(e) より一つずつ選び，その記号を書きなさい。ただし，同じ記号を複数回用いてはならない。

　If you are a lazy person, don't worry; you might be able to blame your brain! At least, that's what the research suggests. Being lazy doesn't just mean you take the elevator instead of the stairs. It can also mean the way you think and make decisions is "lazy." The problem is that this all happens without our even knowing about it. So, what can we do about it? How can we make our brains less lazy?

(1)

(2)

　In fact, research has shown that the brain is trying to save energy all the time. In an experiment at Simon Fraser University in Canada, scientists wanted to test how good the brain was at saving energy. They asked nine subjects to walk on a treadmill. The subjects naturally walked at a pace that saved the most energy. Then the scientists made it more difficult. They added weight at the knees. As a result, the subjects' original pace was not the most efficient anymore. Immediately, they began to walk differently to save as much energy as possible. The brain was saving energy in real time. It happened without them even thinking about it.

(3)

　Lazy thinkers are also more likely to make bad decisions. One research study showed that businesspeople with lazy brains have ended up making terrible financial decisions. They didn't think things through; instead, they made quick decisions based on their emotions. Their companies lost money, and some of them lost everything. This is often because people with lazy brains are too confident. Their lazy thinking makes them think they know everything when they really don't.

(4)

(5)

104

The problem is that many people don't use hard thinking enough, and that is what causes problems. So, the advice from scientists is to fight it. In other words, don't just accept everything you hear as true. Question it, and see if it really makes sense or not. Don't be too confident about what you know; remember that your first thoughts might be wrong, because they're from your lazy brain. Also, don't forget to take the stairs next time.

＜選択肢＞

(a)　So, why does the brain like lazy decisions? When we do things fast and we don't have to think, we save energy. The brain and body are always trying to save energy. If we save energy, we have more of it, and more energy means we can function better in the world. Think about how hard it is to think when we are tired or hungry. We make more mistakes because our brain is too tired.

(b)　So, how can people fight lazy thinking? Luckily, there is a way. Humans also have another kind of thinking— "hard thinking" — but it takes a lot more energy. Hard thinking is slower. It's the kind of thinking we use when we solve a difficult problem, like 17×24. It's the kind of thinking we use when we make more difficult decisions, like when we decide on the career we want or where to live.

(c)　Therefore, it is good that the brain is lazy because it saves energy. But unfortunately, that's not the whole story. When people rely on lazy thinking in situations that require hard thinking, they can run into trouble. For one, lazy thinkers are more likely to believe things without any proof. This means that they may accept that something is true even when it isn't. For example, let's say you meet someone new. He tells you, "I'm an honest person," and you assume he is. But in reality, he lies to people, even his friends. Unfortunately, your lazy brain doesn't let you question his honesty. You believe he's a good person because that was the easiest thought.

(d)　When we use hard thinking, the body isn't so happy because we are demanding a lot more energy from it. That explains why students get so tired after studying for a test. It explains why long conversations make people want to grab a cup of coffee. They need the caffeine because they feel like they're out of energy. They're not using their lazy brain anymore.

(e)　To understand why the brain wants to be lazy, we must understand how the brain works. The brain is very complex, and it actually thinks in two different ways. The first way is the lazy way, and it is a good kind of lazy. It is the thinking we use when we add 1+1. It's the same lazy thinking we use when we drive to school or work. We don't have to think about how to do it; we just do it! According to scientists, we have thousands of these lazy thoughts every day.

(☆☆☆☆◎◎◎)

【3】次の英文を読んで，1〜5の問いに対する答えとして最も適切なものをア〜エの中から一つずつ選び，その記号を書きなさい。

　　In 1907, while enjoying a bowl of soup made with dashi broth and kombu seaweed, the Japanese chemist Kikunae Ikeda had an insight that would change the food world. He noticed a taste that wasn't sweet, salty, sour or bitter. Ikeda gave this hard-to-describe flavorful taste a name—umami—and went on to identify the specific amino acid that caused it. It has become known around the world. However, interest is now growing in another taste first detected in Japan.

　　The newer taste, kokumi, is even harder to describe than umami, but it is potentially just as important for understanding how and why we enjoy food. In Japanese, the term koku describes foods that have the kind of mouthful "thickness" often produced by fats—what English speakers might describe as rich. "It feels like a physical sensation," says the culinary scientist Joshua Evans. It works "by covering the mouth and becoming more intense and being extended in time." When asked what foods have koku, Japanese food experts list wild boar, adult wasps, duck eggs and aged sake, as well as long-simmered and fermented dishes.

The exact nature of kokumi remains the subject of great debate among sensory scientists and chefs, in part because it can't be detected by our tongues on its own; rather, it modifies other tastes and flavors. A Japanese lab claims to have identified the taste receptor on our tongues that is activated by glutathione, which is made up of amino acids. Scientists elsewhere have discovered that glutathione and other compounds appear to activate kokumi in yeasts and in other foods. These include long-cooked meats such as chicken in chicken broth as well as some cheeses and fermented foods like beer, soy sauce and fish paste.

Some scientists remain skeptical. Paul Breslin, a nutritional sciences professor at Rutgers University, contends that the term kokumi will be difficult to understand and use "until the scientific and nonscientific community can agree both on its definition and on the prototypical eliciting stimuli" —that is to say, until we know more.

For all the uncertainty, kokumi has two potentially important implications. The first relates to our understanding of human evolution; the second, human health—especially efforts to create foods with fewer calories but more flavor. In both cases, kokumi may provide a kind of missing link.

Our own research suggests that one key to the adoption of fire by humans, and the invention and adoption of fermentation, was the flavor of cooked and fermented foods. It is known that humans prefer cooked foods over raw foods as well as fermented foods. But it has long been unclear why.

One possibility is that humans evolved a preference for complex aromas and the experience they contribute to flavor, which is much stronger in cooked meats than uncooked meats. It is also notable that cooked meats and fermented foods tend to have kokumi.

We might picture an ancient human ancestor holding up a piece of meat that has been cooked on the fire, pleased by its aromas but also by the rich taste of its kokumi. Our ancestors didn't have to be able to give kokumi a name or know its chemical sources to enjoy it.

107

Chef-researchers employed by top restaurants, such as Nabila Rodríguez Valerón at Copenhagen's award-winning Alchemist, are now eagerly experimenting with the ways in which kokumi could be featured in modern meals to make foods that taste rich but are low in fat. A recent study by Ciarán Forde at the Clinical Nutrition Research Center in Singapore discovered that if the amino acid associated with kokumi is added to beef broth, particularly in combination with umami flavors, consumers perceive the broth to be richer and to have more calories.

Many traditional recipes from cultures around the world appear to already take advantage of this kokumi effect. For example, people add onion and garlic to soup stock to give it a fuller, deeper flavor. Often recipes start with a step in which chopped onions are soaked in fat or oil, which amplifies the flavors of those fats and oils. Kokumi is a taste that asks us to think of food holistically.

If the history of umami is any indication, the market will decide on kokumi's importance before scientists and chefs come to full agreement. After Ikeda discovered umami, he later figured out how to produce a substance that causes the taste: monosodium glutamate, or MSG. He patented the production, and started a company Ajinomoto Co., and long before scientists accepted his discovery, MSG was sold around the world to add the umami taste to foods.

A similar pattern may already be under way with kokumi. To this point, three companies, Ajinomoto itself and the food and flavor companies Kerry and Biospringer, have released kokumi powders that they say add the pleasing kokumi effect without adding calories. You can try them and judge for yourself.

Kokumi is (　A　). Around the world, scientists have leads on many others. Our mouths remain full of mysteries, allowing us to experience surprises and delights each time we eat.

1　Which of the following would make the most suitable title for this passage?

ア How the Human Mouth Evolved

イ Is Kokumi the Next Taste Sensation?

ウ The Great Discoveries of Kikunae Ikeda

エ Umami or Kokumi: Which is more important for taste?

2 Which of the following does the passage imply is a possible benefit of studying kokumi?

ア We can decrease the time it takes to ferment foods and therefore eat more of them.

イ We can develop more foods that contain MSG which will bring health benefits.

ウ We will be able to better understand our evolution and develop tastier and heathier foods.

エ We will be able to enjoy foods such as wild boar, wasps and duck eggs more easily.

3 Which of the following is NOT something talked about in the passage?

ア An amino acid associated with kokumi can make a beef broth's taste richer.

イ A scientist indicates it is still difficult to understand what kokumi really is.

ウ Kokumi is caused by foods such as long-cooked meats and fermented foods.

エ Umami creates a fuller deeper flavor by soaking vegetables in fat or oil.

4 According to the article, based on umami's history, which of the following is likely to occur before scientists and chefs come to agree on kokumi's importance?

ア Companies such as Ajinomoto will stop producing foods with umami taste.

イ Companies will develop and sell food products that cause the kokumi taste.

ウ　New companies will be started in order to create kokumi powders.

エ　Umami will become more widely known around the world.

5　Which are the most suitable words to put into (　A　)?

ア　a highly unique taste that scientists are working hard to reproduce

イ　proving to be a very popular taste in countries where it is sold

ウ　said to be the most important factor that determines taste

エ　unlikely to be the last new taste that we discover

(☆☆☆◎◎)

【4】次の英文を読んで，1～6の問いに答えなさい。

　　People often said that Jerry Boyle was the most boring man in the world. Jerry didn't know why people thought he was so boring. Jerry thought he was quite interesting. After all, he collected stamps. What could be more interesting than stamps? It was true that he didn't have any other hobbies or interests, but that didn't matter for Jerry. He had his job, after all. He had a very interesting job. At least, Jerry thought it was interesting. Everybody else said that his job was boring. But he was an accountant! 'Why do people think that accountants are boring?' thought Jerry. Jerry thought his job was fascinating. Every day, he went to his office, switched on his computer and spent seven and a half hours looking at spreadsheets and moving numbers around on them. What could be more interesting than that?

　　But Jerry was unhappy. He was unhappy because people thought he was boring. He didn't want to be boring. He wanted people to think that he was a very interesting person. He tried to talk to people about his stamp collection. But every time he talked about his stamp collection he saw that people were bored. Because people were bored when he talked about his stamp collection, he talked about his job instead. He thought people would be very interested when he talked about his job, but, no, people thought his job was even more boring than his stamp collection. Sometimes, people even went to sleep when he talked to them.

Jerry thought about how to make himself more interesting. He decided that he needed to be famous for something. He thought about his stamp collection and decided that perhaps his stamp collection could make him famous. Perhaps he had the biggest stamp collection in the world or perhaps he had a very valuable stamp. Yes, this was it, he decided.

He wrote a letter to a local newspaper and asked them if they wanted to come and write an article about a local man with the biggest stamp collection in the world. The local newspaper wrote a letter, back to Jerry telling him that actually the Queen of England had the biggest stamp collection in the world. Jerry was very sad to learn this, but wrote back to the newspaper, telling them that he thought he had the most valuable stamp in the world. The newspaper wrote back to him, telling him that the most valuable stamp in the world cost 2,240,000 dollars, and asking him if he was sure that he had it. Jerry wasn't sure that he had it. In fact, he was sure that he didn't have it. Perhaps his whole collection was very valuable though ...

'Is it worth 10 million dollars?' asked the man from the newspaper on the telephone when Jerry called him.

'Erm, no, I don't think so ...'

'Forget it then,' said the man from the newspaper.

Jerry thought about other things to make himself famous. Perhaps he could be the best accountant in the world! Yes, this was it, he decided. He told a friend that he was the best accountant in the world.

'How do you know?' asked his friend.

'Well,' said Jerry, 'I have a good job, I like it ... it's very interesting ... spreadsheets ... numbers ... taxes ... finance ...' He saw his friend going to sleep. 'Hmmm,' he thought.

'Perhaps I'm not the best or the most interesting accountant in the world.'

'Listen, Jerry,' said his friend when he woke up again. 'Perhaps you don't have the biggest or the most valuable stamp collection in the world. Perhaps

111

you aren't the best or the most interesting accountant in the world. But there is one thing — Jerry, you are probably the most boring man in the world.'

Yes! Of course! This was it. Jerry could be famous because he was the most boring man in the world. Now he saw that his friends were right. He phoned the newspaper again. 'Hello!' he said. 'Would you like to do an interview with the most boring man in the world?'

'The most boring man in the world?' said the man from the newspaper. 'Now that's interesting!'

Next week there was a big article in the newspaper. 'The Most Boring Man in the World!' There was a picture of Jerry in his office. There was a picture of Jerry with his stamp collection. There was an interview with Jerry and interviews with his friends. His friends said they went to sleep when Jerry talked about his job or his stamp collection.

The next day the BBC and CNN called Jerry. They wanted stories about the most boring man in the world. 'The most boring man in the world!' they said. 'That's so interesting!'

And so, finally, Jerry Boyle became the official Most Boring Man in the World. You won't find his name in the *Guinness World Records* book, because they said that it was impossible to decide exactly how boring somebody is, but it was no problem for Jerry. Now he was famous. <u>Now he was so boring that he was interesting.</u>

1 According to the story, why do people think Jerry is the most boring man in the world? Answer in English.

2 Give one reason why Jerry's first attempt to become famous by contacting a local newspaper doesn't go well. Answer in English.

3 Explain what the underlined statement "Now he was so boring that he was interesting." means in your own words. Answer in English.

4 Choose the most appropriate sentence about Jerry.

　(a)　Finally, he could have his name entered into the Guinness World Records book.

(b)　For him his stamp collection was the only interesting thing he did.

(c)　He contacted the Queen of England to talk about his stamp collection.

(d)　His friends thought his job was even more boring than his stamps.

5　Choose the title that least matches the content of the story.

(a)　Everyone Can Be Great at Something

(b)　How a Stamp Collection and an Accountant's Job Can Make You Famous

(c)　Jerry Boyle: The World's Most Boring Man

(d)　The Secret to Building the World's Biggest Stamp Collection

6　Have you ever wanted to be famous? Please explain in English.

(☆☆☆☆○○○)

【5】次の英文を読んで，以下の問いに150語程度の英語で答えなさい。

In developed countries there has been a decline in the number of university students studying the humanities such as history, philosophy, and literature. Actually, in the current situation, students are more likely to major in science related field.

Question :　What do you think about this situation? Write your opinion, with reasons and examples.

(☆☆☆☆☆○○○○)

【6】次の1と2の問いに日本語で答えなさい。

1　次の文章は，「高等学校学習指導要領(平成30年告示)解説　外国語編　英語編」からの抜粋である。空欄(A)～(E)に適する語句を書きなさい。

> 　本目標では，使用する語句や文，対話の展開などについて生徒が支援を活用することを示している。ここでの使用する語句や文における支援を生徒が活用するためには，やり取りにおいて有用な語句や文を示すなどの配慮を教師が行うこと

が考えられる。しかし，使用する語彙や表現を(A)し，それらを正確に使うことを目標とした(B)に終始しないように留意する必要がある。対話の展開における支援を活用するためには，会話の展開の仕方や，会話がうまく続けられないときの対処法を提示するなどの配慮を教師が行うことが考えられる。

また，ティーム・ティーチングによる教師同士のやり取りや，モデルとなる生徒同士のやり取りを見せたり，ペアを(C)やり取りを続けることで，やり取りに慣れさせたりすることなども考えられる。

情報や考え，気持ちなどを話して伝え合うとは，やり取りされる話題に関する情報を交換したり，互いの考えや気持ちなどを伝え合ったりすることである。また，やり取りを続けるとは，互いの考えや気持ちの伝え合いを自然に継続することを意味する。その際，中学校において学習した，会話を継続させるために必要な表現などを繰り返し活用するとともに，会話のきっかけを作って話を切り出したり，会話の流れに応じて関連する質問をしたり，会話の流れを変えたりすることなどができるように継続的に指導することで，(D)力を育成していくことが重要である。

また，2の(3)のエの(ｲ)における本目標の実現のための言語活動例で示しているように，原則としてここでのやり取りは，話すための原稿を事前に用意してその内容を覚えたりそのまま読んだりするのではなく，(E)こととしている。

2 「高等学校学習指導要領(平成30年告示)解説　外国語編　英語編」で示されている「統合的な言語活動」とは何かを説明した上で，そのような言語活動を取り入れた具体的な指導例を書きなさい。

(☆☆☆☆○○○○)

解答・解説

【中高共通】

【1】1 イ　　2 ウ　　3 イ　　4 エ

〈解説〉スクリプトは非公開である。対話と質問文を聞き，問題用紙の選択肢から正答肢を選ぶ問題。放送は1回のみ。選択肢から，時刻，曜日，場所，理由が問われていることがわかるので，該当部分に注力して聴き取るとよい。

【2】1 ウ　　2 ウ　　3 ア　　4 イ

〈解説〉パッセージとその内容に関する4つの質問が放送される。放送は1回のみ。聞き逃さないよう，選択肢内のキーワード(本問では，cacaoなど)を事前にチェックしておきたい。パッセージのトピックは，カカオの栽培についてであろうと推測できる。

【3】1 ア　　2 ウ　　3 ア　　4 エ

〈解説〉本問も放送は1回のみだが，質問文と選択肢は問題用紙に印刷されている。音声が流れる前に最低限質問だけは確認しておきたい。選択肢は文章が長く情報量が多いので，余裕がある場合にだけ確認するようにするとよい。質問文中の疑問詞を確認し，キーワード(本問ではpen, paper, student, cognitiveなど)を押さえておくことで，音声に集中して問題を解くことができるだろう。

【中学校】

【1】1 エ　　2 ア　　3 ウ　　4 ア　　5 ウ　　6 ア　　7 ウ
　　8 イ

〈解説〉1　besidesは「～だけでなく，～に加えて」の意。　2　dedicate A to Bで「AをBに捧げる」の意。　3　ancient civilizationで「古代文明」の意。　4　invalidは「正しくない，無効な」の意。　5　featは「功績」の意。　6　eventuallyは「最終的に，結局は」の意。

2022年度　実施問題

7　withstandは「持ちこたえる」の意。目的語にearthquakesを取っている。　8　forfeitは「没収する，失う」の意。

【2】1　イ　　2　ア　　3　イ　　4　ア　　5　ア
〈解説〉1　Aの2回目の発話で「全くそうではなかった。あなたには私が楽しんでいたことを想像できないでしょう」と否定していることから，イ「それは退屈だったに違いない」が適切。　2　Bの2回目の発話でスーツケースを置いてきた場所を答えていることから，ア「残りはどこにあるのですか」が適切。　3　Aが1回目の発話でチケットの値段を聞いているので，イ「午後の公演と同じ料金です」が適切。　4　Bの2回目の発話で「そんなに長く待てない」と別の歯科医に行く旨を述べていることから，ア「明日の午前10時になら診てもらえます」が適切。　5　A・Bのそれぞれ2回目の発話で待ち合わせ場所をお互いに確認できたことから，当てはまるのはアのみとなる。イは3：45を表すためAの1回目の発話と合致せず不適切。

【3】1　ウ　　2　ア　　3　ウ　　4　ウ　　5　イ
〈解説〉1　人＋of great abilityで「素晴らしい能力を持つ人」を表す。2　主節はShe thoughtと過去形のため，従属節は過去完了形にする。3　funは人を主語に取らない。また，後ろにto不定詞を伴っていることから，ウを形式主語itとする。　4　「学校を終えるか働くかという選択を与えられ，彼は働くことを選んだ」の意の分詞構文。ウを過去形choseとする。　5　仮定法過去完了の倒置。従属節はIf there had been another option「もし他に選択肢があったら」の意なので，主節はI would have made reservations…「予約しただろうに」となる。

【4】1　ア　　2　エ　　3　ア
〈解説〉1　Landline phonesの所持率は年々下がっている。　2　Landline phonesと対照的に，smartphonesは2010年より急激に所持率が上昇している。　3　2011年の所持率は高い順にLandline phones，PCs，Fax

116

machines, Smartphones, Video Games Machinesである。

【5】1　イ　　2　ウ　　3　エ

〈解説〉1　Hanaが述べたい内容は「Emiから学ぶ前はボランティア活動
の重要性について理解していなかった」ということ。　2　第3，4段
落でMs. Okaは，現地の少年が必要としていることを理解し，野菜の
育て方を専門家に聞いてその少年に伝えたことが読み取れる。
3　第5段落3文目でMs. Okaは少年の抱える問題を彼と話すことで理解
できたことが読み取れる。また第6段落1〜4文目でEmiはお金や物を送
るだけでは理解できないこともあり，現地の人々と話すことの重要性
に触れている。Maryは，空所を含む文で，これらの点について述べて
いる。

【6】1　オ　　2　イ　　3　イ

〈解説〉1　最終段落最終文で「Sandraとの友情が損なわれていなかった
のがとても嬉しかった」と述べられていることから，最後の感情は
gladであるとわかる。また，第1段落では友達が少ない寂しさと，
Sandraがカウンティーフェアに誘ってくれたのに驚いていることが読
み取れる。　2　最終段落5文目で，チケット売り場の人はSandraから
電話がありKeikoに自分が病気で来られなくなったことを伝えてほし
いと頼まれていたことがわかる。　3　第2段落より，Keikoは少年た
ちのグループの会話から彼らがお祭りに行くものだと思い込んで後に
ついていったところ，別の場所に行ってしまったことが読み取れる。

【7】To express as a speech, it's necessary to think about the order of facts and
thoughts that students want to convey as a speaker, and to confirm that the
development is in line with the theme of the story. In addition, when giving
a speech in pairs, it's necessary to instruct the listener to make a speech that
is friendly to the listener by confirming difficult-to-understand expressions
and incorporating activities such as examining words and expressions that are

easy for the listener to understand. (84 words)

〈解説〉中学校学習指導要領解説外国語編では，本問の下線部のうち「事実や自分の考え，気持ちなどを整理する」とは「話し手として伝えたい内容や順序，聞き手に分かりやすい展開や構成などを考えたり，事実と考えを分けて整理したりするなど，話す内容を大まかな流れにしてコミュニケーションの見通しを立てることを意味している」と説明しており，「まとまりのある内容を話す」とは「例えば一つのテーマに沿った発表をしたり，内容に一貫性があるスピーチをしたりすることを意味している」と説明している。解答例では話す側の心構えだけでなく，二人一組での活動における聞き手への配慮についての指導にも触れている。日頃から80～100語を目安に自分の意見をまとめる練習をしておくとよいだろう。

【8】① a　　② f　　③ g

〈解説〉外国語科における「思考力，判断力，表現力等」を身に付けるためには，外国語によるコミュニケーションを行う目的や場面，状況などに応じて，情報を捉え，それを整理したり吟味したりしながら思考を深めることで，自らの考えを形成したり深化させたり，さらに表現を選択したりして論理的に表現することが重視されている。選択問題ではあるが，学習指導要領の内容を理解していないと対処は難しいと思われる。繰り返し読み込んでキーワードを把握しておこう。

【9】① まとまり　　② 具体的　　③ 五つ　　④ 活用する

〈解説〉この事項は，外国語科の指導計画の作成に当たり，生徒の主体的・対話的で深い学びの実現を目指した授業改善を進めることとし，外国語科の特質に応じて，効果的な学習が展開できるように配慮すべき内容を示したものである。生徒や学校の実態，指導の内容に応じ，「主体的な学び」，「対話的な学び」，「深い学び」の視点から授業改善を図ることが重要であり，「聞くこと」，「話すこと［やり取り］」，「話すこと［発表］」，「読むこと」及び「書くこと」という五つの領域に

わたる活動を，できるだけ有機的に関連させながら指導計画を考えることが重要であるとしている。記述式問題ではあるが，外国語科の目標および英語科の目標を理解していれば，対処可能な問題であろう。

【10】1 「関心のある事柄」(スポーツ，音楽，映画，テレビ番組，学校行事，休日の計画，日常の出来事など，身の回りのことで生徒が共通して関心をもっていること)について即興で情報を交換したり，お互いの考えや気持ちなどを伝え合ったりする活動を設定する。「即興で伝え合う」ために，話すための原稿を事前に用意してその内容を覚えたり，話せるように練習したりするなどの準備時間を取ることなく，不適切な間を置かずに相手と事実や意見，気持ちなどを伝え合うよう指導する。やり取りを行う際は，相手の発話に応じることが重要であり，それに関連した質問や意見を述べたりして，互いに協力して対話を継続・発展させる。 2 様々な題材の英文(社会で起こっている出来事や問題に関わる話題，広く国内外で起こっている事象で，多様な考え方ができるもの。具体的には自然環境，世界情勢，科学技術，平和など)に関する教師や生徒の発話，映像や音声の教材，ニュースや新聞記事，図表，ポスター，電子メールなどを聞いたり読んだりしたことの内容を理解するだけでなく，その内容に関して自分の意見や感想をもち，その内容をまとめて書かせる活動を設定する。その際，I think やI agreeなどの表現を用いて賛否や自分の意見を述べたり，becauseやsoなどの接続詞を用いて自分の意見や主張とその理由や根拠の関係を明確にしたり，firstやsecondなどの副詞を用いて内容を整理して述べさせる。

〈解説〉学習指導要領の記述が具体的に何を示しているのかは，同解説外国語編に詳述されている。必ず参照して学びを深めてほしい。

1 「関心のある事柄」とは，具体的には，流行している人や物，学校で行われる行事である。そのような話題は生徒も興味関心を持って，積極的に話すことができ，生徒同士がお互いに背景知識を持っている話題であるため，やり取りしやすい。解答例ではそのような事柄をお

互いに話す活動を設定する指導について述べている。「即興で伝え合う」については，準備をすることなく文字通りその場でのやり取りを重視する点を述べている。さらに，対話は双方向の活動である点にも触れ，お互いの協力が必要である点にも触れている。　２　解答例では，書く活動の基となる，中学3年生にとって適切かつ様々な題材についてまず列挙している。その上で英文の組み立て方，自分の意見をわかりやすく表現するための書き方についても触れて指導方法としてまとめている。

【高等学校】

【１】1　(c)　a time　　2　(b)　has held　　3　(b)　for　　4　(a)　who　　5　(b)　annual

〈解説〉1　3カ月という一区切りの期間には不定冠詞aをつけてa timeと表す。なお，3 monthsは，複数形であっても一区切りの期間ととらえ，動詞を単数形で表せるため(b)は正しい。　2　現在完了形の継続用法。「Thompson Corp.は過去60年にわたりニュージーランドの冷凍食品業界第1位の座を維持してきた」。　3　「～に対する志願者」はapplicants for～で表す。　4　the applicantを先行詞とする主格の関係代名詞とするのが正しい。I thoughtは挿入語句である。　5　product「製品」を修飾できるのは副詞annuallyではなく形容詞annual。

【２】1　(e)　　2　(a)　　3　(c)　　4　(b)　　5　(d)

〈解説〉1　空所直前の疑問文How can we make our brains less lazy?に注目する。「どうしたら脳を怠けないようにできるだろうか」に続けるには，(e)「なぜ脳が怠けたがるのかを理解するために，脳の働きを理解しなければならない」が適切。　2　(e)の最終文According to scientists, we have thousands of these lazy thoughts every day.「科学者によれば，私たちは毎日このような何千もの怠けた考えをもつ」に続けるには，(a)「それでは，脳はなぜ怠けた決断を好むのだろうか」が適切。　3　空所直前の文The brain was saving energy in real time. It happened without them even thinking about it.に注目する。エネルギーを節約することについて述べているので，(c)「それゆえ，エネルギーを節約するので脳が怠けるのは良いことである」が適切。　4　空所の直前ではlazy thinkingの具体例が述べられている。残る選択肢(b)と(d)のうち，適切なのは話題を転換してhard thinkingについて述べている(b)となる。

5　4に入る(b)ではhard thinkingがどういうものかが述べられ，続く(d)ではhard thinkingをすると人間の体はどうなるかが述べられている。

【3】1　イ　　2　ウ　　3　エ　　4　イ　　5　エ
〈解説〉1　本文全体を通して，まだはっきり解明されていないkokumiについて詳細に解説されており，今後のさらなる研究が待たれるという内容のため，イが最も適切。　2　本文全体を通して，人間のより良い味を求める探究心が様々なエピソードを交えて述べられているため，ウが最も適切だと判断できる。　3　第10段落参照。この段落で述べられている内容は，umamiについてではなくkokumiについてである。　4　問題文に関連する内容は第11・12段落に述べられている。第12段落でkokumiを生かした製品の開発をする企業について述べられているので，イが最も適切。　5　空所の後で，kokumi以外にも多くの別の味覚を科学者が研究し，人間の口は今でも謎に満ちていると述べて本文が終わっている。ここからkokumiが最後の味覚ではないことが読み取れ，エが適切だと判断できる。

【4】1　Because his talking about his job and hobby was so boring that people often fell asleep.　2　It is because the local newspaper told Jerry that his stamp collection wasn't the biggest in the world.　3　Though his hobby and job were so boring, they showed his uniqueness so that he could get attention in the news, which made him famous.　4　(d)　5　(d)
6　When I was an elementary school student, I wanted to become a Hollywood actor. I thought this would make me famous. I thought that if I could become famous, I would be able to have a lot of money, a nice house

and a happy life. (46 words)

〈解説〉1　第2段落，第5段落の，Jerryが自分の話をすると，あまりに退屈で聞き手が眠ってしまうというエピソードを用いて説明すればよい。　2　第4段落の新聞記者とのやり取りで，Jerryは世界最大の切手のコレクションを所持していなかったことが読み取れる。　3　Jerryの趣味や仕事の話は聞き手にとってあまりに退屈だったが，それが独特の個性となり結果的に有名になったという内容を英語で説明すればよい。　4　(d)は第2段落最後から2文目の内容と一致する。
5　(d)は本文のどこにも述べられていない。(a)～(c)はJerryがあまりに退屈な人間であるいう独自性に触れており適切である。　6　「有名になりたいと思ったことがあるか」という質問に英語で答える問題である。解答例では，幼少の頃の，誰もが一度は思い描くであろう非現実的な夢をエピソードとして挙げている。

【5】 I think this is a problem and that there should be a greater balance between the humanities and sciences. First of all, I think studying the humanities gives us very valuable knowledge of non-scientific things, which are essential for the human race to continue to improve. For example, we must study morals in order to make important decisions in how to use technology such as human cloning. Also, we must study history in order not to repeat the mistakes of the past. In addition, if university students only study science, there is a danger there will be a loss of professionals who encourage the development of our imagination and human expression. For example, there will be fewer artists creating various forms of art or music. There will be fewer writers to inspire the future with their stories. In conclusion, while science is valuable for developing technology and medicine, the humanities are also essential for our future. Humanity needs both. (159 words)

〈解説〉150語程度の自由英作文問題である。語数が多いため内容的にも深いものが求められており難易度は非常に高いだろう。書き始める前に内容や組み立てをじっくり考えておく必要がある。解答例では人文

系の学問を学ぶ必要性，人文系と科学系の両者のバランスが人間にとって大切であるという内容が述べられている。

【6】1　A　限定　　B　練習　　C　何度も変えて　　D　会話を継続する　　E　即興で行う　　2　統合的な言語活動とは，「聞くこと」「読むこと」「話すこと[やり取り]」「話すこと[発表]」「書くこと」の五つの領域のうちの複数の領域を結び付けて行う言語活動のことである。具体的な指導例としては次のようなものが考えられる。①ある日常的な話題について，生徒の興味や理解を促すために，教師とALTが対話を行い，それを生徒が聞く。②聞いた内容について，生徒間で意見を交換し合う。③聞いている間に，または聞いた後に聞き取った内容をメモに取ったり表にまとめたりする。④ペアやグループになって，聞き取ったメモを基に，聞いた内容を口頭で要約する。⑤教師と聞き取った内容について確認する。

〈解説〉1　出題箇所は，「高等学校学習指導要領(平成30年告示)解説　外国語編　英語編」の，英語コミュニケーションⅠの「1　目標　(3)　話すこと[やり取り]　ア　日常的な話題について，使用する語句や文，対話の展開などにおいて，多くの支援を活用すれば，基本的な語句や文を用いて，情報や考え，気持ちなどを話して伝え合うやり取りを続けることができるようにする」の解説の一部である。本問のような記述式問題対策としては，繰り返し読み込み内容をしっかり理解した上でキーワードを把握することが大切である。　2　同じく英語コミュニケーションⅠの「2　内容　(3)　①　言語活動に関する事項」の解説を参照。「統合的な言語活動」とは，五つのそれぞれの領域を扱った言語活動と併せて，他の複数の領域を結び付けた言語活動を指している。中学校においても，「聞くこと」と「話すこと」においては，統合的な言語活動を視野に入れた記載がされているが，高等学校では，五つの領域の全てにわたり，領域間を結び付けた統合的な言語活動を扱うこととしている。具体的な指導例では，解答例のように，五つの領域の中の複数が用いられるような内容にするよう留意したい。

2021年度　実施問題

【中高共通】

【１】これから，会話と質問が5つ放送されます。質問に対する答えとして最も適切なものをア～エの中から一つずつ選び，その記号を書きなさい。なお，会話と質問は一度だけ放送されます。

1

ア　A medium hot soy latte without syrup.

イ　A medium iced soy latte without syrup.

ウ　A small hot soy latte with syrup.

エ　A small iced latte with syrup.

2

ア　Climbing a mountain.

イ　Eating wanko soba.

ウ　Going to a hot spring.

エ　Visiting Koiwai Farm.

3

ア　She is making her first business trip to New York.

イ　She mainly works in the New York office.

ウ　She usually uses the same hotel in New York.

エ　She wants to stay in New York for as short as possible.

4

ア　She didn't like the two movies.

イ　She had her service disconnected.

ウ　She wants to order an additional program.

エ　She was improperly billed.

5

ア　To calculate the bills.

イ　To find a new restaurant.

ウ　To plan the next party.

エ　To play the piano.

(☆☆☆○○○○)

【2】これから，まとまりのある英文が放送されます。英文の後に，その内容について質問が4つ出されます。その質問に対する答えとして最も適切なものをア～エの中から一つずつ選び，その記号を書きなさい。なお，英文と質問は一度だけ放送されます。

1

ア　Almost all of the events.

イ　Almost none.

ウ　Around 20 seconds of events.

エ　2 minute-long events.

2

ア　Cats remember that their owners bring them to the vet.

イ　Chimpanzees pick the correct sample easily after 48 hours or more.

ウ　Elephants never forget a face.

エ　Swallows remember the location of last summer's nest.

3

ア　Because all species adjust well to a laboratory environment.

イ　Because animals have specialized memory systems.

ウ　Because it is important to know where we parked.

エ　Because it is under debate whether animals retrieve memories like humans do.

4

ア　Evolution has a clear order that indicates humans are always at the top.

イ　Evolution is not simple so we should remember humans may not be so smart.

ウ　Humans have improved a lot because evolution is so complicated.

エ　The short-term memory spans of chimpanzees are bad due to their simple evolution.

(☆☆☆○○○○)

【3】これから，まとまりのある英文が一度だけ放送されます。質問に対する答えとして最も適切なものを，ア～エから一つずつ選び，その記号を書きなさい。

1　Until what age should children not be exposed to any screen time at all?

ア　A year and a half.

イ　Eight years old.

ウ　Five years and three months.

エ　Two years and five months.

2　What did children do during the test to check their self-control?

ア　They built a tower of 90 blocks.

イ　They drew a long line on the floor.

ウ　They had a 90-minute break between each session.

エ　They stayed in a room with an unopened present.

3　What did the study find when children got older?

ア　Having continued exposure to computers and TV didn't affect self-control.

イ　Taking a tablet or a phone anywhere made it easier for them to control themselves.

ウ　Using mobile devices was highly addictive.

エ　Using screens made them feel happier.

4　What did parents believe that giving their children screens would do?

ア　They believed mobile devices wouldn't help their children develop.

イ　They believed their children's screen time should be shorter.

ウ　They believed their children wouldn't have any difficulties with self-control.

エ　They believed the screen use could interfere with their interactions with the children.

(☆☆☆○○○○○)

【中学校】

【 1 】次の1～8の英文の(　　)にあてはまる最も適切な英語を，それぞれア～エから一つずつ選び，その記号を書きなさい。

1　Renewable energy sources are very (　　) friendly; for instance, they produce little or no waste.

　　ア　generally　　イ　historically　　ウ　carefully
　　エ　environmentally

2　The doctor explained to the male patient that the new drug prescribed for him was less likely to (　　) unpleasant side effects.

　　ア　submit　　イ　trigger　　ウ　taint　　エ　oppress

3　When Tom first went to elementary school, he was (　　) by his mother and big sister.

　　ア　initiated　　イ　accompanied　　ウ　granted　　エ　struggled

4　The balloon soon caught a (　　) jet stream, which propelled it across the Pacific as fast as at 90 mph.

　　ア　favorable　　イ　equivalent　　ウ　vacant　　エ　sluggish

5　The girl was so (　　) in surfing the Net that she forgot about her dental appointment.

　　ア　enrolled　　イ　engrossed　　ウ　penetrated　　エ　intensified

6　(　　) students complete their assignments on time, take good notes, and allow sufficient time for studying.

　　ア　Jealous　　イ　Cautious　　ウ　Diligent　　エ　Precise

7　All PC users are forced to (　　) security threats as long as they are connected to the Internet.

　　ア　enrage　　イ　address　　ウ　distort　　エ　redeem

8　Joining a club in junior high school is a good way to develop (　　) with

127

other students. Many end up forming lifelong friendships.

　ア　camaraderie　　イ　chivalry　　ウ　cavalry

　エ　consternation

(☆☆☆☆◎◎◎◎)

【2】次の1〜5の会話文中の(　　)に，あてはまる最も適切な英語を，そ
れぞれア〜エから一つずつ選び，その記号を書きなさい。

　1　*A*: Your Spanish is very good, Jane!

　　B: (　　)

　　A: Did you study in Spain?

　　　ア　No, it isn't. I don't speak Spanish at all.

　　　イ　Not at all. Don't mention it.

　　　ウ　Thank you. It's kind of you to say so.

　　　エ　Yes, I know, but I've never been abroad.

　2　*A*: Excuse me. (　　)

　　B: Look, this is a newspaper stand, not a bank.

　　A: O.K. I'll buy a magazine then.

　　　ア　Can I exchange my ticket here?

　　　イ　Can you change this $20 bill for me?

　　　ウ　Is there a bank around here?

　　　エ　Where can I find a change machine?

　3　*A*: Why do you look so happy?

　　B: Because my work has been completed successfully.

　　A: Oh, sounds nice! And what are you going to do now?

　　B: (　　)

　　　ア　I think I should ask you to do the work for me.

　　　イ　I don't think anything will stop me from doing this work.

　　　ウ　Well, I'm going to make every effort to do my work.

　　　エ　I'm thinking of taking a break from work for two or three days.

　4　*A*: Hi! How was your day?

128

B: It was unbelievably busy. I'm exhausted.

A: Well, (　　)

B: I hope it'll be ready soon. I'm really hungry.

　ア　have some dinner and watch TV.

　イ　just finish your dinner.

　ウ　just sit down and eat your dinner.

　エ　sit down and rest while I cook dinner.

5　*A*: I'm glad we went to the class reunion.

　B: Me, too. It was great to see everyone.

　A: I can't believe it's been ten years since we graduated.

　B: I know. (　　)

　ア　I'm looking forward to it.

　イ　It feels like it was yesterday.

　ウ　There's no time like the present.

　エ　There's still plenty of time.

(☆☆☆○○○○)

【3】次の1～3の各文にある下線部ア～エには，英語の文法上または表現上適切ではない語句があります。適切ではない語句をそれぞれア～エから一つずつ選び，その記号を書きなさい。

1　We keep many roses _アthroughout the house, so every _イroom _ウsmells _エsweetly.

2　If we had _アknown her new email address, we _イwould _ウhad _エsent her a message.

3　_アNever before _イone language has _ウbeen spoken by such a _エhigh proportion of people across the world.

(☆☆☆○○○○)

【4】次の英文を読んで，あとの1～3の書き出しに続く内容として，最も適切なものを，ア～エから一つずつ選び，その記号を書きなさい。

129

The telephone rang. It was my sister. She said, "I used your crayon story again." My sister is a librarian in an elementary school. Every now and then, she will tell my story to students who visit her library.

About forty years ago, I sat in my first-grade classroom. My homeroom teacher told me to go to the office of Principal. The PRINCIPAL'S office! What did I do? I was a shy kid. I did my best in my new school life. I hated getting noticed by others. For me, having to go to the principal's office was the biggest shock. I walked ever so slowly to the office.

"Diane, the principal is not ready for you yet. Please have a seat," said the lady at the desk. I climbed up onto a big sofa and wanted to sink lower and lower into the cushions. I wanted the cushions to eat me whole. The phone rang on her desk. "You can go in now," she smiled. I pushed open the heavy door. It was worse than I thought. My parents were already seated in front of the principal's desk. I didn't know why they were there. My father walked straight over to me with my drawings in his hand.

"Why do you only use black crayon when you draw?" he asked. I couldn't speak.

"Show me your desk," said my father.

We went back to my classroom. All my classmates were out on the school grounds. I nervously pointed to my desk. My father took my crayon box out of my desk, and opened it. Only one crayon was in it. It was black.

My father asked, "Where are the other crayons?"

I quietly answered, "I gave all the others .... I used them together with my friends like you and Mom taught me."

My father took a deep breath and let it out slowly. "You were sharing."

I nodded my head. I looked at my father, then at the principal — their faces were both red. The principal said that I could join the classmates. I waved goodbye to my parents. Mom waved back, but I couldn't catch my father's eye; he was too busy looking at the principal.

I learned years later that my father's face was red because he was angry at the principal's mistake. And the principal's was red because he lost face in front of my parents after making a mistake. He thought that all my drawings were full of black and that I had deep problems. To him, my crayon choice showed my "dark and unhappy mind." He called my parents to discuss "my problem."

I was too shy to ask my friends to give my "shared" crayons back.

That night, my father talked to me about "sharing and giving," and how the two are different. He also gave me a new box of crayons and said, "These crayons are for you and you alone, understand?" I held the new box strongly and said, "Yes, Daddy."

Today, my sister tells her students, "Don't be afraid of asking questions. You need to speak up. If you don't, I might not be able to understand what you really think. And that's not a good thing. Let me tell a story about my sister, when she was around your age ...."

1　Diane walked ever so slowly to the principal's office because
　ア　she jumped from a big sofa to the cushions and she hurt her leg.
　イ　her homeroom teacher still didn't notice that the principal had called her.
　ウ　her parents were already waiting for her in front of the principal's desk.
　エ　she was shocked and she had no idea about the reason why she had to go there.

2　The principal's mistake was that he didn't
　ア　know who stole Diane's crayons.
　イ　visit Diane's house to discuss her problem.
　ウ　understand the reason why Diane was using only black crayon.
　エ　take Diane to the hospital immediately when he knew she had a problem.

3　This story tells us when you are in trouble,
　ア　sharing is more important than giving.

イ　it's better to keep silent till your friends notice your feelings.

ウ　your father and mother will get angry and solve the problem.

エ　you should voice your opinions to get to better express yourself.

(☆☆☆○○○○)

【5】次の英文を読んで，あとの質問に答えなさい。

A consumer walks into a store. He stands in front of hundreds of boxes of laundry detergent. He chooses one brand, pays for it, and leaves. Why does he pick that specific kind of soap? Is it truly better than the others? Probably not. These days, many products are nearly identical to one another in quality and price. If products are almost the same, what makes consumers buy one brand instead of another? Although we might not like to admit it, commercials on television and advertisements in magazines probably influence us much more than we think they do.

Advertising informs consumers about new products available on the market. It gives us information about everything from shampoo to toothpaste to computers and cars. But there is one serious problem with this. The "information" is actually misinformation. It tells us the products' benefits but hides their disadvantages. Advertising not only leads us to buy things that we don't need and can't afford, but it also confuses our sense of reality. "Zoom toothpaste prevents cavities and gives you white A !" the advertisement tells us. But it doesn't tell us the complete truth: that a healthy diet and a good toothbrush will have the same effect.

Advertisers use many methods to get us to buy their products. One of their most successful methods is to make us feel dissatisfied with ourselves and our imperfect lives. Advertisements show us who we aren't and what we don't have. Our A aren't white enough. Our hair isn't shiny enough. Our clothes aren't clean enough. Advertisements make us afraid that people won't like us if we don't use the advertised products. "Why don't I have any dates?" a good-looking girl sadly asks in a commercial. "Here," replies her roommate,

"try Zoom toothpaste!" Of course she tries it, and immediately the whole football team falls in love with her. "That's a stupid commercial," we might say. But we still buy Zoom toothpaste out of fear of being unpopular and having no friends. If fear is the [B] motive for buying a product, then wanting a good self-image is the [C] reason for choosing it. Each of us has a mental picture of the kind of person we would like to be. For example, a modern young woman might like to think that she looks like a beautiful movie star. A middle-aged man might want to see himself as a strong, attractive athlete. Advertisers know this. They write specific ads to make certain groups of people choose their product. Two people may choose different brands of toothpaste with the identical price, amount, and quality; each person believes that he or she is expressing his personality by choosing that brand.

Advertisers get psychologists to study the way consumers think and their reasons for choosing one brand instead of another. These experts tell advertisers about the motives of fear and self-image. They also inform them about recent studies with colors and words. Psychologists have found that certain colors on the package of an attractive product will cause people to reach out and take that package instead of buying an identical product with different colors. Also, certain words attract our attention. For example, the words "new," "improved," "natural," and "giant size" are very popular and seem to draw our eyes and hands toward the package.

Many people believe that advertising does not affect them. They know that there is freedom to choose, and they like to think they make wise choices. Unfortunately, they probably don't realize the powerful effect of advertising. They may not clearly understand that advertisers spend billions of dollars each year in aggressive competition for our money, and they are extremely successful. Do you believe that ads don't influence your choice of products? Just look at the brands in your kitchen and bathroom.

1 文中の [A] に共通して入る適切な語を書きなさい。

2 文中の [B], [C] に入る語の組み合わせとして，最も適切な

ものを次のア〜エから一つ選び，その記号を書きなさい。

ア　B：negative　　　　C：positive

イ　B：optimistic　　　 C：pessimistic

ウ　B：constructive　　 C：destructive

エ　B：financial　　　　C：religious

3　本文の内容と一致するものを，次のア〜エから一つ選び，その記号を書きなさい。

ア　Consumers know that one specific kind of soap is better than the others.

イ　One of the problems with advertising is that it doesn't inform us of the disadvantages of products.

ウ　In the Zoom toothpaste commercial, a good-looking girl falls in love with a football player immediately after she uses the toothpaste.

エ　Consumers know that they can buy products without being affected by advertisements because they have the freedom to choose.

(☆☆☆○○○○○)

【6】次の英文を読んで，あとの問いに答えなさい。

A　Many of us have taken personality quizzes in magazines or on the Internet, hoping that they will show us to be one type of person over another. Sometimes it is tempting to influence the result by modifying our answers. Wouldn't we all rather be courageous than cowardly, optimistic rather than pessimistic, relaxed rather than uptight? Many of us like to think of ourselves as extroverted rather than introverted. Extroverts are popular, fun-loving, and cool. Surely it's better to have lots of friends and go to parties than to be a shy nerd? The notion that extroversion is superior is so ingrained in our culture that extroverted parents have even been known to send their children to psychiatrists in an attempt to 'cure' their child's quiet ways. And this happens despite the fact that introverts make up at least one-third of the population.

B　But what exactly is an introvert? An introvert is someone who prefers peace and quiet, and feels uncomfortable in high-stimulus environments. He or she tires quickly at parties, and needs to take frequent 'time-outs' in social situations. Signs of introversion appear at the earliest stage of life. Studies have shown that babies who react strongly to stimuli, such as hand-clapping, are more likely to grow up as introverts while those who react less are more likely to become extroverts. Many people believe introversion is about being shy or antisocial, but that's a misconception. Shyness derives from the fear that society will react negatively toward you. You can be introverted without having that fear at all. It is also possible to be a shy extrovert who performs well socially but experiences discomfort at the same time.

C Western society seems obsessed with turning us into extroverts from the get-go. Picture the modern classroom. The days when kids sat at their desks and worked individually are long gone. Nowadays students sit facing each other as they work on countless group projects, even in subjects like math and creative writing. Kids who prefer to work by themselves don't fit in, and research shows that most teachers believe the ideal student is an extrovert—even though introverts tend to get higher grades. Colleges similarly focus on the extrovert. U.S. colleges, especially, grade you on your ability to speak out. When they are not in the classroom, students are encouraged to take part in sports clubs or study groups that leave them little time to themselves.

D Do we just have to accept that the extroverts will win all the spoils, leaving the introverts to slink away into a corner and deal with the situation as best they can? Luckily, the answer is 'No.' Despite the best efforts of the education system, a full 40% of executives describe themselves as introverts. While extroverts have the gift of the gab, the introverts' very lack of dominance can help them succeed within a certain type of business environment. Charismatic extroverts may be better at leading people who are prepared to accept the boss' word without question, but introverted leaders often produce better outcomes when their teams are proactive. In such setups, extroverted leaders might dominate discussions, preventing good ideas from coming to the fore.

[E]　Introverted leaders are also better listeners, and tend to think before they speak. This tendency to be more careful with words is an asset in a position where it is costly to make mistakes. Introverted leaders like to dig deep, investigating issues and ideas thoroughly before moving on to new ones. They are drawn to meaningful conversations, not chit-chat, and they know how to ask great questions and really listen to the answers. Introverted leaders also prepare well, rehearsing speeches and delivering them in measured tones. Former President Obama is a good example of just such a leader. They also tend to be comfortable with the written word, which helps them better articulate their positions and document their actions. Finally, they embrace solitude, and these regular timeouts actually fuel their thinking, creativity and decision-making.

[F]　So if you ever have the time to take a personality test and it indicates that you are an introvert, don't be dismayed. Don't say to yourself, 'I am shy and inhibited, and will never make it to the top.' Instead, you can reassure yourself that you are probably careful and reflective, and be proud that you share a personality trait with many of the great achievers, not just in the world of business, but across the spectrum of professions. Who wouldn't want to be in the company of distinguished individuals such as the writer J.K. Rowling, actor Harrison Ford, entrepreneur Bill Gates, and physicist Albert Einstein? Perhaps introversion carries the key to success, after all.

1　本文は[A]～[F]の6段落で構成されている。次の内容を含んでいるのはどの段落か，最も適する段落を，[A]～[F]から一つ選び，その記号を書きなさい。

　　　the difference between shyness and introversion

2　本文の内容と一致するものを，次のア～エから一つ選び，その記号を書きなさい。

　ア　Introversion is a personality trait that many prefer to have.

　イ　People who grow up to become introverts reacted less to stimuli as babies.

ウ　Wanting to be alone is a weak point for a leader.

エ　Some of the most accomplished people have been introverts.

(☆☆☆☆○○○○○)

【7】次の文は，中学校学習指導要領解説　外国語編(平成29年7月)　第2
章「第2節　英語」における「3　指導計画の作成と内容の取扱い」を
一部抜粋したものです。

　アの事項において，下線部のような学習の充実を図るためには，ど
のような指導が考えられるか，あなたの考えを80語以上の英語で書き
なさい。

　なお，最後に語数を記入すること。語数については，同じ語を2回
使用した場合，2語と数えること(のべ数)とします。

> (1)　指導計画の作成に当たっては，小学校や高等学校における
> 指導との接続に留意しながら，次の事項に配慮するものとす
> る。
> 　ア　(略) 英語の音声や語彙，表現，文法の知識を<u>五つの領域</u>
> <u>における実際のコミュニケーションにおいて活用</u>する学習
> の充実を図ること。

(☆☆☆○○○○○)

【8】次の文は，中学校学習指導要領(平成29年3月)　第2章「第9節　外
国語」における「第2　各言語の目標及び内容等」の「1　目標」を一
部抜粋したものです。文中の(①　)～(③　)にあてはまる語句とし
て，最も適切なものを，あとのa～iから一つずつ選び，その記号を書
きなさい。

> (1)　聞くこと
> 　ア　（　①　）と話されれば，日常的な話題について，必要な情
> 　　　報を聞き取ることができるようにする。
> 　イ　（　①　）と話されれば，日常的な話題について，（　②　）
> 　　　を捉えることができるようにする。
> 　ウ　（　①　）と話されれば，社会的な話題について，（　③　）
> 　　　を捉えることができるようにする。

a　ゆっくり　　　　　　　　b　はっきり
c　ゆっくりはっきり　　　　d　話の概要
e　具体的な情報　　　　　　f　簡単な語句や表現
g　短い説明の要点　　　　　h　まとまりのある文の内容
i　十分に慣れ親しんだ表現の意味

(☆○○○○○)

【9】次の文は，中学校学習指導要領(平成29年3月)　第2章「第9節　外
　　国語」における「第2　各言語の目標及び内容等」の「3　指導計画の
　　作成と内容の取扱い」を一部抜粋したものです。文中の（　①　）～
　　（　④　）にあてはまる適切な語句を書きなさい。

> (2)　2の内容に示す事項については，次の事項に配慮するものと
> 　する。
> 　ク　各単元や各時間の指導に当たっては，コミュニケーショ
> 　　　ンを行う（　①　），場面，状況などを明確に設定し，
> 　　　（　②　）を通して育成すべき（　③　）を明確に示すことによ
> 　　　り，生徒が学習の（　④　）を立てたり，振り返ったりする
> 　　　ことができるようにすること。

(☆☆○○○○○)

【10】次の文は，中学校学習指導要領(平成29年3月)　第2章「第9節　外国語」における「第2　各言語の目標及び内容等」の「1　目標」を一部抜粋したものです。

> (3)　話すこと[やり取り]
> 　ア　関心のある事柄について，簡単な語句や文を用いて即興で伝え合うことができるようにする。

1　下線部の関心のある事柄とはどのような事柄か，具体を示しながら日本語で説明しなさい。

2　下線部の即興で伝え合うとはどのようなやり取りか，留意点を挙げながら日本語で説明しなさい。

(☆☆☆◎◎◎◎◎)

【11】次の文は，中学校学習指導要領(平成29年3月)　第2章「第9節　外国語」における「第2　各言語の目標及び内容等」の「1　目標」を一部抜粋したものです。

> (5)　書くこと
> 　ア　関心のある事柄について，簡単な語句や文を用いて正確に書くことができるようにする。

1　この目標で示されたことができるようにするために，中学校第1学年の初期段階で指導する際，どのようなことに留意する必要があるか，小学校の外国語科の「書くこと」の活動を踏まえ，日本語で書きなさい。

2　「書くこと」が苦手な生徒や，「書くこと」につまずきが見られる生徒に対し，具体的にどのような指導が必要であるか，日本語で書きなさい。

(☆☆☆☆◎◎◎◎◎)

【高等学校】

【1】次の英文1～5にはそれぞれ誤りや不適切なところがある。修正が必要な箇所を(a)～(c)の内から一つ選び，適切な形に直しなさい。

1　This morning, I (a)<u>left</u> all the windows (b)<u>opening</u> (c)<u>to let</u> some fresh air in.

2　(a)<u>As far as</u> you talk with someone new (b)<u>for a while</u>, you might begin to feel as if you (c)<u>have known</u> them for decades.

3　If you can (a)<u>explain a doctor</u> how (b)<u>you feel</u> when you get ill in a foreign country, your language ability (c)<u>is</u> perfect.

4　I didn't know what (a)<u>to do</u> when my cat (b)<u>was kidnapped</u> (c)<u>during</u> I was away on a business trip.

5　Every year, the Happy Farm produces (a)<u>five-sixth</u> of the towns'rice, (b)<u>which</u> is (c)<u>used</u> to feed hundreds of people.

(☆☆☆○○○○○)

【2】次の空所(1)～(5)に入れるのに最も適切な段落を，あとの(a)～(e)より選び，その記号を書きなさい。ただし，同じ記号を複数回用いてはならない。

According to a 2018 survey, 51 percent of high school students don't believe their schools have done enough to help them deal with stress. 49 percent feel their schools don't help in dealing with emotions. 46 percent feel this about their school's support in helping deal with disagreements. Meanwhile, fewer than half of the graduates surveyed feel prepared for life after high school.

(1)

Why? Teens need more opportunities to dig deeper—to actively explore who they are, what drives them, and who they want to be in the world. So how can we better address teens'developmental needs?

Researcher David Yeager and his colleagues argue that it's important to address teens'needs for status and respect, allowing them to contemplate questions such as "How do others treat me?" and "Am I granted the rights I expect to be granted as a student?" . If teens feel competent, autonomous, and valued in their community—if they have a sense of high status and respect, in other words—they're likely to be more motivated and engaged. There are some ways you can help teens to develop greater self-awareness—and ultimately enhance their sense of status and respect among peers and adults.

(2)

After they learn about some of their key strengths, ask them to choose one strength to focus on every day for a week. Have them describe the strength in writing and propose several different ways they might use it each day, and challenge them to act on that strength throughout the week.

For example, if a student wants to capitalize on kindness as a strength, he might perform a random act of kindness for a peer, write a thank-you note to a teacher, or volunteer to care for abandoned animals at a local shelter over the weekend.

As an alternative to focusing on one strength all week, they might choose to focus on a different strength each day. Whichever option they choose, have them write about what they did, how it made them feel, and what they learned from the experience.

(3)

Another way to help students clarify who they are and who they want to be in the world is to invite them to envision their ideal future.

Ask your students to respond to the following questions in a 15-minute free-write: What is the best possible life yon can imagine? Consider all the areas in your life that are important to you—relationships, school, career, hobbies and interests, etc. Be as creative and imaginative as you want, and don't worry about spelling and grammar.

Ask them to be as specific as possible, and tell them that it's easy to focus on current obstacles to reaching goals, so they should let go and simply dream about the future and exactly what it could look like.

(4)

We can't challenge adolescents to make a difference in the world without offering them opportunities to lead and be heard. High schools aren't simply holding spaces for teens. They can be places where students test their wings, raise their voices, and learn how to effect change. In fact, students in schools with strong Social and Emotional Learning programs and positive learning environments are more likely to report that their "voice" matters.

(5)

However, you might also offer more students advisory roles on boards or in district-level committees. Invite their feedback and input on school policies, programs, assemblies, and even hiring decisions.

Many of our students face significant obstacles in their lives due to factors beyond their control, like health challenges, poverty, and institutionalized racism. Prompting students to connect with their strengths, identify what matters most to them, and envision ways they might contribute to the world may ultimately help them to feel more respected and empowered.

(a)   Researchers suggest that it's important to create mindsets that blunt the power of perceived threats to teens'status and respect, and this exercise can help students feel a greater sense of control as they clarify a vision of their future self.

(b)   Research tells us that this activity can increase well-being and reduce symptoms of depression. It's easy for us to focus on our weaknesses and personal challenges, but when we spend time making the most of our positive qualities, we can build greater self-esteem and confidence.

(c)   What does this look like beyond classroom-based suggestions? This means holding student-led conferences and class meetings, student-led instruction, and student choices in curriculum. You can extend student influence at your school through peer mediation, mentoring, and buddy programs, as well as student-led community engagement and service learning opportunities.

142

(d)　We're learning that some social and emotional learning approaches simply aren't as effective with teens as they are with children. When teaching relationship skills, teens can sometimes find direct teaching through lectures, videos, and homework to be patronizing and heavy-handed.

(e)　If teens crave respect, it's important to create a school climate where their strengths are recognized and valued. Take time in class to have your students identify their personal strengths, such as hope, humility, honesty, kindness, and perseverance. You can begin by asking them to take a 10-minute online survey designed by positive psychology researchers.

(☆☆☆☆◎◎◎)

【3】次の英文を読んで，1～5の問いに対する答えとして最も適切なものをア～エの中から一つずつ選び，その記号を書きなさい。

Early last year, NASA announced an ambitious plan to return American astronauts to the Moon and establish a permanent base there, with an eye toward eventually placing astronauts on Mars. The Artemis Moon Program has plenty of critics, including many in the US House of Representatives, who appear to prefer a stronger focus on a crewed mission to Mars. As Eric Berger reported last August, "NASA has a very real risk of turning the Artemis Program into a repeat of the Apollo Program—a flags-and-footprints sprint back to the Moon with no follow-through in the form of a lunar base or a sustained presence in deep space."

But if the Artemis Program's ambitious objectives survive the budget allotment process, materials science will be crucial to its success, particularly when it comes to the materials needed to construct a viable lunar base. Concrete, for instance, requires a substantial amount of added water in order to be usable in that area, and there is only a small supply of water on the moon. In a new paper in the Journal of Cleaner Production, an international team of scientists suggests that astronauts setting up a base on the moon could use the urea in their urine, that is the liquid or semi-liquid waste produced by

143

the kidneys of humans or other animals, as a plasticizer to create a concrete-like building material out of lunar soil.

There's certainly a strong argument to be made for using existing materials on the Moon itself to construct a lunar base. NASA estimates that it costs around $10,000 to transport one pound of material into orbit, according to the authors. Past proposals have called for 3D printing with Sorel cement, which requires significant amounts of chemicals and water, and a rocklike material that would require both water and phosphoric acid as a liquid binder. The latter might be better suited to constructing a base on Mars.

Spiking lunar regolith, a fine powdery soil on the surface of the Moon, with geopolymers could provide a solution. Geopolymers bring several advantages to the concrete mix: they are resistant to fire and have low thermal conductivity, provide radiation shielding, and can withstand the elements of the harsh lunar environment, which includes high amounts of sulfates, for example, as well as attacks from acid and salt. They typically show good freeze/thaw resistance and high compressive strength, too.

3D printing is favored for lunar construction to minimize risks to humans on the Moon during construction, but that layer-by-layer manufacturing approach requires a material that is pliable enough for extrusion, among other desirable properties. On Earth, one could just add extra water, but this is not feasible on the Moon. There are so-called super-plasticizers that would be ideal for this purpose, but there are no naturally occurring super-plasticizers on the Moon either, so this, too, would require expensive transport. Plasticizers are chemical additives that serve to soften concrete mixtures so that they are soft enough to pour or shape before hardening.

But there will be human astronauts on the Moon during construction, producing organic waste, i.e., urine and feces. And the urea component in urine might serve as an effective super-plasticizer for 3D printing building materials for lunar bases. Scientists from Norway, Spain, the Netherlands, and Italy conducted a study on the effectiveness of this principle with the

European Space Agency's blessing. Along with its Chinese counterpart, the ESA is also interested in establishing a lunar base.

"To make the geopolymer concrete that will be used on the Moon, the idea is to use what is there: regolith—loose material from the Moon's surface—and the water from the ice present in some areas," said co-author Ramón Pamies of the Polytechnic University of Cartagena. "With this study we have seen that a waste product, such as the urine of the personnel who occupy the Moon bases, could also be used. The two main components, of this body fluid are water and urea, a molecule that allows the hydrogen bonds to be broken and therefore reduces the thickness of many water-based mixtures."

The team used a synthetic material designed by the ESA with similar characteristics as lunar regolith, adding urea, a polycarboxylate-based super-plasticizer, and a naphthalene-based super-plasticizer to different batches, as well as making a control group batch without any super-plasticizer. Then the researchers used a 3D printer to make mud cylinders out of each batch. They tested each batch for the ability to support heavy weights while maintaining shape, including after each of eight freeze/thaw cycles, mimicking as much as possible the harsh lunar conditions.

The results: the batches with no super-plasticizer and the polycarboxylate-based super-plasticizer proved too stiff for 3D printing and were prone to cracking. The batches with urea- and naphthalene-based super-plasticizers, in contrast, proved malleable enough for extrusion with few fractures in the case of naphthalene to none in the case of urea. They also retained their shape under heavy external loads. Both those batches showed a decrease in compressive strength and some microcracks, after eight freeze/thaw cycles, however. Nonetheless, "Overall, urea exhibits promising properties as a super-plasticizer for 3D printing of lunar geopolymers," the authors concluded.

The research of this principle is still in the early stages, and more experiments are needed. The materials were not subjected to a vacuum, for instance, which could cause crack formation due to the evaporation of volatile components. The team also has not yet evaluated how well lunar regolith geopolymers would hold up under meteorite bombardment or how well they would shield humans from high radiation levels.

There's also (　A　). "We have not yet investigated how the urea would be extracted from the urine, as we are assessing whether this would really be necessary, because perhaps urine's other components could also be used to form the geopolymer concrete," co-author Anna-Lena Kjøniksen said. "The actual water in the urine could be used for the mixture, together with that which can be obtained on the Moon, or a combination of both."

1　Which of the following sentences best summarizes this passage?

　ア　Building lunar bases is a vital step to prepare for crewed missions to Mars.

　イ　3D printing shows promise as a reliable method for building lunar bases.

　ウ　Urea found in astronauts' urine could be used to help build lunar bases.

　エ　Water on the moon may be used as a plasticizer for building lunar bases.

2　According to the passage, which of the following is NOT a reason why materials already existing on the moon would be more practical for building a lunar base?

　ア　Lunar regolith can be mixed with geopolymers to make concrete.

　イ　Substances commonly found on Earth such as water and phosphoric acid are scarce on the moon.

　ウ　3D printing with Sorel cement from the moon can be done more easily.

　エ　Transporting materials from Earth would be much more costly.

3　According to the passage, what do the results of the study conducted by the team of European scientists indicate?

ア　Non-urea based super-plasticizers were more malleable and without cracks.

イ　3D printing was more feasible with the polycarboxylate super-plasticizer.

ウ　Urea-based plasticizers showed no microcracks throughout the testing.

エ　Urea showed effectiveness as a super-plasticizer for 3D printing concrete.

4　Which of the following "unknowns" requiring further research is NOT mentioned in the passage?

ア　Whether it is necessary for urea to be extracted from the astronauts' urine.

イ　Whether the material could be used similarly to build a base on Mars.

ウ　Whether the material could protect humans from high radiation levels.

エ　Whether the material would crack when exposed to the vacuum of space.

5　Which are the most suitable words to put into (　A　)?

ア　a potential disadvantage

イ　a practical concern

ウ　a promising breakthrough

エ　a sharp criticism

(☆☆☆☆○○○○)

【4】次の英文を読んで，1～6の問いに答えなさい。

　　Once upon a time there lived in China a young man named Chang. He was intelligent and sincere, and more than anything, he loved flowers. Nothing pleased him more than watching the lilacs, lilies and peonies as they bloomed in the springtime. In the winter he anticipated the appearance of the beautiful narcissus. He could not choose a favorite flower, for he loved morning and evening glories, pomegranate and peach flowers, and the summer lotus that floated on the ponds. He enjoyed fragrant roses, hardy chrysanthemums, dazzling dahlias.

Chang admired the emperor of the land because he had heard he also loved flowers and supervised a beautiful garden on the palace grounds.

Now the emperor was growing old. He had no son, and so he had no successors. For many years he had carefully considered how to choose a man he might name as the next emperor. Then one day in early spring as he wandered through his garden, he came up with a most marvelous plan.

The very next day the emperor sent word to all the young men in the land, announcing that at the end of that week he would hand out seeds to anyone who wanted to grow a flower.

"Whoever grows the finest flower from among all those brought before me," the emperor decreed, "will be my successor."

When Chang heard the news, he filled a bright blue pot with moss and compost, topsoil and sandy loam. Satisfied that his soil was rich and moist, he carried it to the palace. There he stood in line among hundreds of others. Each young man held a pot - some huge, some tiny, some round, some tall and slender and each received a seed from the emperor's own hand.

Chang pressed the seed into the soil and carefully covered it with a light coating to keep it warm. Then he hurried home.

There Chang tended his seed with the same devotion he offered all his other plants. He was careful not to give it too much water or too little. At the proper times he treated it with fertilizers, and was careful to protect it, like all the others, from insects, dust and mold.

As the months passed, Chang's other plantings burst through the soil and began to grow, but he was disappointed that nothing sprouted in his bright blue pot. "That's odd," he said. "Perhaps it does not need so much sun." So he moved the pot to another room, but nothing happened. "Perhaps this room is too cool," he said, and so he carried his blue pot into a warmer room. Still, nothing happened.

Now the time was nearing to visit the emperor again, and Chang's bright blue pot stood empty. He was filled with despair each time he looked at it. "What could I be doing wrong?" he wondered. He visited every gardener he knew, and to each he told the tale of his seed. They shook their heads. No one knew what could be wrong.

Some said it was obvious that he was not meant to be the next emperor. Others told him he must add more soil, or more water, or to fertilize less. Others told him to forget his foolish plan.

But Chang's parents listened to his worries and only smiled. "Do'not worry, son. You are doing your best," they said. "That is all any of us can do."

"But I have failed," Chang sighed as he stared down at the barren soil in his pot. "It is time to see the emperor, and I have let him down."

"Simply tell him what has happened," his father said. "Your only duty is to tell the truth."

His heart nearly breaking with disappointment, on the appointed day one year later, Chang walked to the palace. When he arrived, tears fell from his eyes, for before him stood a sea of young men, each one holding a flower more exquisite than the one before. The orchids were delicate and elegant, the lilies fragrant and full, the peonies bursting with color. Their owners held them proudly. "Look at mine!" they called, holding their plants high as the emperor walked through the crowd. He nodded pleasantly as he passed by, noting the bellflowers, the forget-me-nots, the foxgloves, flowers in every shade of the rainbow.

Chang had never seen a sight so beautiful, and some of his sadness left him as he inhaled the fragrances and marveled at the size and variety of the blooms.

At last the emperor reached him. Chang bowed his head. "Where's your flower, young man?" the emperor asked.

Chang looked up and saw a gleam in the man's eye that surprised him. "Sir, I have failed you," he said sadly. "I cared for my seed, but as you, see, I was not able to grow a flower for you. I hope you'll forgive me."

But the emperor's face lighted up with a smile brighter than even the flowers all around him. "You are my successor," the emperor said, taking Chang's hands in his.

"But sir, I am the only person here who failed."

The emperor shook his head. "On the contrary," he explained. "You see, I boiled these seeds before I handed them out. None of the seeds should have grown, but all these people were so eager for my position that they wanted only to please me with the beauty of their flowers and thereby gain my throne. They did not care enough for honesty, for truth. You alone have proven you are a worthy leader."

And so it was that the boy with the empty pot became successor to the emperor of China.

1 How would you describe Chang and his parents? Answer in an English sentence(s).

2 Why did Chang believe he had failed the Emperor? Answer in an English sentence(s).

3 Why did the other men's flowers grow while Chang's did not? Answer in an English sentence(s).

4 Choose the sentence which is false.

   (a)　The Emperor chose Chang as his heir because of his honesty

   (b)　The Emperor decided to choose an heir with a flower growing competition

   (c)　Chang could not get his flower to grow because he lacks skill in gardening

   (d)　Chang's father encouraged him to be always be truthful, even if it means failure

   (e)　The Emperor tricked the men into using boiled seeds

5 Choose the best title for this story.

   (a)　A Year with No Flowers

   (b)　Chang's Magical Flower

(c)　The Emperor's Garden

(d)　The Value of Truth

6　The Emperor was deceitful in order to find an honest heir. Do you believe that telling a lie to benefit a greater cause is okay? Why or why not? Answer in an English sentence(s).

(☆☆☆◎◎◎◎◎)

【5】次の英文を読んで，以下の問いに150語程度の英語で答えなさい。

At a recent TED Conference, AI expert Noriko Arai gave a talk presenting her Todai Robot, a machine that has been programmed to take the entrance exam to one of Japan's most prestigious universities, Tokyo University.

While Arai discovered Todai wouldn't have passed the exam, the robot still beat 80% of the students taking the exam, which has seven sections, such as math, English, science, and a 600-word essay writing portion.

However, instead of celebrating, Arai is troubled by the results. She worries that in preparing for the future where AI may replace many jobs, education is flawed. Instead of getting meaning from their studies, Arai has observed students behaving more like her Todai robot. They ingest facts and spit them out, without comprehension. The problem is, Todai and other forms of AI will ultimately surpass human memory and cognition, research has suggested. The human brain can never compete with the rote fact-checking power of a computer.

Question:　What kind of education reform do you think is necessary to co-exist with AI?

(☆☆☆☆◎◎◎◎)

【6】次の1と2の問いに日本語で答えなさい。

1　次の文章は，「高等学校学習指導要領(平成30年告示)解説　外国語編　英語編」からの抜粋である。空欄(　A　)～(　E　)に適する語句を書きなさい。

151

　　なお，今回の改訂では，領域として「話すこと」が「話すこと［（　Ａ　）］」と「話すこと［（　Ｂ　）］」に分かれているが，両者を示すことで，複数の話者が相互に話し伝え合う場合（「話すこと［（　Ａ　）］」）と一人の話者が連続して話す場合（「話すこと［（　Ｂ　）］」）という特性の違いを明確にしている。

　　今回の改訂において，小学校外国語活動・外国語科，中学校外国語科，高等学校外国語科の目標は，外国語で聞いたり読んだりして得た知識や情報，考えなどを的確に理解したり，それらを活用して適切に表現し伝え合ったりすることで育成される「知識及び技能」と「（　Ｃ　）等」について，高等学校卒業時において求められる資質・能力を見据えた上で，設定されている。このために小学校から中学校，高等学校に至るまで，児童生徒の発達の段階に応じて，五つの領域ごとに設定された言語活動を通して，「知識及び技能」と「（　Ｃ　）等」を一体的に育成するよう目標を設定している。

　　また，第1節でも述べたとおり，「知識及び技能」及び「（　Ｃ　）等」の育成の過程を通して「（　Ｄ　），人間性等」に関する資質・能力を育成することを目指す必要があり，ここではこのことを明確に示している。

　　各学校において作成される学習到達目標は，五つの領域別の目標を踏まえながら，2の内容に記述された，より具体的な言語材料と言語活動を参照して設定されたものにすることが望ましい。同一の学習到達目標について，複数の単元で異なる言語材料を活用した異なる言語活動を行うことにより，五つの領域別の目標をよりよく達成できるような（　Ｅ　）や課題設定が望まれる。

2　「高等学校学習指導要領(平成30年告示)解説　外国語編　英語編」では「実際のコミュニケーションの過程で考えられる様々な配慮などを，目標において「支援」と総称することとした。」と示されて

いるが，それぞれの領域において，どのような「支援」があるのか，「聞くこと」「読むこと」「やり取り」「発表」「書くこと」の各項目に沿って具体的に説明しなさい。

(☆☆☆◎◎◎◎)

解答・解説

【中高共通】

【1】1　ア　　2　エ　　3　ウ　　4　エ　　5　ウ
〈解説〉スクリプトが公表されていないが，会話と質問は1回しか流れないため，選択肢をあらかじめ読んでおくことで，トピックは予測しておくとよいだろう。例えば，選択肢に飲み物の名前が並んでいれば，カフェやレストランなど場所を予測することができるだろう。また，選択肢の主語を確認することで，男性と女性どちらの発話に集中すべきかもわかる。

【2】1　イ　　2　イ　　3　エ　　4　イ
〈解説〉本問も英文と質問は1回しか流れないため，選択肢をあらかじめ確認しておく必要がある。本問では，まとまりのある英文1つとそれに対する質問が4つ放送されるため，聞き逃さないよう，選択肢内のキーワード(本問では，動物の名前やEvolutionなど)を事前にチェックしておきたい。英文のトピックは，動物の進化についてであろうと推測できる。

【3】1　ア　　2　エ　　3　ア　　4　ウ
〈解説〉本問では，他のリスニング問題と異なり，質問と選択肢が印刷されている。音声が流れる前に最低限質問だけは確認しておきたい。情報量が多くなってしまうため，選択肢は余裕がある場合にだけ確認す

るようにするとよい。疑問詞を確認し，質問中のキーワード(本問では childrenやself-controlなど)を押さえておくことで，音声に集中して問題 を解くことができるだろう。

【中学校】

【1】1　エ　　2　イ　　3　イ　　4　ア　　5　イ　　6　ウ　　7　イ　　8　ア

〈解説〉1　空所を含む文の文意は，「再生可能エネルギー源は(　　　)や さしい」である。environmentally friendlyで「環境にやさしい」という 意味。　2　空所の後ろのunpleasant side effects「不快な副作用」につ ながるのは，trigger「(反応などを)引き起こす」である。　3　空所を 含む文の文意は「トムが最初に小学校に行ったとき，お母さんやお姉 さんに(　　　)された」である。これに適する動詞は，過去分詞形で accompanied「〜に付き添われる」。　4　空所を含む文の文意は「風船 はすぐに　(　　　)なジェット気流をとらえた。それは90mphほどの 速さで太平洋を渡って風船を前に進めた」である。これに適する形容 詞はfavorable「有利な，役立つ，好都合な」である。mph(miles per hour)は「マイル毎時」。　5　that節以降に「その女の子は歯医者の予 約について忘れた」とあるため，この文意に合うのはengrossed「〜に 没頭する，夢中になる」である。　6　空所を含む文の文意は 「(　　　)な生徒は時間通りに宿題を完成させ，ノートをしっかりと取 り，勉強に十分な時間を取る」である。よって，形容詞はdiligent「勤 勉な，熱心な」が適切。　7　空所後ろのthreats「脅威」につながる動 詞はaddress「〜に対応する」。addressはこの意味の他にも「述べる」 という意味を持つ多義語である。　8　空所を含む文の文意は「中学 校でクラブに参加することは他の生徒と(　　　)を発展させるよい方 法である」。これに適する名詞はcamaraderie「友情，仲間意識」で，2 文目にあるfriendshipと同義語である。

【2】1　ウ　　2　イ　　3　エ　　4　エ　　5　イ

〈解説〉1　空所前のAの称賛に対する返答が入る。正解はウ「ありがと
う。そう言ってくれてご親切に」である。　2　空所後にBは「ここは
新聞売り場であって，銀行ではありません」と答えている。したがっ
て，空所には銀行で使われる表現であるイ「この20ドル紙幣を両替し
てもらえますか」が入る。　3　仕事が成功裏に終わったと喜ぶBに対
し，Aは「これから何をする予定ですか」と尋ねている。したがって，
この文意に合うのはエ「2，3日仕事を休むことを考えています」。
4　空所後にBは「空腹だから，それがすぐ支度できればいいなあ」と
述べている。この文意に合うのはエ「私が夕食を作る間，座って休ん
でて」。　5　空所前のAの「卒業してから10年も経ったなんて信じら
れない」という発話に対し，Bは同意している。したがって，空所に
入るのはイ「昨日のことのように感じる」である。

【3】1　エ　　2　ウ　　3　イ

〈解説〉1　smellの後ろに形容詞を置いて「〜のにおいがする」という意
味。sweetlyは副詞なので適切ではない。sweetly→sweetが正しい。
2　本問は仮定法である。wouldは助動詞であるため，後ろに動詞の原
形がくる。had→haveが正しい。　3　Neverなどの否定語が文頭に来る
と，その後ろでは倒置が起こり疑問文の語順となる。したがって，
one language has→has one languageの語順が正しい。

【4】1　エ　　2　ウ　　3　エ

〈解説〉1　設問の訳は「Dianeは校長先生の部屋へかなりゆっくりと歩い
て向かった。なぜなら〜」である。第2段落4文目より，校長に呼ばれ
た理由がわからないこと，同段落8文目より，校長に呼ばれたことが
ショックだったことがわかる。したがって，エ「彼女はショックを受
け，なぜそこに行かなければならないのか理由がわからなかった」が
適切。　2　設問の訳は「校長先生の間違いは彼が〜しなかったこと
だった」である。第8段落2文目より，校長先生は面目を失って顔を赤

155

くしたこと，同段落3文目より，校長先生はDianeが黒いクレヨンだけ使った理由を勘違いしていたことがわかる。したがって，ウ「Dianeが黒いクレヨンだけを使った理由を理解する」が適切。　3　設問の訳は「この話は，あなたがもしトラブルに巻き込まれたとき，〜ということを私たちに教えてくれる」である。第10段落の筆者の姉(妹)の「質問をすることを恐れないで。声を上げなさい。もしそうしなければ，私はあなたたちが本当に考えていることを理解できないかもしれない。それはよくないことよ」という言葉から，エ「自分の考えをよりよく表現することができるように，意見を述べるべきである」が適切。

【5】1　teeth　　2　ア　　3　イ
〈解説〉1　第2段落のAを含む文は「Zoom歯磨き粉は虫歯を防ぎ，白い(A)を与えてくれる」，第3段落のAを含む文は「私たちの(A)は十分に白くない」という意味。したがって，この文意にあてはまる単語はteeth「歯」である。空所の前にaといった冠詞がないので，toothpaste「歯磨き粉」につられて，単数形のtoothにしないこと。
2　BとCを含む文は「もし心配が，ある製品を買う(B)な理由であるとすれば，よい自己イメージを求めることはそれを選ぶ(C)な理由になる」である。広告の戦略として，第3段落2文目に「私たちが自分自身や自身の不完全な生活に不満を持たせること」が挙げられている。したがって，Bにnegative「否定的な」，Cにpositive「前向きな」を入れれば文意に合う。　3　第2段落5文目の「それは私たちに製品のよい点を教えてくれるが，悪い点は隠す」から，イ「広告の問題点の1つは私たちに製品の悪い点を教えてくれないことである」が適切。ア　第1段落4〜6文目に「消費者はある石鹸がもう一方よりもよいということはおそらくわかっていない」と述べられているため不適。ウ　第3段落10文目に「(選手一人ではなく)チーム全員が彼女に恋をする」とあるため不適。　エ　第5段落3文目に「多くの人々は広告の効果(広告に影響を受けているということ)に気づいていない」とあるた

め不適。

【6】1 　B　　2　エ

〈解説〉1　内容の文意は「内気と内向性の違い」である。段落Bでは，まず内向的な人についての説明がされ，その後，内気であることの説明がされている。　2　段落Dから内向的な人のよい点が述べられており，段落Fの3文目に多くの成功者(achievers)が内向的であるという点で共通しているとある。したがって，エ「成功者の中には内向的である人もいる」が適切。　ア　段落Aの4文目に「多くの人が自分は内向的ではなく，外向的であると考えたがる」と述べられているため不適。　イ　段落Bの5文目に「内向的に育つのは，拍手に強く反応する赤ちゃんである」と述べているため不適。　ウ　段落Eの最後の文で，孤独について肯定的に述べられているため不適。

【7】In listening activities, it is important to consider purpose, scene and situation. We need to think about how we frame activities based in natural communication. Speaking activities should be divided into two parts; "interaction" and "presentation". So, we have to make a flexible teaching plan that alternates from presentation to interaction. We need to give the students the opportunity for impromptu interaction. Reading and writing are also communicative activities, so we should consider our audience (readers and writers). It is important to think of teaching plans which encompass the five parts of language skills and are based in real communication. (100 words)

〈解説〉指導計画に関して，中学校学習指導要領に基づいて自分の意見を述べる問題である。本問の下線部中の「五つの領域」は，新学習指導要領(平成29年3月告示)の外国語科における重要な改訂箇所である。従来1領域であった「話すこと」が，今回の改訂により「話すこと[やり取り]」と「話すこと[発表]」の2領域に分けられ，「読むこと」，「聞くこと」，「書くこと」と合わせて，「五つの領域」を学ぶことと示された。新学習指導要領では，領域ごとの目標がより詳しく具体的に示さ

れている。それぞれの領域と，実際のコミュニケーションにおける活
用の関連を，しっかり把握しておくこと。なお，語数は80語以上との
指定があるが，解答例は100語程度でまとめられているので，日頃か
ら100語を目安に自分の意見をまとめる練習をしておきたい。

【8】① b　② d　③ g
〈解説〉小学校からの段階的な変化に留意しよう。例えば，①は小学校の
　　外国語活動・外国語では「ゆっくりはっきり」となっているが，中学
　　校では「はっきり」である。また，小学校では「短い話の概要」であ
　　る箇所が，中学校では「話の概要」となっている。さらに，小学校で
　　は，日常的な話題のみ扱われるが，中学校では，発展させ，社会的な
　　話題も扱われる。用語は似ているが，明確に区別して覚えること。

【9】①　目的　②　言語活動　③　資質・能力　④　見通し
〈解説〉活動が単なる繰り返しにならないよう，生徒自身がコミュニケー
　　ションを行う目的や場面，状況を意識して活動できるようにするよう，
　　教師は働きかけを行う必要がある。なお，本問で出てくる「目的，場
　　面，状況」や「資質・能力」といった言葉は，学習指導要領全体で頻
　　出の重要なキーワードである。学習指導要領の内容を完全に暗記する
　　ことはできなくても，繰り返し読み，キーワードをしっかりと押さえ
　　ておきたい。

【10】1　スポーツ，音楽，映画，テレビ番組，学校行事，休日の計画，
　　日常の出来事など，身の回りのことで生徒が共通して関心を持ってい
　　ることである。具体的には，今流行りのお笑いタレントや歌手，学校
　　で行われる体育祭や文化祭など，どの生徒にとっても興味関心が高く，
　　話題にしやすい事柄のことである。　2　話すための原稿を事前に用
　　意してその内容を覚えたり，話せるように練習したりするなどの準備
　　時間を取ることなく，不適切な間を置かずに相手と事実や意見，気持
　　ちなどを伝え合うことである。やり取りを行う際は，相手の発話に応

じることが重要であり，それに関連した質問や意見を述べたりして，互いに協力して対話を継続させる。

〈解説〉学習指導要領の記述が具体的に何を示しているのかは，同解説に詳述されている。必ず参照して学びを深めてほしい。　1　関心のある事柄とは，具体的には，流行している人や物，学校で行われる行事である。そのような話題は生徒も興味関心を持って，積極的に話すことができ，生徒同士がお互いに背景知識を持っている話題であるため，やり取りしやすい。　2「即興で伝え合う」ということは，「話すこと[やり取り]」の特徴であり，これに対して，「話すこと[発表]」では，「即興で話す」ことが目指されている。今回の重要な改訂箇所であるので，しっかり押さえておきたい。

【11】1　小学校で，大文字，小文字を活字体で書いたり，音声で十分に慣れ親しんだ簡単な語句や基本的な表現を書き写したり，例文を参考に自分のことなどについて書いたりする活動をしてきたことを踏まえ，自分が好きなことや嫌いなこと，日常的に行っていることなどについて，生徒が自己紹介を行ったり，休日の過ごし方などについて話したりするなどの言語活動を経て，簡単な語句や文を用いてその内容を書く活動に取り組ませるなど，「話すこと」と「書くこと」のバランスに留意する必要がある。　2「書くこと」が苦手な生徒には，何をどのように書けばよいかを指導する必要がある。例えば，自分の考えや気持ちをペアやグループで簡単な語句や文を用いて口頭で伝える活動をした後に，その内容を書いてまとめる，といった言語活動を設定することが考えられる。「書くこと」におけるつまずきには，綴りや語順，文法，語彙だけでなく，発想や情報整理，文章構成など，様々なものが見られる。個の習熟度に応じて，ヒントを示したり，辞書の使用を促したり，直接的・間接的に誤りの修正を行ったりすることが大切である。

〈解説〉今回の改訂では，校種間の接続がより重視されるようになっているため，小学校の学習指導要領にも目を通しておくことが望ましい。

小学校の外国語活動における「書くこと」では，アルファベットや単語を書くという活動が中心で，文章を書く活動はあまり行われない。したがって，中学校第1学年の初期段階では「話すこと」に関する活動を踏まえて，うまく文を書くことに移行させたい。また，中学生が英文を書く際に，具体的にどのようなつまずきが多いか把握しておくことで，指導計画へと発展させやすいだろう。

【高等学校】

【1】1　(b)　open　　2　(a)　When／If　3　(a)　explain to a doctor／tell a doctor　　4　(c)　while／when　　5　(a)　five-sixths

〈解説〉1　leave O Cで「OをCのままにしておく」という意味である。Cに形容詞が来る場合は状態の継続，現在分詞が来る場合は動作の継続となる。今回は窓が開いているという状態の継続であるため，Cに現在分詞のopeningではなく，形容詞openを置く。　2　as far as ～は「～する限りでは」という意味であり，文意に合わない。「～した場合に」のifや「～するとき」のwhenを使うとよい。　3　explainは人を目的語に取ることができず，explain to A (人)のようにtoが必要となる。もしくは，人を目的語に取ることができるtellを用いるとよい。4　duringは前置詞なので，後ろに主語と動詞を含んだ文を取ることができない。したがって，whenやwhileといった時を表す接続詞を用いるとよい。　5　分子が1より大きい場合，分母の序数を複数形にする必要がある。本問は分子がfiveであるため，分母のsixthをsixthsとする必要がある。

【2】1　(d)　2　(e)　3　(b)　4　(a)　5　(c)

〈解説〉1　空所1の前段落では，調査の結果，生徒たちが「学校では，ストレスや感情，意見の不一致への対処方法を教えてくれない」と答えていると述べている。それを受け，選択肢(d)では，教師側の立場から「生徒たちが抱える問題に対処する方法を学ぶsocial and emotional learning approaches(社会と情動の学習アプローチ)は，10代にはそれほ

ど効果的ではない」と述べている。　2　空所2の前段落では，David Yeagerとその同僚の主張を取り上げ，「10代が自己認識を高め，最終的に地位や敬意への感覚を強める方法がいくつかある」と述べている。したがって，敬意を育てる方法について述べている選択肢(e)が適切。3　空所3の前の部分では，生徒たちの強みを育てていく活動がいくつか紹介されている。したがって，この活動の研究結果について述べている選択肢(b)が適切。　4　空所4の前段落では，自身の理想的な将来について生徒たちに考えさせる活動を提示している。したがって，同様にa vision of future「将来の展望」について述べている選択肢(a)が適切。　5　空所5の前段落では，生徒自身で主導していくことについて述べられている。したがって，生徒主導の活動について述べている選択肢(c)が適切。

【3】1　ウ　　2　ウ　　3　エ　　4　イ　　5　イ
〈解説〉1　設問は「本文を最もよく要約している文は次のうちどれか」。本文全体で月面基地を建設するための材料について述べられている。第7段落目以降ではurine「尿」から採取できるurea「尿素」がその材料として有力であることが述べられている。したがって，ウ「宇宙飛行士の尿中の尿素が月面基地建設の一助として使用される可能性がある」が適切。　2　NOT問題であることに注意する。設問は「本文によれば，月にすでに存在している材料が，月面基地建設のためにより実用的である理由として，適切ではないものは，次のうちどれか」。第3段落3文目にソーレルセメントと岩のような材料が挙げられており，4文目に後者(岩のような材料)のほうが「火星」の基地を作る材料として適切であると述べられている。したがって，ウ「月から採れるソーレルセメントを使った3Dプリンティングがより容易になされる」は本文の内容と一致しない。　3　設問は「ヨーロッパの科学者のチームによって行われた研究結果は何を示しているか」。第6段落2文目に「尿中の尿素が月面基地の3Dプリンティング用の材料の効果的な可塑剤として役立つ可能性がある」と述べられ，3文目に「ノルウェー，

スペイン，オランダ，イタリアの科学者がこれについて研究した」と
ある。この研究結果は第9段落に述べられており，尿素の有効性が証
明されている。したがって，エ「尿素は3Dプリンティング用のコンク
リートの可塑剤として効果的であることが示された」が適切。

4　NOT問題である。設問は「さらなる研究が必要な『未知のこと』
として，本文中で述べられていないことは，次のうちどれか」。アは
第11段落2文目，ウは第10段落3文目，エは第10段落2文目で述べられ
ている。イ「その材料が火星基地の建設にも同様に利用できる可能性
があるかどうか」は述べられていない。　5　設問は「空所Aに当ては
まる最も適切な語句はどれか」。第11段落の2文目以降では，実際に尿
素を材料として使用する上でまだ検証されていないこと(懸念点)が述
べられている。したがって，イ「実際的な懸念点」が適切。

【4】1　Chang and his parents are hardworking and trustworthy./Chang and his
parents are honest.　　2　Chang believed he had failed because his flower
did not grow.　　3　The other men's flowers grew because they used
flowers that didn't grow from the seed./The other men's flowers grew because
they switched their seed with a different flower.　　4　(c)　　5　(d)

6　Yes. It is more important to think of others before yourself. Sometimes
you need to lie to protect people./Yes. Small or white lies don't always have
major consequences, especially if they are used to protect someone's
feelings.　　No. If you justify telling a lie for "good" anyone could lie as
long as they believe their reason is good./No. Lying is morally wrong, and
anyone who lies could potentially hurt people.

〈解説〉記述問題は英文で答える問題であることに注意すること。

1　Changと彼の両親がどのような人かを説明する問題である。本文中
のどこかに答えが記述されているわけではなく，Changと彼の両親の
行動から推測する必要がある。Changが「花を咲かせるために懸命に
作業していたこと」や「花を咲かせるのに失敗したが，皇帝に正直に
報告したこと」，また彼の両親は「失敗したことを皇帝に正直に言う

ようにChangに助言したこと」から，解答例では，hardworking「勤勉な」，trustworthy「信頼に値する」，honest「正直な」が挙げられている。

2　Changが皇帝を失望させてしまったと考えた理由を答える問題である。第18段落3文目より，皇帝から命じられた花を咲かせることができなかったからである。この理由を英語でまとめるとよい。

3　Chang以外の人の花が成長した理由を答える問題である。この問題も本文中に明示的に答えが述べられているわけではない。第21段落より，皇帝が配った種は一度茹でられていたため，育つはずがないと述べられている。したがって，Chang以外の人は皇帝からもらった種ではなく，別の育った花を持ってきたり，別の種を使用したりしたと推測できる。この内容を英語でまとめるとよい。　4　本文の内容と一致しない文を選ぶ問題。先述したように，Changの花が咲かなかったのは，一度種が茹でられていたからである。したがって，(c)「Changは園芸の技術がなかったため，花を成長させることができなかった」は本文の内容と一致しない。　5　本文は，花を咲かせることができたと嘘の報告をした人々が皇帝になれず，正直に花を咲かせることができなかったと話したChangが後継者に選ばれたという内容である。したがって，(d)「真実の価値」がタイトルとして適切。　6　「より大きな目標の利益のためなら嘘をついてもよいか」という質問に対する意見を英語で述べる問題。解答例ではYesとNoどちらの意見も挙げられているので，書きやすい方で書くとよい。なお，Yesの解答例中のwhite lieとは，人の害にならない他愛のない嘘のことである。

【5】 I believe that in order to coexist with AI in education in the future we will need to develop a kind of education that maximizes opportunities for students to analyze and think critically about facts they are presented in class. Being able to simply recall memorized facts won't be enough. We need to include activities that allow students to use their abilities in pattern recognition, problem solving, and be able to do creative projects. For example, in a history class, students should look at known facts and discuss what factors most likely led to a particular historical event and also compare it with current conditions in order to determine if history is being repeated. In language classes, more emphasis should be placed on expression such as through creative writing or speaking opportunities. Such activities are something that AI machines cannot do. Therefore, I believe that we must focus education on these areas, which humans excel in versus AI machines. (158 words)

〈解説〉質問は「AIと共存するためにはどのような教育改革が必要であると考えるか」である。英文はAIに関する実験結果とその結果から導かれる示唆について述べている。解答例では，「授業中に提示された事実について，生徒が批判的に分析したり考えたりする機会を最大限にいかす教育を発展させるべき」と述べられ，それに対する理由と歴史と言語の授業における活動の具体例が示されている。AIは事実を答える問題には優れているが，「批判的に」分析したり，考えたり，推論したりすることは不得手である。したがって，それに沿った論を展開させるとよいだろう。このような教育に関する時事問題に対応できるよう新聞等で情報を得ておきたい。

【6】1　A　やり取り　　B　発表　　C　思考力，判断力，表現力　D　学びに向かう力　　E　カリキュラム・マネジメント
2　聞くこと…聞き手に合わせて話す速度や情報量を調整する。読むこと…読み手に合わせて使用する語句や文や情報量を調整する。やり取り…対話の例を示すため，教師が実際のやり取りを見せる。発表…話し手に，使用する語句や会話や発表の仕方などを与えたりする。　　書くこと…書き手に，書く際に有用な語彙や表現などを与えたりする。

〈解説〉1　学習指導要領の改訂が行われたときは，現行版と比較して，改訂に至った経緯や具体的な改訂点を確認しておく必要がある。外国語科では，「話すこと」が[やり取り]と[発表]の2つの領域に分けられたことが大きな改訂点である。しっかりと押さえておきたい。
2　「支援」に関しては，学習指導要領解説　外国語編・英語編の「第

2章　外国語科の各科目　第1節　総論　3　支援について」を参照されたい。解答例に挙げられた支援以外にも，各領域の節において詳述されているので，確認しておくとよい。

2020年度　実施問題

【中高共通】

【1】これから，会話と質問が5つ放送されます。質問に対する答えとして最も適切なものをア～エから一つずつ選び，その記号を書きなさい。なお，会話と質問は一度だけ放送されます。

1
- ア　Come with some new ideas.
- イ　Meet the client for the woman.
- ウ　Reschedule the meeting.
- エ　Take the woman home.

2
- ア　Buying another book.
- イ　Checking the records.
- ウ　Coming back next week.
- エ　Trying another store.

3
- ア　By bus.
- イ　By car.
- ウ　By train.
- エ　On foot.

4
- ア　Check out new products.
- イ　Request a catalog.
- ウ　Set up a Web site.
- エ　Subscribe to a fan club.

5
- ア　It is affordable.
- イ　It is customizable.
- ウ　It makes other beverages.

エ　It takes less time.

（☆☆☆○○○）

【2】これから，まとまりのある英文が放送されます。英文の後に，その内容について質問が四つ出されます。その質問に対する答えとして最も適切なものをア～エの中から一つずつ選び，その記号を書きなさい。なお，英文と質問は一度だけ放送されます。

1

   ア　A guide for future visitors

   イ　An introduction for new foreign leaders

   ウ　A report about a government announcement

   エ　A report on research findings

2

   ア　For getting assistance from his secretary

   イ　For greeting special visitors from overseas

   ウ　For having fun with his family

   エ　For working with his advisers

3

   ア　Less than 40 presidents have lived in the White House since it was built.

   イ　The President has dinner in the West Wing of the White House.

   ウ　The White House was built after the Civil War in the 1860s.

   エ　The White House's first family started to live there from 1800.

4

   ア　The presidents aimed to create a place for basketball.

   イ　The president is usually a big fan of bowling.

   ウ　The president can change the White House as he likes.

   エ　The president gives away whatever he wants from the White House.

（☆☆☆○○○）

【３】これから，まとまりのある英文が一度だけ放送されます。質問に対する答えとして最も適切なものをア～エの中から一つずつ選び，その記号を書きなさい。

1　Why did the host mother put her belongings into a clear bag?

　　ア　Because she had to show what was inside.

　　イ　Because she needed to work.

　　ウ　Because she preferred a clear plastic bag.

　　エ　Because she wanted to show off her things.

2　What is the meaning of "an ambulance at the bottom of the cliff"?

　　ア　It means disregarding the real cause of the problem.

　　イ　It means solutions to problems concerning stealing things.

　　ウ　It means the emergency service that people need at cliff sides.

　　エ　It means the end of the story about preventing school shootings.

3　Why do employees want to work overtime?

　　ア　They want their company to have high profits.

　　イ　They want their family to be financially stable.

　　ウ　They want to enjoy work culture.

　　エ　They want to support their coworkers.

4　What should we do to prevent ambulances at the bottoms of cliffs?

　　ア　We should consider recycling plastics.

　　イ　We should force people to go home early.

　　ウ　We should solve business problems.

　　エ　We should understand the background behind problems.

(☆☆☆◎◎◎◎)

【中学校】

【１】次の1～8の英文の(　　)にあてはまる最も適切な英語を，それぞれア～エから一つずつ選び，その記号を書きなさい。

1　We will (　　) the exact date and time of your arrival at a later date.

　　ア　repeal　　イ　permit　　ウ　expel　　エ　designate

2 Laura ( ) great satisfaction from the fact that she had been accepted into one of the top universities in the United States.

ア derived イ detached ウ dedicated エ depreciated

3 Jeff is in the ( ) of drinking tomato juice with all his meals.

ア manner イ trait ウ habit エ custom

4 English learners are often perplexed by the frequent lack of ( ) between spelling and pronunciation.

ア conductivity イ correction ウ correlation

エ concavity

5 Young people often enjoy the present and make no ( ) for the future.

ア compliment イ consignments ウ provisions

エ pretension

6 The number of working women is particularly ( ) among those in their late 20s.

ア countable イ noticeable ウ workable エ available

7 I don't have any plans to go anywhere during the ( ) summer holidays.

ア subsequent イ consecutive ウ consequent

エ progressive

8 Even though our company is doing well, let's not be ( ). We shouldn't just rest on our success.

ア complacent イ zealous ウ contentious エ profuse

(☆☆☆☆○○○○○)

【2】次の1〜5の会話文中の( )にあてはまる最も適切な英語を，それぞれア〜エから一つずつ選び，その記号を書きなさい。

1 *A :* Do you know a good hotel in this city?

B : The Leaf Hotel is good.

A : ( )

B : It's quite close...about three blocks.

ア How far is it from here?

イ　Why is it so good?

ウ　What did you say?

エ　How long is it from here?

2　A：What is that silver thing moving above the building over there?

　　B：（　　）

　　A：That tall one next to the bank.

ア　It must be an airplane.

イ　Which building?

ウ　I can't see anything moving.

エ　Maybe it's a balloon.

3　A：It has been many years since I saw you last.

　　B：（　　）

　　A：I wouldn't have, either, if someone had not mentioned your name.

ア　I hardly thought I would miss you so much.

イ　I recognized you at first sight.

ウ　You haven't changed very much.

エ　I didn't recognize you at first.

4　A：You don't seem to mention Sarah these days. Do you still see her?

　　B：（　　）

　　A：But you were such good friends that I envied you both.

ア　She's no longer important to me.

イ　We met just before I came to this class.

ウ　She's somewhere in Hokkaido now on business.

エ　Yes, I see her almost every day except on Mondays.

5　A：Are you ready?

　　B：Yes, I finished packing. But I misplaced my passport.

　　A：Your passport? （　　）

　　B：I know. I am certain I packed it but I can't remember in which bag.

ア　That's why you have to leave.

イ　That's not something you should carry on you.

ウ That's the one thing you mustn't leave behind.

エ That's the one thing you should leave behind.

(☆☆☆○○○○○)

【3】次の1～3の各文にある下線部ア～エには，英語の文法上または表現上適切ではない語句があります。適切ではない語句をそれぞれア～エから一つずつ選び，その記号を書きなさい。

1 Would you mind $_{ア}$to keep $_{イ}$an eye $_{ウ}$on my luggage while I make $_{エ}$a phone call?

2 Ryan $_{ア}$heard a strange noise while he $_{イ}$was driving his car, so he took it $_{ウ}$to a garage to get it $_{エ}$to repair.

3 If you $_{ア}$go abroad, you will realize how inconvenient $_{イ}$is it $_{ウ}$not to be able to make yourself $_{エ}$understood in a foreign language.

(☆☆☆○○)

【4】次の英文を読んで，あとの1～3の書き出しに続く内容として，最も適切なものを，ア～エから一つずつ選び，その記号を書きなさい。

　Once there were two brothers. The older one was a greedy miser always chasing after money. He was waiting for his father to die to get all his possessions. The younger brother was different. He was a good honest man, fair and just in every way, and was very fond of both his father and his brother. At last their father passed away, leaving his sons all his possessions. A few days later the older brother offered a deal to the younger brother saying, "The time has come for us to divide our father's things between us. Let us go and plow our father's land tomorrow morning, and the one who succeeds in plowing the larger area will keep all the land. But let us add one condition — neither of us should eat or drink during the whole day." The younger brother, who always listened to his older brother, agreed to the plan. The following day the older brother got up very early, and while his younger brother was still sleeping, he had a big breakfast and lots of water. Then he

171

woke up his younger brother and took him out to the field. Without eating or drinking, the younger brother could not win the match, and the older brother won everything that their father had owned.

The following day the younger brother left the house and went to the mountains to earn his daily bread. He found a cave among the rocks and stayed there and became a woodcutter. He cut down trees and took the wood to town to sell and bought bread and meat. His days passed in poverty, while his older brother became richer with his father's money. By now he had forgotten his younger brother.

One day the younger brother went out as usual to cut trees in the forest. When he came near a certain tree, he raised his eyes to the treetop and saw among the branches a bird's nest. He picked up a stick and threw it at the nest, once, twice and three times, but each time he missed the mark. At last a big black crow flew from the nest and called out, "Do not destroy my nest. I built it myself for my beautiful babies. If you do me this favor, I will take you to the Mountain of the Sun in return."

"What is there on the Mountain of the Sun?" asked the younger brother.

To this the crow answered, "Many treasures. Come to me tomorrow morning before sunrise. Bring a small bag with you, and you will know what I mean."

The next morning before sunrise, the younger brother took a small bag and followed the big black crow to the Mountain of the Sun. When they got to the mountain peak, the younger brother stood in surprise and wonder, not believing his own eyes, Gold, diamonds and other precious stones were lying on the ground.

"Do not wait," said the bird. "Take as much as you want, but remember to go before sunrise."

The younger brother did not stay long. He filled his little bag with treasures, thanked the crow and went back to his cave. The same day he left the mountains and returned to his home town. He had a beautiful house built

172

there, bought rich land, and lived a happy life.

When the older brother found out how his younger brother had gained his riches, he was very jealous. He, too, took a big stick in his hand and ran to the forest. There he found the crow's nest and began to throw the stick at it. Soon the crow jumped out of the nest and started to beg, "Please do not try to break my nest. If you do as I ask you, I will take you to the Mountain of the Sun. Take with you a small bag and be ready before sunrise."

The older brother came to the big black crow early in the morning carrying a huge bag on his shoulder. When they arrived at the mountain peak, he forgot about everything else and fell upon the treasures and began to fill his huge bag. He put one precious stone after another into the bag, trying to fill it up.

"Enough, enough. Do not stay any longer," warned the crow. "Run home quickly, or the sun will rise and burn you." But the greedy man would not listen. He continued to collect the gold and jewels. Finally the sun rose with its horrible heat and burned the older brother so that he was turned into ashes.

1 The reason why the older brother got up very early was that
　ア　he tried to let his younger brother have a big breakfast.
　イ　he wanted to inherit a large fortune from his father.
　ウ　he looked for the person who could plow the larger area.
　エ　he hoped to be a good honest man, not a greedy miser.

2 Soon after the younger brother found a bird's nest,
　ア　a big black crow flew from the sky, and called out "Do not destroy the nest."
　イ　a big black crow jumped out of the nest, but he kept throwing some sticks.
　ウ　he jumped into the nest, and the crow started to beg to stop breaking the nest.
　エ　he threw a stick at the nest several times, but each time he missed the mark.

3　At the Mountain of the Sun, the crow told the older brother not to

ア　carry a huge bag to the cave, because the sun will burn him.

イ　fill his little bag with treasures, then he thanked the big crow.

ウ　stay any longer and run home quickly, but he would not listen.

エ　continue to collect the gold and jewels, so he left the mountain.

(☆☆☆◎◎◎◎)

【5】次の対話文を読んで，あとの質問に答えなさい。

(Satoshi is an exchange student at an American university where Taylor is also a student.)

Taylor：Hey, Satoshi! What are you watching there?

Satoshi：It's a YouTube video of the Debate Club Roast.

Taylor：Oh yeah, everyone was talking about it in the cafeteria tonight at dinner. It was really funny.

Satoshi：My dictionary says a "roast" is an event at which the guest of honor undergoes "severe banter or criticism," but I'm having a hard time understanding why everyone thought it was so funny.

Taylor：Really? Why?

Satoshi：It seems pretty (　①　) to me. I mean that's the leader of the club they're making fun of! And he's sitting right there!

Taylor：Well Satoshi, it seems to me he gave it as good as he got it.

Satoshi：He did get a lot of laughs. His English was easier to understand, but I couldn't understand all of what he said.

Taylor：Yeah, like what?

Satoshi：OK, listen to this part.

VOICE on video："... and furthermore, thanks to my membership campaign, we now have more club members than any

174

other time in our club's history. You're welcome."

Satoshi : Why does he say "you're welcome" ? Nobody said "thank you."

Taylor : Oh, that's just a cheeky way of patting yourself on the back.

Satoshi : What?

Taylor : You know, kind of like showing off. Like, "I know you want to thank me... You're welcome!"

Satoshi : I could never imagine anyone saying that in Japanese.

Taylor : Really? So, what would you say in that case?

Satoshi : Well, that's *"dō itashimashite."* it means "It was nothing."

Taylor : Yeah, that wouldn't work. "Thanks to my great membership campaign, we've got all these new members, blah, blah, blah... it was nothing." "It was nothing" is kind of the opposite of "you're welcome" ... But what about "thank you" ?

Satoshi : "Thank you" is *"arigatō."*

Taylor : What does that mean?

Satoshi : Literally, it means "it is very rare."

Taylor : Hmm, so when someone says *"arigatō,"* it must be very special. You must reserve the expression for times when someone really does you a service.

Satoshi : No, not really. Actually, people say it all the time.

Taylor : In the same way as "thank you" ?

Satoshi : Almost. I've noticed that, in America, when the shop clerk says "thank you" at the counter, customers say "thank you" back to him. In Japan customers don't often say it back when they pay for something.

Taylor : You mean Japanese people don't think that's rude?

Satoshi : Not usually. There's this idea that as a customer you're doing the shop a favor by giving them your business.

Taylor : Huh.

Satoshi : Hey, instead of learning about American humor, I ended up giving you a lesson in cross-cultural understanding. (　②　)

Taylor : You're a quick learner, Satoshi.

1　対話文の内容にあうように，文中の(　①　)に入る適切な語句を，次のア～エから一つ選び，その記号を書きなさい。

ア　respectful　　イ　disrespectful　　ウ　reasonable

エ　understandable

2　対話文の内容にあうように，文中の(　②　)に入る適切な文を，次のア～エから一つ選び，その記号を書きなさい。

ア　Do you want to thank me?

イ　It's nothing to me.

ウ　You're welcome.

エ　Thank you.

3　対話文の内容と一致しないものを，次のア～エから一つ選び，その記号を書きなさい。

ア　Satoshi didn't think it was funny to make fun of the leader of the Debate Club Roast in public.

イ　At first, Satoshi couldn't understand why the leader of the Debate Club Roast said "you're welcome".

ウ　Satoshi doesn't think Japanese people must reserve the expression of "*arigatō*" for the times when they get a special service.

エ　Satoshi thinks that Japanese people regard it as rude not to say "thank you" back to the clerk when they buy something at a shop.

(☆☆☆◎◎◎◎)

【6】次の英文を読んで，本文の内容と一致するものを，あとのア～オから二つ選び，その記号を書きなさい。

Artificial intelligence is intelligence which does not occur naturally, it is intelligence that has been created. In recent history, it has often been used in science fiction to describe computers or robots which can think as humans do, which is to say they can learn by themselves, make plans for the future, and interact with society and the world around them. However, the concept of artificial intelligence has been around far longer than computers have, For examples, there is a story from over 2000 years ago of a large metal animal which was created and brought to life to protect a city.

Currently, artificial intelligence is fairly well-known. It has appeared in popular action movies and TV series, some famous examples being The Matrix and The Terminator movie series, and has even been the object of a few movies about love. In many cases, the artificial intelligence in these movies seeks to control the world, and either uses humanity as an object to be controlled or sees them as an enemy to be eliminated.

However, the reality of artificial intelligence is very different from what is displayed on the movie screen. Current progress in artificial intelligence research has led to computers beating the best players in the world in Chess and *Go*, increasingly accurate speech recognition and personal assistant programs such as Siri on smart phones, and it is driving the technology used in self-driving cars. Tesla, a maker of electric cars, released a statement in 2016 saying that their research showed their self-driving cars were 50% less likely to get in accidents than human drivers.

While these are very exciting developments, upon analysis it is easy to see where one of the critical difficulties with artificial intelligence lies. For instance, a single human is able to play chess, be an assistant, drive a car, and do many other things by him or herself. Programs or robots with artificial intelligence, however, are currently only able to perform one of those tasks at a time.

The limitations of artificial intelligence comes both from the processing

177

power of computers today and from the limitations of computer programs The K computer in Kobe Japan, the fastest computer in the world in 2011, ran an experiment and found that it was only able to run at 0.04% the speed of the human brain when it processed information in the same way. Furthermore, the programs used to play chess, drive cars, or to do other artificial intelligence related tasks are not created the same way. They often utilize different programming languages. If the goal of artificial intelligence is to create something like a human, it will require coordinating all of these separate programs and combining them into one large system.

Nonetheless, Stephen Hawking, a famous scientist, and Elon Musk, the president of Tesla, and many others recently wrote an open letter calling for increased research into the impacts of artificial intelligence on society. They say that artificial intelligence can bring enormous benefits if used correctly, but that it could also end human life if used incorrectly. If these people felt it necessary to write this letter, maybe true artificial intelligence is coming soon.

Indeed, at the current rate that processing power increases, which is doubling its speed every 18 months, we will begin to see computers " think" at the same speed as humans by 2030. This leaves us with three questions. Is true artificial intelligence possible? Will this intelligence be like humans? And will it benefit society? Reality may be even stranger than the movies.

ア　According to the article, artificial intelligence refers to computers.

イ　One thing that artificial intelligence cannot do with current technology is to beat humans in strategy games.

ウ　The reason why computers are not able to act like humans yet is that computer programs do not always work well together.

エ　An open letter was written about artificial intelligence because many people want to know how artificial intelligence will affect society.

オ　Computers won't be able to process information as quickly as humans do.

(☆☆☆○○○○○)

【7】次の文は，中学校学習指導要領解説　外国語編(平成29年7月)第2章「第2節　英語」における「3　指導計画の作成と内容の取扱い」を一部抜粋したものです。

　　ウの事項において，下線部のような指導が必要とされる趣旨は何なのか，またその際に考えられる留意事項としてどのようなことが考えられるのか，あなたの考えを80語以上の英語で書きなさい。

　　なお，最後に語数を記入すること。語数については，同じ語を2回使用した場合，2語と数えること(のべ数)とします。

---

(1)　指導計画の作成に当たっては，小学校や高等学校における指導との接続に留意しながら，次の事項に配慮するものとする。

　ウ　実際に英語を使用して互いの考えや気持ちを伝え合うなどの言語活動を行う際は，2の(1)に示す言語材料について理解したり練習したりするための指導を必要に応じて行うこと。また，<u>小学校第3学年から第6学年までに扱った簡単な語句や基本的な表現などの学習内容を繰り返し指導し定着を図ること。</u>

(☆☆☆○○○○○)

【8】次の文は，中学校学習指導要領(平成29年3月告示)第2章「第9節　外国語」における「第1　目標」です。文中の(①)〜(③)にあてはまる語句として，最も適切なものを，あとのア〜ケから一つずつ選び，その記号を書きなさい。

　外国語によるコミュニケーションにおける見方・考え方を働かせ，外国語による聞くこと，読むこと，話すこと，書くことの言語活動を通して，簡単な情報や考えなどを理解したり表現したり伝え合ったりするコミュニケーションを図る資質・能力を次のとおり育成することを目指す。

　(1)　外国語の音声や語彙，表現，(①)，言語の働きなど

179

　　　を理解するとともに，これらの知識を，聞くこと，読むこと，話すこと，書くことによる実際のコミュニケーションにおいて活用できる技能を身に付けるようにする。

(2) （　②　）に応じて，日常的な話題や社会的な話題について，外国語で簡単な情報や考えなどを理解したり，これらを活用して表現したり伝え合ったりすることができる力を養う。

(3) （　③　）を深め，聞き手，読み手，話し手，書き手に配慮しながら，主体的に外国語を用いてコミュニケーションを図ろうとする態度を養う。

ア　文法
イ　文字
ウ　文構造
エ　コミュニケーションを行う楽しさや大切さなど
オ　コミュニケーションを行う目的や場面，状況など
カ　コミュニケーションを行う相手や事柄など
キ　言語や文化に対する理解
ク　外国語の背景にある文化に対する理解
ケ　外国語の背景にある言語や文化に対する理解

(☆☆○○○○○)

【9】次の文は，中学校学習指導要領(平成29年3月告示)第2章「第9節　外国語」における「第2　各言語の目標及び内容等」の「3　指導計画の作成と内容の取扱い」を一部抜粋したものです。文中の（　①　）～（　④　）にあてはまる適切な語句を書きなさい。

(2) 2の内容に示す事項については，次の事項に配慮するものとする。
　　エ　文法事項の指導に当たっては，次の事項に留意すること。
　（イ）文法は（　①　）を支えるものであることを踏まえ，

> （　①　）の目的を達成する上での必要性や有用性を実感させた上でその知識を（　②　）させたり，繰り返し使用することで当該文法事項の規則性や構造などについて（　③　）を促したりするなど，（　④　）と効果的に関連付けて指導すること。

(☆☆☆◎◎◎◎)

【10】中学校学習指導要領(平成29年3月告示)第2章「第9節　外国語」における「第2　各言語の目標及び内容等」の「1　目標」を一部抜粋したものです。

> (5)　書くこと
> 　　イ　<u>日常的な話題</u>について，事実や自分の考え，気持ちなどを整理し，簡単な語句や文を用いて<u>まとまりのある文章を書く</u>ことができるようにする。

1　下線部<u>日常的な話題</u>とはどのような話題か，日本語で説明しなさい。
2　下線部<u>まとまりのある文章を書く</u>とはどのようなことか，日本語で説明しなさい。

(☆☆☆◎◎◎◎)

【11】次の1と2は，中学校学習指導要領(平成29年3月告示)の第2章「第9節　外国語」における「第2　各言語の目標及び内容等」を一部抜粋したものです。以下の目標で示されたことができるようにするために，具体的にどのような言語活動が考えられるか日本語で書きなさい。

1

> (2)　読むこと
> 　　ウ　社会的な話題について，簡単な語句や文で書かれた短い文章の要点を捉えることができるようにする。

181

2

> (3)　話すこと[やりとり]
> 　イ　日常的な話題について，事実や自分の考え，気持ちなど
> 　を整理し，簡単な語句や文を用いて伝えたり，相手からの
> 　質問に答えたりすることができるようにする。

(☆☆☆◎◎◎)

【高等学校】

【1】次の1〜5の各文の(　　)に入る最も適切なものをア〜エの中から一つずつ選び，その記号を書きなさい。

1　Kevin Smith (　　) the first prize for the project he displayed at the science fair held last week in Windsor.
　ア　awarded　　イ　had awarding　　ウ　was awarded
　エ　was awarding

2　The Ministry of Education will increase the educational budget by more than ten percent (　　) the next five years.
　ア　beside　　イ　over　　ウ　since　　エ　under

3　It is expected to take a few years, (　　) a decade, to repair the historical cathedral which was damaged by the fire last month.
　ア　after all　　イ　if not　　ウ　nevertheless　　エ　while

4　(　　) the financial burden, I simply didn't like traveling by air.
　ア　Above all　　イ　Aside from　　ウ　Despite　　エ　In addition

5　It is important to give the person in charge a clear (　　) for choosing equipment when you make a presentation at an new place.
　ア　fraction　　イ　inception　　ウ　outfit　　エ　rationale

(☆☆☆◎◎◎◎)

【2】次の英文を読んで，1〜5の問いに対する答えを英語で書きなさい。
　Language is one of the bases of identity and culture. As the world becomes

increasingly globalised and reliant on technology, English has been reinforced once again as the lingua franca.

The technological infrastructure that now dominates our working and private lives is overwhelmingly in English, which means minority languages are under threat more than ever.

But it might also be true that technology could help us bring minority languages to a wider audience by using it to help linguistic diversity rather than damage it. This is one of the main suggestions of a series of papers, the most recent of which looks at the Welsh language in the digital age.

Welsh was granted official status in Wales in the UK by the Welsh Language Measure 2011. This builds on previous legislation that sought to ensure that bodies providing a service to the public in Wales—even those that are not actually based in Wales—must provide those services in Welsh.

As more public services go online, the language in which those services are presented is important. Language technology advances mean it will be possible for people to communicate and do business with each other, even if they don't speak the same language.

These language technology and speech processing tools will eventually serve as a bridge between different languages. We already have question answering services and natural language interfaces, but they often focus on the big languages such as Spanish or French.

At the moment, many language technologies rely on imprecise statistical approaches that do not make use of deeper linguistic methods. Sentences are translated by comparing a new sentence against thousands of sentences previously translated by humans.

This is bad news for minority languages. The automatic translation of simple sentences in languages with sufficient amounts of available text material can achieve useful results, but these shallow statistical methods will fail in the case of languages with less sample material.

The next generation of translation technology must be able to analyse the deeper structural properties of languages if we want to use technology as a force to protect minority languages.

Minority languages have traditionally relied on informal use to survive. The minority language might be used at home or among friends but speakers need to switch to the majority language in formal situations such as school and work.

But where informal use once meant speaking, it now often means writing. We used to chat with friends and family in person. Now we talk online via email, instant messaging and social media. The online services and software needed to make this happen are generally in the majority language, especially English. That means that it takes extra effort to communicate in the minority language, which adds to its vulnerability.

Enthusiasts are thinking of solutions to this problem. Volunteers have produced a version of Facebook's interface in Welsh, so who knows what might be next?

Unless an effort is made, technology could serve to further disenfranchise speakers of minority languages. David Cameron is already keen on a sentiment analysis app to monitor social networks and other live data, for example. But if that app only gathers information and opinions posted in English, how can he monitor the sentiments of British citizens who write in Welsh, Gaelic or Irish?

All this is going to be a big job. We need to carry out a systematic analysis of the linguistic particularities of all European languages and then work out the current state of the technology that supports them. But it's a job worth doing.

1 What is the main idea presented in the papers on the Welsh language in the digital age?

2 What is important as more public services go online?

3 What does the underlined "This" refer to?

4 What are the examples of how informal language is used now?

5　What could be a potential problem of a sentiment analysis app?

(☆☆☆○○○○)

【3】次の英文を読んで，1〜5の問いに対する答えとして最も適切なもの
をア〜エの中から一つずつ選び，その記号を書きなさい。

　　Lying is an accepted part of daily life, from our usual response of "good" when asked how we are, to the praise we give when a friend asks if we like her awful new haircut.

　　Yet despite lies being everywhere in our lives, most of us are not very good at detecting them. What would happen, though, if we could suddenly tell, without a doubt, when we were being lied to?

　　Many researchers believe humans began lying to each other almost as soon as they invented language, mostly as away to get an advantage. Throughout human history, lying has also served as "an evolutionary necessity to protect ourselves from harm," says Michael Lewis, a distinguished professor of child studies and psychiatry at Rutgers University.

　　Lying also benefits us when the risks are lower, including at work. If we told our boss what we really thought of him, or why we actually didn't make our deadline, we might be fired or demoted. We also lie to make ourselves look better and to seem professional.

　　On the other hand, there are times at work when it would be beneficial to know when we're being lied to, says Clark Freshman, a professor of law at the University of California, Hastings, and a specialist in lie detection. By asking the right questions in negotiations and being assured of accurate answers, minority employees, for example, could more easily get salaries and positions equal to employees of the majority.

　　"For me, a world in which people could know the truth that mattered to them would be a great world," Freshman says. "We'd have less discrimination and more equality."

　　We'd also have more hurt feelings. For most of us, a world without lies would harm our self-image, says Dan Ariely, professor of psychology and behavioral economics at Duke University. "Living with the truth means you would get more honest, brutal feedback about your work, the way you dress, the way you kiss — all kinds of things like that," he says.

This damage to our self-image might begin from childhood — harming our development in unpredictable ways. "Imagine a child comes over and says 'Daddy, Mommy, look at my painting!' and you respond, 'It's horrible!' " Lee says. "The negative impacts would be immediate." Some of the innocence of childhood would also be lost, including magical stories such as Father Christmas, the Tooth Fairy and the Easter Bunny.

"There's a lot of things that if children knew about, they'd find hard to understand," says Paul Ekman, a retired professor of psychology at the University of California, San Francisco.

Children themselves learn the social value of lying from a very young age. "Mom might say to the child, 'Listen, grandma is going to give you a present for Hanukkah, and you've got to tell grandma that you like it, otherwise it'll hurt her feelings,' " Lewis says. By the age of three or four, studies show that many children have mastered the art of the polite lie.

By the time we're adults, most of us are lying on a regular basis. "Lying is a total and complete necessity in a culture in which the moral understanding is you don't want to hurt the feelings of other people," Lewis says.

We all have little white lies. At the end of a dinner party, for example, we typically tell our hosts that we had a great time — even if we hated every moment. Our hosts tend to believe this, having no desire themselves to know just how awful we found their company and food.

In a world without such polite lies, friendships would be broken, professional relations would be strained, and family gatherings would be even more difficult than they already are.

Our closest romantic relationships are not without lies, either. In a now-classic 1989 study conducted by Sandra Metts at the University of Illinois, just 33 of 390 people were unable to recall a situation in which they were "not completely truthful" with a romantic partner. Likewise, in 2013 Jennifer Guthrie and Adrianne Kunkel from the University of Kansas found that just two of 67 participants in a study did not deceive their romantic partners over the course of a single week.

In both studies, most people said they said something dishonest in order to avoid hurting their partner or damaging their relationship. If romances suddenly involved total truthfulness about everything from the way our partner looks in the morning to whether we ever engaged in cheating, many relationships likely would not last.

A world without lies would likely benefit police and criminal justice. Police violence and bias would decrease—officers could simply ask suspects if they are carrying a weapon or if they are responsible for a crime—and trials would be replaced with a simple set of questions to determine guilt. "We want the criminal to be found and we don't want to misjudge an innocent person and punish someone for a crime they didn't commit," Ekman says.

It's impossible to predict all the ways we would benefit and suffer if all lies were known, but what is for certain is that the world would be a very different place to the one we live in today. Humans, however, are adaptable, and "over time, we would develop new norms and acceptable codes of social conduct," says Vian Bakir of Bangor University in Wales.

At the same time, she says, we would likely do all we could to develop new ways of lying and dishonesty, whether through technology, drugs, social behavior or mental training. "I'm 100% certain we'd continue to (A) somehow; we'd just find a different way to do it. It's a life necessity."

1 According to the passage, which of the following is NOT an example of how lying benefits us?

ア Minorities can use it to get salaries or positions equal to others.

イ Parents can tell magical stories such as the Tooth Fairy to children.

ウ We can make our grandmother feel good about a gift she gave us.

エ　We can use it to explain to our boss why we missed a deadline.

2　According to the passage, what do the studies by Metts, Guthrie and Kunkel show?

　　ア　Being truthful in romantic relationships is less likely to be harmful.

　　イ　Most people in romantic relationships tend to lie to their partner.

　　ウ　Romanic relationships that involve lying do not last very long.

　　エ　The percent of people who are truthful is about the same as those who lie in relationships.

3　According to the passage, which of the following would be an advantage of being able to detect lies?

　　ア　Our friendships and professional relations would last longer.

　　イ　There would be greater justice in police matters and court trials.

　　ウ　We would be less likely to hurt the feelings of others.

　　エ　We would still maintain the same norms and codes of conduct.

4　Which are the most suitable words to put into (　A　)?

　　ア　be kind in our relationships

　　イ　conceive new ways to detect lies

　　ウ　deceive each other

　　エ　search for the truth

5　Which of the following titles is the most suitable for this passage?

　　ア　How does telling the truth benefit society?

　　イ　What if we knew when people were lying?

　　ウ　When is the best time to tell the truth?

　　エ　Why do people lie so much?

(☆☆☆☆○○○○○)

【４】次の英文を読んで，1〜5の問いに答えなさい。

　　Fashion shoppers spent about ￡3.5 billion on Christmas party clothing this year－but 8 million of those sparkly items will be on their way to landfill after being worn just once.

So-called fast fashion has introduced throw-away culture into the clothing business.

Now, however, some fashion experts believe the end could be coming to, disposable clothing and a backlash could occur, (1   ).

In the past 15 years, global clothing production has doubled. But it has left a trail of waste, with more than half of fast fashion items thrown away in less than a year.

In 2015, greenhouse gas emissions from textiles production globally totaled 1.2 billion tons of CO_2 equivalent. This is more than the emissions of all international flights and maritime shipping combined.

(2   ), with 12% recycled into other products such as insulation or mattress stuffing.

With a parliamentary committee set to produce a report on the issue in February and concerns about plastic pollution, industry insiders believe a backlash against fast fashion is on the way.

Mike Barry, director of sustainable business at Marks & Spencer, said: "The signals are fashion is on the same trajectory as plastics and forests and alternatives to meat.

"There is not an obvious consumer backlash against fast fashion today, but it would be a very brave business leader who didn't look into the next 12 to 18 months and say we are not heading there. Every business leader in the fashion industry knows that clothing will have the same level of questioning and challenging that food has had for years.

"It is going from being a business-to-business and risk-management issue behind the scenes to a consumer issue, (3   )."

His theory is backed up by research that suggests shoppers have already begun buying clothing less frequently.

In 2018, one-third of consumers bought clothing once a month, down from 37% in 2016.

Samantha Dover, senior retail analyst at Mintel, says nearly half of consumers say they prefer to buy clothing from companies trying to reduce their impact on the environment, and that rises to 60% among people under 24.

"People are far more interested than before in knowing exactly where products are coming from and how they are being made," Dover says. She says (　4　), but that change is coming.

With that in mind, clothing companies are considering how to make their entire range more sustainable.

The UK's government also wants to introduce extended producer-responsibility for textiles and clothing which would force companies to pay for the recovery of waste. But it is a slow process, with consultation promised only by 2025.

Mary Creagh Member of Parliament, chair of the parliamentary environmental audit committee, which has been investigating (A)fashion industry sustainability, says the timetable is too slow.

"We have only got 12 years to tackle damaging climate change," she says. "These are massive companies run by some of the world's richest men. Someone is doing OK out of it."

Creagh adds that (B)cheap fashion comes with a social as well as an environmental cost—with low-paid workers overseas unable to provide for their families. "We are not saying to people on a low income you can't buy cheap clothes. We are saying it is time that the cost should reflect the true cost of the minimum wage and decent working conditions and growing stuff without pesticides.

Environmental campaigners say people who want to be more sustainable should choose quality clothes and make them last as long as possible by learning to repair them. Buying secondhand clothing, considering renting outfits rather than buying, and washing garments less often at lower temperatures in a full machine can all help.

Even cleaning and mending services are becoming popular. Earlier this month, H&M brought its free mending service to the UK, making it a key part of a store revamp in Hammersmith.

Recycling is also becoming mainstream, with the Primark brand set to launch a clothing take-back scheme in 2019, joining similar efforts by M&S and H&M that have been in operation for several years.

Reprocessing fiber is (　C　), according to Mark Sumner, a lecturer in sustainable fashion at the University of Leeds.

Most fabrics are a mix of different kinds of thread and there are currently no commercial-scale facilities that can separate and reprocess such fabrics. Modern dyes are also difficult to remove, meaning that recycled threads cannot be recolored.

Sumner says: "The more you process and play with them the worse they are and the quality reduces. "Recycled fibers through traditional routes are poor quality."

Sumner and Barry say the government and businesses need to fund research into how good-quality fibers can be reprocessed on a large scale. "If we can find a way of recycling, we can think about the UK being an exporter of those fabrics or rescuing our textile industry. There is an economic story there," Sumner says.

1　本文中の空所(　1　)～(　4　)に入れるのに最も適切なものをア～エの中から一つずつ選び，その記号を書きなさい。なお，文頭にくる語も小文字にしてある。

ア　consumers are still more interested in the price and style of the clothing than where and how it has been made

イ　just as it has against takeaway coffee cups, plastic packaging and meat

ウ　in the same way as plastics and deforestation linked to palm oil have been in the last 12 months

エ　less than 1% of the material used to produce clothing globally is recycled into new clothing

2　本文中の下線部(A)の内容に合致しないものを，次のア～カから二
　　つ選び，その記号を書きなさい。
　　ア　To make the price of fashion items lower
　　イ　To pick out quality clothes
　　ウ　To provide mending or cleaning service
　　エ　To purchase old clothing
　　オ　To send unwanted clothes to a landfill
　　カ　To rent clothes

3　本文中の下線部(B)の内容を，具体的に日本語で説明しなさい。

4　本文中の空所(　C　)に入れるのに最も適切なものを次のア～エの
　　中から一つ選び，その記号を書きなさい。
　　ア　doubtful　　イ　serious　　ウ　tricky　　エ　understandable

5　本文のタイトルとして最も適切なものをア～エの中から一つ選び,
　　その記号を書きなさい。
　　ア　Can Recycling Make the Fashion Industry Sustainable?
　　イ　How is Fashion Hurting the Environment?
　　ウ　How Unethical is the Fashion Industry?
　　エ　Is Fast Fashion Giving Way to the Sustainable Wardrobe?

(☆☆☆○○○○○)

【5】次の英文を読み，あとの問いに150語程度の英語で答えなさい。

　　I believe that the results of a study on language learning presented in the
journal *Cognition* have been misrepresented in newspapers. The newspapers
claimed that the findings show that after the age of about 10, the "critical
period" of language acquisition, it is impossible to become fluent in a foreign
language. The results of the study actually show that this "critical period" can
extend to about 17 years old. However, what I want to stress is that while
younger learners have an advantage in mastering certain complex grammar
features and in acquiring a native-like accent, foreign language learners of any
age can still become fluent in their target language.

Question : Do you agree with the writer's opinion that it is possible to become fluent in a foreign language after the "critical period"? Use specific reasons and examples to support your opinion.

(☆☆☆☆◎◎◎)

【6】次の1と2の問いに日本語で答えなさい。

1　次の文章は，高等学校学習指導要領解説　外国語編・英語編(平成21年12月)である。空欄(　A　)〜(　E　)に適する語句を書きなさい。

第2節　コミュニケーション英語Ⅰ

この科目は，高等学校外国語科で英語を履修する場合，(　A　)生徒に履修させる科目であり，中学校における「英語」や高等学校における「コミュニケーション英語基礎」の学習を踏まえ，情報や考えなどを的確に理解したり適切に伝えたりする基礎的な能力を養うために設定されたものである。

「コミュニケーション英語Ⅰ」の目標は，次の二つの要素から成り立っている。

①　英語を通じて，(　B　)コミュニケーションを図ろうとする態度を育成すること。

②　英語を通じて，情報や考えなどを的確に理解したり適切に伝えたりする基礎的な能力を養うこと。

①は，「外国語科の目標」に準ずる。

②は，(　C　)読んだりして得た情報や考えなどを的確に理解したり，自分が伝えたい情報や考えなどを(　D　)に対して適切に伝えたりする基礎的な能力を養うことを意味する。

「基礎的な能力を養う」とあるのは，この科目が中学校における「英語」や高等学校における「コミュニケーション英語基礎」の学習を基礎に，比較的平易な内容を学習させ，高等学校における英語の学習の(　E　)を培うことをねらいとしているからである。

2　英語の授業を他教科の学習内容と関連づけて行うこと(教科横断的な学習等)にはどのような効果があると思いますか。次の欄にある語を使用し，具体例を挙げながら，あなたの考えを述べなさい。

「内容」「言語」

(☆☆☆○○○○○)

解答・解説

【中高共通】

【1】1　イ　　2　エ　　3　ウ　　4　ア　　5　イ

〈解説〉スクリプトは公開されていない。選択肢のみが印刷されているリスニング問題では，必ず音声が流れる前に選択肢に目を通しておくこと。全てを覚える必要はないが，音声の内容と質問を，選択肢から予測しておくのがポイントである。その上で，音声が流れている間は，図を見るような感じで，選択肢全体を眺めておき，注意の99％を音声に向けて聴く。正答がわかった瞬間に正答の記号に印をつける。

【2】1　ア　　2　イ　　3　エ　　4　ウ

〈解説〉本問でも，選択肢のみが与えられているため，音声が流れる前に選択肢に目を通し，音声の内容と質問を予測しておきたい。ただし，本問ではまとまりのある英文1つと，それに対する質問が一度に放送される。音声の最中に正答の記号を書くと，書くことに注意が削がれて他の質問の答えになっている箇所を聞き逃す恐れがある。このため，正答がわかっても音声が流れている間は選択肢に鉛筆で印をつけるだけにし，音声終了後，解答用紙に正答選択肢の記号を書くとよい。

194

【3】1　ア　　2　ア　　3　イ　　4　エ

〈解説〉本問では，質問と選択肢が印刷されている。この場合，質問に目を通しておき，音声が流れる前に何が問われるのかを把握しておくのがポイントである(情報量が多くなるので選択肢は無理に読む必要はない)。その際，質問を短い日本語に要約すると，記憶を保持しやすい。1　「ホストマザーが持ち物をカバンに入れたのはなぜ？」が保持する内容。　2　「"an ambulance at the bottom of the cliff" って何？」を覚えておく。　3　「従業員が残業したいのはなぜ？」を保持する。4　「an ambulances at the bottoms of the cliffsを防ぐには？」を保持する。

【中学校】

【1】1　エ　　2　ア　　3　ウ　　4　ウ　　5　ウ　　6　イ　　7　イ　8　ア

〈解説〉空欄に適切な意味の語を選ぶ問題であるが，選択肢の中にはかなり難しい語彙も含まれている。英検準1級から1級の単語集を全て覚えるつもりで対策が必要だろう。　1　空欄を除く文意は，「後日，到着の正確な日時を～する」。ここに適する動詞はdesignate「～を指定する」。なお，repealは「廃止する，無効にする」。　2　空欄の3語後に，fromがあることに注目。derive A from Bで「BからAを得る」という成句を作り，「アメリカの最高の大学の1つに合格したことから，Lauraは大きな満足を得た」という文を完成させる。　3　空欄を除く文意は「Jeffは毎食トマトジュースを飲む」である。よって，habit「習慣」が適切。be in the habit of doing「～することを習慣にしている」。　4　空欄を除く文意は「英語学習者はしばしば，綴りと発音の～が無いことがよくあることに混乱する」である。ここに最適なのはcorrelation「相関」である。なお，conductivityは「伝導性」，concavityは「凹面，くぼみ」のこと。　5　the presentが「現在」であることを見抜くのがポイント。「若者はしばしば現在を楽しみ，将来に向けた～を作らない」の空欄に適切な選択肢はprovisions「準備」。make provision(s) for A「Aへの準備をする」。なおconsignmentsは「委託販売品」。　6　空欄を除く文意

は，「働く女性の数は，20代後半において特に〜である」なので，noticeable「顕著な，目立つ」が適切。なおcountableは「数えられる」。　7　文意は「夏期休暇の間，どこへも行く計画が無い」。consecutive「連続して」。なお，consequentは「当然の」。　8　空欄を除く文意は「私たちの会社は順調だが，〜しないようにしましょう。成功に安んずるべきではない」。2文目の意味を考慮すると，complacent「自己満足の，独りよがりの」が適切。なお，zealous「熱心な」，contentious「論争好きな」，profuse「豊富な」。

【2】1　ア　2　イ　3　エ　4　ア　5　ウ
〈解説〉1　会話問題では，会話の流れをおさえる必要があるが，特に空欄の直後の発言がポイントとなる。空欄後のBの発言で「すぐ近く」と答えているため，距離を尋ねる「ここからどのくらい？」が正解。2　空欄後にAは「銀行の隣りの高い方」と答えている。これが返答となるのは「どのビル？」である。　3　空欄後には「もしあなたの名前が言われなければ，私も〜しなかったでしょう」という仮定法過去完了の発言がある。not…eitherで「〜も…ない」の意味をおさえることがポイント。これに話がつながるのは，「最初誰かわかりませんでした」である。　4　空欄後に逆接のButがあり，But you were such good friends…. 「だけど，あなたたちはあんなに良い友だち同士だった…」と続いている。よって，空欄にはgood friendsと対照的な内容がくると考え，「彼女はもう私にとって大切ではない」を選ぶ。　5　空欄前までの会話からパスポートが話題になっていることに注目。パスポートに関する発言として最適なものは，「それは忘れてはいけないもの」である。空欄後のI know.「わかってる」ともうまくつながる。

【3】1　ア　2　エ　3　イ
〈解説〉1　mindは後ろに動詞の〜ing形をとりWould you mind doing〜?「〜しても差し支えないですか？」という成句を作る。正しくはkeeping。　2　車を修理してもらうという文意である。「get＋A＋動詞

の過去分詞形」で「Aを〜してもらう」なので，正しくはrepaired。修理された状態の車を手に入れると考えると理解しやすい。　3　文中に疑問文が入った間接疑問文において，疑問詞の後の語順は平叙文の「主語(S)＋述語動詞(V)」となる。正しくはit is。

【4】1　イ　　2　エ　　3　ウ
〈解説〉1　兄が朝早く起きた理由をおさえる。第1パラグラフにある兄の発言の2, 3文目で「明日父の土地を耕しに行って，より広い面積を耕せた方が土地の全てを得ることにしよう。ただ，2人とも1日何も食べてはいけないという条件をつけよう」と提案している。そして，その後，兄は朝早く起きて朝食をたくさんとり，反対に飲まず食わずの弟は，兄に勝つことができなかったというストーリーである。以上のことから，「彼は父から多くの財産を相続したかった」が適切。
2　文頭にSoon afterとあるので，弟が鳥の巣を見つけた「直後」の行動をおさえる。これは，第3パラグラフの3文目He picked up a stick〜に該当する。したがって，「彼は棒を巣に向かって何度か投げたが，毎回的を外した」が適切。　3　the Mountain of the Sunで，カラスが兄にやめるよう伝えたことをおさえる。最終パラグラフの1, 2文目で，カラスは，長居せずにすぐ帰宅するよう兄に警告している。続く3文目で，兄はこの忠告に耳を貸していなかったことがわかる。したがって，「それ以上留まる(ことがないよう伝えたが)，彼は聞かなかった」が適切。

【5】1　イ　　2　ウ　　3　エ
〈解説〉1　会話問題は，それまでの会話の流れをおさえるとともに，問われている箇所の直後に注意して解答する。*Satoshi*の直前の発言から，ゲストがからかわれるroastというパーティー(具体的にはthe Debate Club Roast)が話題であるため，空欄がある文の主語Itはこれを指していることがわかる。また，空欄直後の文で，*Satoshi*は「参加者がからかっているのはクラブのリーダーだよ！」と説明している。以上を考慮

すると，*Satoshi*にとってパーティーはdisrespectful「失礼な」に見えたと判断できる。　2　空欄の直前で，*Satoshi*は「アメリカのユーモアを学ぶ代わりに，君に異文化理解のレッスンをしていた」と発言している。空欄はこれを受けて，*Satoshi*から*Taylor*に向けた発言である。ただし，正答には，ここまで話されている日米の文化の違いを考慮し，アメリカ文化から適切な選択肢を考える必要がある。*Taylor*の7つ目の発言において，(I know you want to thank me…) You're welcome. という表現が紹介されている。これはつまり，「(あなたが私に感謝したいのをわかっています。そして私はそれを)歓迎します」という意味で，異文化理解を*Taylor*に教えていた*Satoshi*からTaylorに向けた発言として最適である。　3　*Taylor*は最後から3つ目の発言で，店員からの「ありがとう」に「ありがとう」と返さないことを日本人は失礼と思わないか，と尋ねている。それに対して*Satoshi*はNot usually.「普通はそのようなことはないです」と答えている。この部分が，エの「*Satoshi*は日本人が店員に『ありがとう』を返さないのを失礼に思っている」と矛盾している。

【6】ウ，エ

〈解説〉正誤問題では，本文を一度全て読み，全体的な内容を把握してから選択肢の正誤を検討する。　ア　人工知能とはコンピューターであるという選択肢だが，第1パラグラフ3文目「人工知能のコンセプトは，コンピューターよりも遥かに長く存在してきた」という記述から判断すると，人工知能とコンピューターは必ずしもイコールではないと考えられる。　イ　第3パラグラフ2文目において，「人工知能研究の進歩は，チェスや碁の最も優れたプレイヤーに勝つコンピューターを生んだ」という記述に矛盾する。選択肢では，チェスや碁がstrategy gamesに言い換えられている。　ウ　人工知能の限界点が述べられているのは，第5パラグラフである。Furthermoreから始まる3文目にある「人工知能関係の課題の遂行に使われるプログラムが，同じように作られているわけではない」という限界点が，「コンピューターのプロ

グラムは，常にうまく協働できるわけではない」という選択肢の内容と一致する。　エ　第6パラグラフ1文目にあるopen letter calling for increased research into the impacts of artificial intelligence on society. から，公開状は，人工知能が社会に及ぼす影響についての研究を求めたものとわかり，選択肢のbecause以下と一致する。　オ　選択肢には，未来を示す助動詞willの否定形が使われており，「将来において」コンピューターは人と同じ速度で情報を処理することはできないと述べている。これは，最終パラグラフの1文目にあるwe will begin to see computers "think" at the same speed as humans by 2030. と矛盾する。

【7】Foreign language activities were introduced in the third grade of elementary school, and foreign language studies were introduced in the fifth grade. So it is necessary to establish a smooth connection to junior high school, especially in the first grade of junior high school.

We should consider the content of foreign language activities and foreign language studies in elementary school where the students were enrolled. And also, it is necessary to check the teaching system and timetable organization in elementary school.

And then, it is necessary to grasp the interests of the students. (93 words)

〈解説〉指導計画について自分の考えを制限語数内で述べる英作文問題である。中学校学習指導要領と並行して同解説を複数回熟読し，その背景や趣旨を適切に把握し，英語で考えをまとめる練習が必須となる。本問については，学習指導要領において規定される，小学校第3, 4学年での外国語活動と，第5, 6学年での教科としての外国語を踏まえた，英語科における小中接続が趣旨となる。併せて，小中接続に関する留意事項を，平易な英語で書く。

【8】①　ア　　②　オ　　③　ク
〈解説〉学習指導要領の中で，目標は最も重要な事項である。少なくとも，中学校と高等学校の目標は暗記しておくこと。　①　目標のうち，こ

の(1)は「知識及び技能」に関わる事項である。基礎的・基本的な知識として習得すべきものとして，「外国語の音声や語彙，表現，文法，言語の働き」があげられている。　②　ここで問われている「目的や場面，状況」というキーワードは必ずおさえておくこと。これらは，外国語によるコミュニケーションを行う際に意識すべき，コミュニケーションの前提というべきものである。これを踏まえて，情報や考え等を伝えたり，表現したりすることで，外国語による「思考力，判断力，表現力等」の育成を目指す。　③　この(3)は，「学びに向かう力，人間性等」の涵養に対応している。人が言葉によって意思を伝え合う背景には，個々人の文化があり，異文化の理解が目標の1つとしてあげられている。

【9】①　コミュニケーション　②　活用　③　気付き　④　言語活動
〈解説〉学習指導要領において，中学校での外国語科の大きな目標として「コミュニケーションを図る資質・能力」が示されており，文法事項は「コミュニケーションを支えるもの」と位置づけられている。ただし，文法事項の重要性が低いというわけではない。コミュニケーションのために学習言語を使う中で，文法事項を導入し，その必要性を実感させることが大切である。その上で，文法の知識をコミュニケーションに活用させたり，規則性や構造に気づかせたりすることで，使える技能として文法事項を身につけさせていくことが求められている。

【10】1　生徒の日々の生活に関わる話題のうち，生徒自身や家族に関すること，生徒の興味・関心の対象となることや社会生活で必要なことなどである。具体的には，例えば基本的な個人的な情報から始まり，住んでいる場所や部屋の様子，行きたい場所，家族や友人，所有しているもの，好きな動植物や飼っているペット，学校生活や家庭生活における出来事などが考えられる。　2　文と文の順序や相互の関連に注意を払い，全体として一貫性のある文章を書くこと。導入－本

論－結論や，主題－根拠や具体－主題の言い換えや要約，など文章構成の特徴を意識しながら，全体として一貫性のある文章を書くことができるようにすることが重要である。

〈解説〉本問のように，「日常的な話題」や「まとまりのある文章」などのキーワードが何を意味しているかは，学習指導要領の「解説」に詳述されている。必ず目を通して理解を深めておくこと。 1 「日常的な話題」とは，具体的には住んでいる場所，趣味，好きなもの，学校生活や家庭生活における出来事のことである。「書くこと」の指導にあたっては，生徒にとってこのような身近なことを題材にするよう示されている。 2 「まとまりのある文章」のキーワードとして「一貫性」をおさえておきたい。一貫性とは，文章全体で述べていることが矛盾なく一体となっていることである。一貫性の高いまとまった文章を書かせるには，ひとつひとつの文を正確にさせるだけでなく，文と文のつながりや順序に注意を払わせたり，文章の構造を意識させたりすることが求められる。

【11】 1 簡単な語句や文で書かれた社会的な話題に関する説明などを読んで，イラストや写真，図表なども参考にしながら，文章全体としての構成や論理の展開を押さえさせたうえで，読む目的に応じた要点を把握する活動を設定する。 2 日常的な話題について，伝えようとする内容を整理し(整理するための時間を設定)，(詳細なメモやキーワードのみのメモなど，)自分で作成したメモなどを活用しながら相手と口頭で伝えあう活動を設定する。

〈解説〉言語活動の例についても学習指導要領解説に示されているので，確認しておくこと。 1 「社会的な話題」とは，具体的には地球温暖化等の環境問題や，世界経済等の社会問題等を指す。これらを扱った文章を教材とする場合，このような文章の個々の語句や文を解釈させるだけでなく，文章全体の構成や展開，主張を理解させたり，読む目的に応じて要点を把握させたりする活動が望ましい。 2 「事実や自分の考え，気持ちなどを整理し，」は，伝える内容について考えさせ

たり，メモを作らせたりすることで，話す内容を事前に整えさせることである。このような活動を含めて，「話すこと(やりとり)」の指導例について述べる。

【高等学校】

【1】1　ウ　　2　イ　　3　イ　　4　イ　　5　エ

〈解説〉1　awardは「(賞等)を贈る」の意味をもつ他動詞で，主語のKevin Smithが賞を「贈った」側なのか，「贈られた」側なのかを判断する。ポイントは，for the project...のforの部分。forは理由を表し，「Kevin Smithは，そのプロジェクトのために，最優秀賞を『贈られた』」と受動態と解釈する。　2　助動詞willと空欄後のthe next five yearsから時制は未来で，教育予算を増額するのは今後5年に「かけて」と判断できる。この期間を表す前置詞は，over「〜にわたって，〜を通して」が適切。　3　空欄前に「数年はかかると予測される」，空欄後は「10年」と，年数が増えている。このことから，「10年『ではないにしても』，数年はかかると予測される」という意味と解釈できる。if not「〜でないとしても」。　4　後半の節に関し，副詞のsimplyから「私は『単純に』飛行機で旅をしたくない」という意味である。ただ飛行機が嫌いなだけ，という文脈に自然につなげるには，「金銭的な負担は『さておき』」という語が望ましい。aside from「〜は別として」。

5　空欄に入るのは，形容詞clearで修飾でき，かつ，前置詞forを後ろにとる語である。rationale forで「〜の(論理的)根拠」という意味。

【2】1　Technology could help us bring minority languages to a wider audience by using it to help linguistic diversity.　2　The language in which those services are presented (is).　3　Many language technologies rely on imprecise statistical approaches (that do not make use of deeper linguistic methods).　4　Email, instant messaging and social media (are).

5　It would only gather information and options posted in English. / It could not monitor the sentiments of British citizens who write in Welsh, Gaelic or

Irish.

〈解説〉1　設問にあるデジタル時代のウェールズ語については，第3パラグラフ2文目にthe Welsh language in the digital ageと記述がある。この直前の英文からtechnology...diversityの部分を抜き出す。文意は「技術は少数言語をより多くの人々に届け，言語的多様性の一助になる」。　2　公共サービスがオンライン化するという文言は，第5パラグラフの最初に述べられている。大切なこととして，the language...presentedとある。　3　第8パラグラフの冒頭で，Thisは少数言語にとって悪いニュースであると述べている。続くThe automatic translation...の文では，この悪いニュースの内容として，「サンプルとなる材料が少ない言語では，自動翻訳の統計手法がうまく機能しない」と述べている。よって，Thisが指しているのは，「少数言語に有害になり得る技術的な情報」と判断できる。すると，直前の第7パラグラフのmany language technologies rely on imprecise statistical approaches「多くの言語技術は不正確な統計手法に頼っている」が，Thisの指示対象とわかる。　4　インフォーマルな言語の用法は，第11パラグラフに述べられている。同パラグラフ3文目Now we talk online via email, instant messaging, and social media.から，具体的な用途を抜き出す。　5　感情分析のアプリは，第13パラグラフに述べられており，このパラグラフから問題点としてあげられている記述を探す。問題とはっきり書かれてはいないが，最後のBut if that app only gathers information...の文は，「アプリが英語による情報や意見しか収集しない場合，少数言語を使用するイギリス人の感情がわかるのか？」と反語的な表現になっており，これが問題になり得ることだとわかる。

【3】1　ア　　2　イ　　3　イ　　4　ウ　　5　イ
〈解説〉1　ア　第5パラグラフにマイノリティに関する記述があるが，ここで述べられているのはマイノリティが「嘘をつかれている」場合の話であって，彼らが「嘘をつく」のではない。　イ　第8パラグラフの最後の文「(嘘の無い世界では)歯の妖精やイースターのウサギを含

む魔法の物語もなくなってしまうかもしれない」という部分から，物語はある意味嘘によって存在していると考えられるため，一致する。　ウ　第10パラグラフのpolite lieの例として述べられる "Mom might say..." の引用部分に注目。「おばあちゃんがプレゼントをくれるから，それを気に入ったと言わなきゃだめよ...」が一致する。　エ　第4パラグラフに職場での嘘の役割について述べられている。この2文目「もし上司に本心や，締切を守れなかった本当の理由を伝えたら，解雇か降格されるだろう」が一致する。　2　Metts, Guthrie, Kunkelらの研究については，第14および第15パラグラフに述べられている。これらの研究結果では，「恋仲にあるカップルでは嘘が非常に頻繁につかれる」ことが示されている。　3　嘘を見抜くことの利点に関する設問。第16パラグラフに，「嘘を見抜くことが治安や刑事司法に役立つ」と述べられている。　4　最終パラグラフ1文目から，「人は嘘をつく方法をなんとしてでも開発する」という主張が読み取れる。よって，空欄には人が「互いに嘘をつき続ける」という内容がくると判断できる。　5　嘘には，人間関係を損なわないようにするための配慮があることが述べられている。「嘘がこの世からなくなったら，世界はどうなってしまうだろう」「嘘は人生に必要なものだ」となどの見解が引用されていることから，イ「他人の嘘に気付いたらどうしますか」が適切。

【4】1　1　イ　　2　エ　　3　ウ　　4　ア　　2　ア，オ
3　殺虫剤を使用しない原材料の栽培や，理にかなった最低賃金，そして相応な労働条件を反映した価格を犠牲にして，安価なファッションが成り立っていること。　　4　ウ　　5　エ
〈解説〉1　1　空欄の直前に注目。ここでは，disposable clothing「使い捨ての服」に終わりが訪れ，backlash「反動」が起こる可能性があると述べられている。この続きとして，backlashをitで受けたイが適切。イは，just as it has (occurred) against...と動詞が省略されており，「ちょうど持ち帰りのコーヒーカップや，ビニール包装とその中身に対して反動が起きたように」という意味。　2　空欄の直後に付帯状況を示す

withがあり，「その12％は，絶縁体やマットレスの詰め物等の製品にリサイクルされる」とある。このことから，空欄はリサイクルされる物についてであると考え，エ「新しい服としてリサイクルされるのは…1％に満たない」を選ぶ。　3　空欄より1つ前の文「服飾は，食品が抱えてきたものと同レベルの疑問や困難に直面する」をおさえるのがポイント。これを踏まえ，食品の例を提示しているウを選ぶ。空欄がある文で「(服飾は)舞台裏でのビジネス間やリスク管理の問題から，消費者の問題になっている」とあり，ウはこの動きの例として，パーム油に伴うプラスチックや森林伐採をあげている。　4　後ろに逆接のbutがあることから，空欄にはchangeに対比的な内容がくると考える。このchangeは，空欄前の発言にある「人々は，製品がどこからきているか，どのように作られているかについて，以前よりはるかに関心がある」という「変化」のことで，これの対比となる内容の選択肢は，ア「顧客はまだ，服がどこでどのように作られたかよりも，値段やスタイルに関心がある」である。　2　「ファッション業界の持続可能性」に関しては，下線部(A)より3つ後ろのパラグラフのpeople who want to be more sustainable should…以降の部分に述べられている。具体的には「quality clothesを選ぶ」「服を修復して可能な限り長持ちさせる」「中古の服を買う」「買うのではなく借りることを検討する」「気温が低いときは洗濯の頻度を低くする」とある。選択肢のうち，アとオはいずれにも該当しない。　3　説明すべきは，安価なファッションに伴う社会的，環境的なcostである。このcostは2文後の(We are saying it is time that) the cost should reflect…以下で詳述されており，この部分に基づき解答する。　4　reprocessing fiberがどのようなものかは，後続する2つのパラグラフで述べられている。ここでは，生地は多くの種類の糸がまとまって出来ており，それを商業的規模で分離して再処理するような施設は現状存在しないことや，染料を落とせないこと，処理をして手を加えれば加えるほど生地の質は下がってしまうこと等，生地を再処理することの困難について述べられている。この内容を1語で表すのは，ウのtricky「扱いにくい，手のかかる」。　5　英文は全体を通し，

ファストファッションに終わりが近づいており，持続可能なファッションに関心が集まっていることを述べている。

【5】 Yes...I think that it is possible to become fluent in a foreign language after their critical period has passed. Firstly, as the speaker in the article says, while it may be difficult to master some complex grammar patterns or develop a native-like accent, I think many older people can still become fluent in their foreign language. For example, many of my English teacher friends did not begin studying English intensively until their adulthood. Yet, they can still communicate fluently in conversation or writing. Secondly, the critical period has not been scientifically proven. Each person's ability to become fluent in a foreign language depends on many other factors than age, such as environment and motivation. For example, people who can use the Internet might be more likely to become fluent than people who do not have access. Therefore, I agree that anyone can become fluent in a foreign language at any age. (152)

No... I don't think it is possible to become fluent in a foreign language after a person has reached their critical period. First of all, it is often said that when children are young they tend to learn many things more easily, for example, playing the piano, singing, or figure skating. Usually the people who do well in these started learning them when they were a young child. I think the same is true for foreign language. In addition, young children are better at imitating others. So, if they have a lot of experience listening to or reading a foreign language when they are young, they will be able to imitate that and acquire fluency more easily. For example, many parents try to send their children to a foreign country or to a language school for lessons with native speakers so that they can learn to imitate their use of the language. Therefore, I disagree with the writer's opinion. (158)

〈解説〉本問のような特定分野の理論(第二言語習得の臨界期仮説)に関して，うまく作文するためには，関連する知識がある程度は必要である。

高校英語では，英語教授法や第二言語習得に関する理論が出題されることが多い。英語科教育法のテキストを何度も読み，基本的な理論やモデルを必ずおさえておくこと。「臨界期仮説」とは，それを過ぎるとネイティブスピーカーと同程度の言語能力を習得するのが不可能になってしまう年齢が存在するという仮説である。この記事の著者は，複雑な文法やアクセント習得において，年齢の若さがある程度アドバンテージとなることは認めているものの，外国語学習者は年齢を問わず学習言語で流暢になれると主張している。これについて，同意するかどうかを，理由とともにわかりやすい英語でまとめる。

【6】1　A　すべての　　B　積極的に　　C　聞いたり　　D　受け手
E　基礎　　2　中身のある内容や目的のある活動により，学習への動機付けが高まる。例えば，理科や社会の内容の中から生徒が興味のあるトピックについて実験・観察や調査をし，英語で発表する場合，その内容を学んだり伝えたりするためのツールとして，積極的に英語を使うことが期待される。また，深い思考を伴う活動の中で，インタラクションやアウトプットなどの言語活動が活発になる。例えば，国際問題や異文化理解について学ぶ際，ペアやグループで話し合い，互いの意見を共有する必要がある。その中で，様々な表現方法に互いに気付き，理解を深めることにより，より高い言語能力を身に付けることができる。以上のように，思考力や表現力の育成が重視される中，教科横断的な英語学習を行うことには大きな効果があると考えられる。
〈解説〉1　学習指導要領と同解説は併せて複数回熟読し，各文言の趣旨や背景を正確に把握しておくこと。なお，本問は現行の高等学校学習指導要領(平成21年3月告示)に関する出題であるが，新学習指導要領(平成30年3月告示)がすでに出されていることから，今後は新学習指導要領・同解説からの出題の可能性がある。必ずそれらに目を通しておこう。　2　他教科と関連づけた授業では，英語という言語そのものに加えて，理科や社会といった科目の「内容」が対象となる。生徒の興味関心に応じたトピックについて話し合わせたり，発表させたりす

れば，学習への動機づけを高めたり，インタラクションやアウトプット等の言語活動を促すことができる。

2019年度　実施問題

【中高共通】

【1】これから，会話と質問が5つ放送されます。質問に対する答えとして最も適切なものをア〜エの中から一つずつ選び，その記号を書きなさい。なお，会話と質問は一度だけ放送されます。

1
ア　She is going to sell her motorcycle.
イ　She is going to stay home all day long.
ウ　She is going to take a look at the man's motorcycle.
エ　She is going to work on her motorcycle.

2
ア　He will arrive at 2:30.
イ　He will arrive at 2:55.
ウ　He will arrive at 3:00.
エ　He will arrive at 3:25.

3
ア　Claire is going back to Japan.
イ　Claire is leaving for Kyoto.
ウ　Claire is moving to Osaka.
エ　Claire is returning to the U.S.

4
ア　Around 1,000 people visited their booth.
イ　Around 1,500 people visited their booth.
ウ　Around 2,000 people visited their booth.
エ　Around 2,500 people visited their booth.

5
ア　She wants to do domestic chores.

イ　She wants to live by herself.

ウ　She wants to pay bills.

エ　She wants to buy the man's shoes.

(☆☆☆◎◎◎)

【２】これから，まとまりのある英文が放送されます。英文の後に，その内容について質問が4つ出されます。その質問に対する答えとして最も適切なものをア～エの中から一つずつ選び，その記号を書きなさい。なお，英文と質問は一度だけ放送されます。

1

ア　Children greet each other.

イ　A human teacher greets the class.

ウ　A robot greets children.

エ　A robot greets a human teacher.

2

ア　It takes children to the classroom.

イ　It teaches English to children.

ウ　It waits for a human teacher at the chalkboard.

エ　It shows children gestures in the classroom.

3

ア　To develop robot technology.

イ　To reduce the budget for human teachers' salaries.

ウ　To replace teachers with robots.

エ　To deal with the lack of English teachers.

4

ア　Help teachers and parents.

イ　Help parents and friends.

ウ　Replace teachers and parents.

エ　Replace parents and friends.

(☆☆☆◎◎◎)

【3】 これから，まとまりのある英文が一度だけ放送されます。質問に対する答えとして最も適切なものをア～エの中から一つずつ選び，その記号を書きなさい。

1　According to the passage, how many places did Japan drop in the gender equality ranking for 2017 from the year before?

ア　By one.

イ　By three.

ウ　By four.

エ　By seven.

2　According to the passage, which of the four categories is the main factor for Japan's fall in the 2017 ranking?

ア　Economy.

イ　Education.

ウ　Health.

エ　Politics.

3　According to the passage, which of the four categories is the main factor for the global gender gap widening in 2017?

ア　Economy.

イ　Education.

ウ　Health.

エ　Politics.

4　Which of the following is true about the passage?

ア　Gender equality in Japan is the second to last among the world's 7 big economies.

イ　The World Economic Forum is a think tank which is based in Japan.

ウ　The World Economic Forum survey started in 2006 and it has never shown a widening gender gap before.

エ　For the last ten years women have made little progress in seeking gender equality.

(☆☆☆☆◎◎◎)

【中学校】

【１】次の1～8の英文の(　　　)にあてはまる最も適切な英語を，それぞれ
ア～エから一つずつ選び，その記号を書きなさい。

1　Getting enough sleep and exercising regularly are said to be (　　) to one's health.

　　ア　perfect　　　　　イ　bountiful　　　　ウ　beneficial

　　エ　memorable

2　The President (　　) her as the next Secretary of State.

　　ア　allowed　　　　　イ　designated　　　　ウ　reversed

　　エ　convinced

3　In order to be promoted in this company, you should be (　　) with the concepts of time management.

　　ア　conceded　　　　　イ　retired　　　　ウ　authorized

　　エ　acquainted

4　Since the student had a fever, his teacher gave him (　　) to go home.

　　ア　forbearance　　　　イ　fortitude　　　　ウ　declaration

　　エ　permission

5　People often say that the best (　　) for a person to have is honesty.

　　ア　attribute　　　　　イ　concern　　　　ウ　creativity

　　エ　perception

6　The wedding planner had made (　　) for bad weather by reserving a reception hall.

　　ア　provision　　　　　イ　expense　　　　ウ　foresight

　　エ　necessary

7　The volleyball team was delighted because after losing many games they now had three (　　) wins in their last three games.

　　ア　consignment　　　　イ　imprudent　　　　ウ　developing

　　エ　consecutive

8　You should not be (　　) about your small victories; there is still much more to be done.

ア　unwary　　　　イ　complacent　　ウ　irritated

エ　controversial

(☆☆☆☆◎◎◎◎)

【2】次の1～5の会話文中の(　　)にあてはまる最も適切な英語を，それ
ぞれア～エから一つずつ選び，その記号を書きなさい。

1　A: Do you have a moment?

　　B: (　　　　)

　　A: I want to tell you in private.

　　B: Let's go to my office, then.

　　　ア　How do you pronounce it?

　　　イ　I think she left.

　　　ウ　There are no more.

　　　エ　What's the problem?

2　A: I'll meet you at the station at 5:15 the day after tomorrow.

　　B: Which station do you mean?

　　A: Ichinoseki Station, where we've always met.

　　B: Oh, of course! (　　　　)

　　　ア　I'll try to get there on time.

　　　イ　OK. I'll see you at a quarter to five.

　　　ウ　Till tomorrow, then.

　　　エ　I don't know where you mean.

3　A: I suppose you didn't see my phone on the table?

　　B: (　　　　)

　　A: What? You shouldn't touch things that don't belong to you!

　　　ア　Yes, I did.

　　　イ　No, I didn't.

　　　ウ　I broke it.

　　　エ　I left it on the table.

4　A: Darling, do you mind if I make a phone call before we leave?

B: (　　　　)

A: I am, but this is important.

 ア I do mind. I'm leaving.

 イ Of course not. I'll wait here.

 ウ Do we have enough time?

 エ I thought you were in a hurry.

5 A: What are your plans for this weekend?

 B: (　　　　)

 A: I'm having a party on Friday night. Would you like to come?

 B: I'm afraid I can't. I promised my parents I'd stay home and do something with my little brother.

 ア I will try not to.

 イ I want to, but I can't.

 ウ Yes, I'll try.

 エ Nothing much.

(☆☆☆○○○)

【3】次の1～3の各文にあるア～エの下線部には，英語の文法上または表現上適切ではない語句があります。適切ではない下線部をそれぞれア～エから一つずつ選び，その記号を書きなさい。

1 ア<u>It is said that</u> Americans are good at イ<u>to make friends</u> with ウ<u>new people</u> and often have エ<u>high</u> communication skills.

2 We tried ア<u>for hour</u> to solve our problem; Lisa came up イ<u>with</u> an answer after she ウ<u>studied</u> the problem エ<u>alone</u>.

3 If every one of us ア<u>had made</u> greater イ<u>efforts</u> to remedy the state of things at that time, we wouldn't ウ<u>have been</u> エ<u>criticized</u> so severely now.

(☆☆☆○○○○○)

【4】次の英文は，Sarahが野球について述べたものです。あとの1～3の書き出しに続くものとして，内容に最も一致するものを，ア～エから

214

一つずつ選び，その記号を書きなさい。

My father was an avid baseball fan. Many Saturdays were spent with my dad cheering on our favorite team. As much as I loved the game of baseball, I was born female at a time when girls watched more than they played. Dad often took me out to the park in which the Little League played, and threw balls for me to hit. Baseball became a big part of my life.

One Saturday at the park, a woman pushing a young boy in a wheelchair stopped to watch us play. My dad went to them at once to ask if the child could join our game. The woman explained that the boy was her son and that he had polio and wouldn't be able to get out of the chair. That didn't stop my dad. He pushed him out to home plate and assisted him in holding the bat. Then he yelled out to me on the mound, "Sarah, pitch one in to us." The ball made contact with the bat with an assist from my dad and the child screamed with joy. The ball flew over my head. I ran to catch up with it and, as I turned, I heard my dad singing "Take Me Out to the Ball Game" while he pushed the wheelchair around the bases. The mother clapped and the boy begged to be allowed to continue the game.

An hour later, when we all left the field, dad told the mother to bring the boy back next Saturday and we would play another game.

Dad and I were at the field the next Saturday but the mother and son never came. I felt sad and wondered what had happened to change their minds about joining us.

Many years passed and my beloved father died at the age of fifty-nine. With my dad gone, things changed so much that the family decided to move to Seattle.

I decided to take one last walk around the park where Dad and I had spent so many happy moments. Two Little League teams were on the field just about to start a game. I sat down to watch for a while.

"Bob, protect your base," one coach yelled. I cheered the runner on when the ball was hit far into the outfield. One coach turned and smiled and said,

"The kids sure love a rooting section, Miss." He continued, "I never thought I'd ever be a coach playing on this field. You see, I had polio as a child and was confined to a wheelchair. One day a man was playing baseball with his daughter. He stopped playing when he saw us watching and asked my mother if I could join them in their game. He helped me to hold the bat and his daughter pitched to me. I was able to hit the ball with man's assistance and he ran me around the bases in my wheelchair singing the song "Take Me Out to the Ball Game." I went home happier that night than I had been in years. I believe that experience gave me the desire to walk again. We moved to Los Angeles the next day ― that's why my mother had taken me to the park, so I could say good-bye to my friends. I never forgot that man and his daughter or that day. I dreamed about running around the bases on my two feet and the dream, with a lot of work, came true. I moved back here last year, and I've been coaching Little League since then. I guess I hope that some day I'll look up in the stands and see that man and his daughter again. Who knows, I might find him on one of the fields pitching to one of his grandkids ― a lot of years have come and gone. I sure would like to thank him."

As the tears ran down my face, I knew that my dad had just been thanked and even more I knew every time I heard "Batter up!" my dad would always be right beside me. That simple act of kindness that spring day had changed a life forever, and now twenty years later the memory of that day had changed my life forever. "Batter up, Dad," I said as I left the field, "I know you're still playing the game we love ― baseball!"

1　When Sarah was little,
　　ア　girls often played baseball with boys.
　　イ　there were few girls who played baseball.
　　ウ　girls were not allowed to play baseball with boys.
　　エ　there were many girls who played baseball with their fathers.
2　The coach's childhood experience made him
　　ア　look for the man and his daughter ever since.

イ　want to play baseball in a wheelchair.

ウ　work hard to become a baseball coach.

エ　want to get out of the wheelchair.

3　The coach told Sarah that he hoped

　ア　to help children in wheelchairs so they could have a dream.

　イ　to play baseball with one of the man's grandkids.

　ウ　to tell the man and his daughter how much they had encouraged him.

　エ　to explain to the man why he had not shown up.

(☆☆☆◎◎)

【5】次の対話文を読んで，あとの質問に答えなさい。

Nick : Hey, Kate!

Kate : Hi, Nick! Oh, you're all wet! It is raining outside?

Nick : Yes, it's pouring out there. Do you mind if I sit here for a while till the rain stops?

Kate : Of course not. If you want, you can have some of this chocolate cake. It's a big piece.

Nick : Sure, thanks. Wow, this cake is delicious. I've never been to this coffee shop. I was cycling to my part-time job and I wanted to (①) the rain.

Kate : It should let up soon. Have some more cake while you're waiting.

Nick : No, thank you. I've had enough. It's very quiet here.

Kate : Yes, that's why I like to come here to study. Right now, I'm writing an article for the student newspaper about where you can get vegetarian food in and around the university.

Nick : I don't suppose there are many places selling that kind of stuff around here, are there?

Kate : Actually, there are quite a few. You would be surprised how popular vegetarian food is these days. Take this coffee shop, for example. Everything they serve here is vegetarian.

Nick : Oh, I didn't know that. Now, you said you come here often. Does that mean (②) ?

Kate : Yes, I am. I gave up eating meat five years ago. It was a little difficult at first, but it's not anymore. In fact, I'm really glad that I made the effort. Being a vegetarian has so many advantages.

Nick : Really? What kind of advantages?

Kate : Well, apart from the obvious fact that no animals are being killed, it's also good for your health.

Nick : So, why did you become a vegetarian? Was it the health or moral aspects that attracted you?

Kate : To be honest, I didn't really think much about those things at first. I would have to say the main influence was my elder brother.

Nick : What do you mean?

Kate : He's a really wonderful person I've always looked up to and tried to be like. He took a trip to Nepal where he was influenced greatly by Buddhist culture. Because of that, he became a vegetarian and because I respect his opinion, I decided to become a vegetarian as well.

Nick : How interesting!

Kate : What about you, Nick? Have you ever thought about becoming a vegetarian?

Nick : Oh, look at the time! I'm sorry, but I've got to get going.

Kate : But it doesn't look like the rain has stopped yet.

Nick : I know, but I've got to be at work in 10 minutes. If I'm late, I could lose my job.

Kate : Where do you work?

Nick : I'm a little embarrassed to tell you, but in fact I work at MacArthur's Hamburger Restaurant on High Street.

Kate : What? You must be joking!

1　対話文の内容にあうように，文中の(①)に適する語句を，次のア～エから一つ選び，その記号を書きなさい。

ア　take down　　イ　come around　　ウ　get out of

エ　give rise to

2　対話文の内容にあうように，文中の(　②　)に適する文を，次のア
　　～エから一つ選び，その記号を書きなさい。

ア　you love to have a good time here

イ　you wrote a wonderful article

ウ　you are a vegetarian

エ　you are so busy

3　次のア～エから，本文の内容と一致しないものを一つ選び，その
　　記号を書きなさい。

ア　Kate often comes to the coffee shop because she enjoys eating
　　vegetarian food there.

イ　Kate's brother became a vegetarian and that had a profound influence
　　on Kate's life.

ウ　Nick thought there are few restaurants for vegetarians around his
　　university.

エ　Nick felt a twinge of embarrassment for Kate because he works at a
　　hamburger shop.

(☆☆☆◎◎)

【6】次の英文を読んで，本文の内容と一致するものを，あとのア～オか
　　ら三つ選び，その記号を書きなさい。

　　According to the study by psychologists at Lancaster University, led by Dr.
Katie Alcock in 2006, children who can lick their lips, blow bubbles and
make various things with building blocks are most likely to find learning
language easy. They found strong links between these movement and thinking
skills and children's language abilities. In the study, they looked at more than
120 children aged 21 months because that's the time when they are learning
new words at a faster rate than at any other stage of their life. It included
questionnaires for parents and special tests of motor and cognitive abilities.

Dr. Alcock said they got some interesting findings. Most surprising was that there were relationships between children's skill moving their mouths and their language abilities. She thought that the findings could help child experts identify very early on those youngsters most likely to have problems with their understanding of words and speech in later life.

They divided the children into four groups, and examined motion capability of movement, understanding, language and hearing. The study found that some skills had closer relationships to language abilities than others. For instance, there was no relationship when it came to easier movements, such as walking and running.

To assess spontaneous speech in a familiar place, researchers recorded everything said by children, and the person looking after them, during a half-hour free play session in each child's home. This was then analyzed in terms of the range of words produced, and the length of sentences.

In a second group, children were assessed on a wide variety of thinking and reasoning skills: matching pictures and colors, interacting with adults to get their attention, and 'pretending' that one object is another, such as using a block for a car, or a box for a doll's bed, or giving a doll a tea party. Children who were good at this were also better at language, but there was no relationship with more general thinking skills, such as doing puzzles.

In another group, children were tested on their ability, for instance, to say a new or unfamiliar word or to work out which of two character pictures the sound they were hearing went with. Children who could say new words an adult asked them to repeat were best at language. Being able to listen to a new word or a funny sound and work out which picture it went with also distinguished between children with advanced and not so strong abilities.

Dr. Alcock said: "We have found relationships between non-language and language skills in children at a time of very rapid development. We plan to follow-up this study when the children are older, to find out which skills give the best indication of later language abilities and problems. We have already examined how much parents talk to their children at home. Now we are also going to look at parents' levels of education, and the children's home environments, such as the number of books they have, to see what influences these have."

ア Children aged 21 months were assessed in this study because it's the best time of life to learn new words.

イ The children who could repeat the words according to requests by their parents were best at language.

ウ The children who are good at blowing bubbles, repeating a new word, or running fast, could be a fast language learner.

エ The researchers found some relationships between doing puzzles and learning language.

オ The researchers thought they should take account of the home environments when assessing children's language abilities.

(☆☆☆◎◎)

【7】中学校学習指導要領(平成29年3月告示)の「第2章　第9節　外国語　第2　各言語の目標及び内容等　英語　3　指導計画の作成と内容の取扱い」に，次のような配慮事項が掲載されています。

> (1)　指導計画の作成に当たっては，小学校や高等学校における指導との接続に留意しながら，次の事項に配慮するものとする。
> (ア〜ウ　省略)
> エ　生徒が英語に触れる機会を充実するとともに，授業を実際のコミュニケーションの場面とするため，授業は英語で行うことを基本とする。その際，生徒の理解の程度に応じた英語を用いるようにすること。

　この下線部の事項に関して，このような指導が必要とされるねらいは何なのか，またその際に考えられる留意事項としてどのようなことが考えられるのか，ねらいと留意事項についてあなたの考えを80語以

221

上の英語で書きなさい。

　なお，最後に語数を記入すること。語数については，同じ語を2回使用した場合，2語と数えること(のべ数)とします。

(☆☆☆☆◎◎◎◎)

【8】次の文章は，中学校学習指導要領(平成29年3月告示)の「第2章　第9節　外国語　第1　目標」です。これを読んで，下の問いに答えなさい。

第1　目　標

　外国語によるコミュニケーションにおける見方・考え方を働かせ，外国語による聞くこと，読むこと，話すこと，書くことの言語活動を通して，簡単な情報や考えなどを理解したり表現したり伝え合ったりするコミュニケーションを図る(　①　)を次のとおり育成することを目指す。

(1)　外国語の音声や語彙，表現，文法，言語の働きなどを理解するとともに，これらの知識を，聞くこと，読むこと，話すこと，書くことによる実際のコミュニケーションにおいて(　②　)できる技能を身に付けるようにする。

(2)　コミュニケーションを行う目的や場面，状況などに応じて，日常的な話題や社会的な話題について，外国語で簡単な情報や考えなどを理解したり，これらを活用して表現したり(　③　)することができる力を養う。

(3)　外国語の背景にある文化に対する理解を深め，聞き手，読み手，話し手，書き手に(　④　)しながら，主体的に外国語を用いてコミュニケーションを図ろうとする態度を養う。

1　文中の(　①　)～(　④　)にあてはまる言葉を書きなさい。

2　下線部「主体的に外国語を用いてコミュニケーションを図ろうとする態度」とはどのような態度か，日本語で説明しなさい。

(☆☆☆☆◎◎◎◎)

222

【9】中学校学習指導要領解説外国語編(平成29年7月)の「第2章　外国語
　科の目標及び内容　第1節　外国語科の目標」に，「外国語によるコミ
　ュニケーションにおける見方・考え方」について，次のように述べら
　れています。文中の(　①　)(　②　)にあてはまる言葉を書きなさい。

　「外国語によるコミュニケーションにおける見方・考え方」と
は，外国語によるコミュニケーションの中で，どのような視点
で物事を捉え，どのような考え方で思考していくのかという，
物事を捉える視点や考え方であり，「外国語で表現し伝え合うた
め，外国語やその背景にある文化を，社会や世界，(　①　)との
関わりに着目して捉え，コミュニケーションを行う目的や場面，
状況等に応じて，情報を整理しながら考えなどを形成し，
(　②　)すること」であると考えられる。

(☆☆☆☆◎◎◎◎)

【10】次の文章は，中学校学習指導要領(平成29年3月告示)の「第2章　第
　9節　外国語　第2　各言語の目標及び内容等　英語　1　目標」から
　の抜粋です。文中の(　①　)〜(　③　)にあてはまる語句を下のア〜ケ
　から一つずつ選び，記号を書きなさい。

---

(5)　書くこと
　ア　関心のある事柄について，簡単な語句や文を用いて
　　(　①　)書くことができるようにする。
　イ　日常的な話題について，事実や自分の考え，気持ちなど
　　を整理し，簡単な語句や文を用いて(　②　)文章を書くこ
　　とができるようにする。
　ウ　社会的な話題に関して(　③　)したことについて，考えた
　　ことや感じたこと，その理由などを，簡単な語句や文を用
　　いて書くことができるようにする。

ア　ある程度長い　　　　イ　聞いたり読んだり

ウ　身近な　　　　　　エ　正確に

オ　まとまりのある　　カ　聞いたり話したり

キ　話したり読んだり　ク　その場で

ケ　適切に

(☆☆☆☆◎◎◎◎)

【11】次の文は，中学校学習指導要領(平成29年3月告示)の「第2章　第9節　外国語　第2　各言語の目標及び内容等　英語　2　内容　(3)　言語活動及び言語の働きに関する事項」からの抜粋です。これを読んで，下の問いに答えなさい。

> エ　話すこと[やり取り]
>
> （ア）　関心のある事柄について，相手からの質問に対し，その場で適切に応答したり，関連する質問をしたりして，互いに会話を継続する活動。

1　今回の学習指導要領改訂において，「話すこと[やり取り]」の領域が設定されました。その理由について，日本語で書きなさい。

2　この事項は，小学校の外国語科の「話すこと[やり取り]」の言語活動(ウ)「自分に関する簡単な質問に対してその場で答えたり，相手に関する簡単な質問をその場でしたりして，短い会話をする活動」を踏まえたものです。このことから，指導する際にどのようなことを心掛ける必要があるか，日本語で書きなさい。

(☆☆☆☆◎◎◎◎)

【高等学校】

【１】次の1～5の各文の(　　)に入れるのに最も適切なものをア～エの中から一つずつ選び，その記号を書きなさい。

1　He liked Morioka and decided to stay there (　　) few days.

ア　another　　イ　more　　ウ　one more　　エ　other

2　John signed a contract to buy a car without reading it (　　). Now he has

224

discovered that he is paying a high interest rate.

ア absolutely

イ certainly

ウ roughly

エ thoroughly

3 Since there was only one microwave oven, we had to (   ) using it.

ア change in

イ exchange for

ウ take place

エ take turns

4 Green Search Associates, one of our important clients, (   ) its corporate headquarters in San Francisco, California.

ア has

イ have

ウ having

エ to have

5 Engineers are designing a bridge that will connect cities on (   ) sides of the river.

ア alternate

イ either

ウ opposite

エ similar

(☆☆☆◎◎◎)

【2】次の英文を読んで，あとの1〜5の問いに対する答えを英語で書きなさい。

A small part of Shanghai is turning greener, street by street.

In the Lingang district, pavements are lined with trees, gardens and public squares full of plant beds. Between cranes and construction sites, plans display new buildings enveloped in the green and blue of parks, streams, and water features.

Shanghai faces long-term risks from rising sea levels. So Lingang is on a mission. Known as a "Sponge City", it is leading an ecologically-friendly alternative to traditional flood defences and drainage systems in Shanghai.

Rapid concrete development in China has often blocked the natural flow of water with hard, unaffected surfaces. To reverse this, the Sponge City concept focuses on green infrastructure, such as wetland areas, rooftop plants and rain gardens.

"In the natural environment, most rain sinks into the ground or is received by surface water, but this is disrupted when there are large-scale hard pavements," says Wen Mei Dubbelaar, director of Water Management China at Arcadis. "Now, only about 20-30% of rainwater sinks into the ground in urban areas, so it breaks the natural water circulation and causes waterlogging and surface water pollution."

In Lingang, the wide streets are built with absorptive pavements, allowing water to drain into the soil. Central areas are used as rain gardens, filled with soil and plants. The large manmade Dishui Lake helps control the flow of water, and buildings feature green rooftops and water tanks.

Since the disastrous large-scale flooding in Beijing in 2012, flood prevention has rocketed up the state agenda. The Sponge City initiative was launched in 2015 with 16 model Sponge Cities, before being extended to 30, including Shanghai.

"The first thing is to try and preserve or restore natural waterways, because that is the natural way to reduce the flooding risk," says Prof Hui Li at Tongji University. "In Wuhan, for example, the main problem is that a lot of small rivers were filled in during building. That is a benefit the Lingang area has, as there is still a lot of agricultural land and a manmade lake which has the capacity to hold more water during heavy rain."

But it is difficult to create room for new green space. Even existing parks are largely a missed opportunity, says Li, usually built higher than an street level and failing to offer a natural escape route for runoff floodwater. Most of the focus is on green roofs — the Shanghai government wants 400,000 square metres of new rooftop gardens — or gradually replacing pavements.

1   What has prevented water from flowing naturally in big cities in China?

2   What disaster caused the Chinese government to take actions for flood prevention?

3   What beneficial capacity do agricultural land and a manmade lake have in the Lingang area?

4   Why does the Shanghai government want more rooftop gardens?

5   According to the passage, what does "Sponge City" imply?

(☆☆☆☆○○○○)

【3】次の英文を読んで，あとの1～5の問いに対する答えとして，最も適切なものをア～エの中から一つずつ選び，その記号を書きなさい。

When I was a child my parents told me that I was a winner, and for the first six years of my life I believed them.

I was slow to start talking, but my first year of school went smoothly. In the second grade we were supposed to learn to read. For me it was like a Chinese newspaper. I remember praying at night, saying, "Please Lord, let me know how to read tomorrow when I get up."

I ended up in the dumb row with a bunch of other kids who were having a hard time learning to read. I didn't know how I got there. I didn't know how to ask for help either. By the seventh grade I had basically given up. I was sitting in the principal's office most of the day for fighting or disrupting class. But I didn't feel like a "bad student" inside — I wanted to be a good student. I just didn't know how.

In the eighth grade, I decided to do whatever it took to pass my classes. I had social skills. I dated the student with the highest grades, and I had people do my homework for me. I cheated on all of my tests. Why didn't I ask for help? I didn't believe there was anybody out there who could teach me to read. I never told anybody that I couldn't read. That was my well-guarded secret.

When I graduated from college there was a teacher shortage and I was offered a job. I taught a lot of different things: athletics, social studies, and even typing. (I could copy-type even though I couldn't read it.) I never wrote on the blackboard and there were no handouts in my classroom. We watched a lot of films and had a lot of discussions.

I remember how fearful I was. I couldn't even take the roll. I always had two or three students to help me. They didn't suspect anything because I was the teacher. Sometimes I felt like a good teacher. I worked hard and I really cared about what I was doing but I wasn't. I didn't belong in the classroom and sometimes what I was doing made me physically sick, but I was trapped. I couldn't tell anybody.

I got married while I was a teacher. Getting married is a commitment to be truthful with another person and this was the first time I thought, "OK, I'm going to trust this person, I'm going to tell her." One evening I said, "Cathy, I can't read." She thought I meant I didn't like reading. She didn't realize how serious it was until she heard me reading to our three-year-old daughter. I was reading a new book, Rumpelstiltskin, and my daughter said, "You're not reading it like mama."

I had always asked Cathy for help with writing, in life and for work, but she hadn't realized how severe my problem was. When she found out, there was no confrontation, and she just carried on helping me get by. I taught high school from 1961 to 1978. Something finally changed eight years after I quit my teaching job.

I was 47 when I saw Barbara Bush talking about adult literacy on TV. I'd never heard anybody talk about adult literacy before; I had thought I was alone. I felt desperate. I wanted to tell somebody and get help. So, one Friday afternoon I walked into the library and asked to see the director of the literacy programme. I told her I couldn't read. That was the second person in my adult life that I had ever told.

I had a volunteer tutor who was 65 years old. She loved to read and didn't think anybody should go through life without knowing how. We started with writing poems because you don't have to write in complete sentences. She got me to about a sixth-grade reading level, but it took seven years until I felt literate. It was hard but it filled a big hole in my soul. Adults who can't read are suspended in their childhoods: emotionally, psychologically, academically, spiritually. We haven't grown up yet.

She encouraged me to tell my story to motivate others and promote literacy. At first, I said "No way!" but eventually agreed. I had guarded this secret for decades so it was hard to share with the world.

I want people to know there is hope and it's never too late. Unfortunately, we are still pushing children through school without teaching them basic reading and writing skills. But we can break this cycle of failure if instead of blaming teachers we make sure teachers and students (A   ).

For 48 years I was in the dark. But I finally buried the ghost of my past and now I am reading in the light.

1　According to the passage, which of the following is NOT true?

　ア　His parents were sure that he was talented when he was a child.

　イ　He had no difficulty at school in the first grade.

　ウ　He was in the "dumb row" and asked teachers for help.

　エ　He was far from a good student by the eighth grade though he wanted
　　to be.

2　According to the passage, what was on John's mind while he was a
teacher?

　ア　He was proud of himself because he could teach several things well.

　イ　He thought there must be someone who could teach him to read.

　ウ　He was fearful because some students noticed that he couldn't read.

　エ　He thought he was doing wrong though he worked hard as a teacher.

3　According to the passage, which of the following is true about John's family?

ア　It was his wife to whom he told his secret for the first time in his life.

イ　It didn't take long for his wife to notice how serious his problem was.

ウ　He managed to read children's books to his daughter.

エ　His wife helped him write things and taught him how to read.

4　According to the passage, which of the following is NOT true about john after quitting his teaching job?

ア　At the age of 47, he learned there were people with the same problem as him.

イ　His tutor had helped lots of her students to acquire reading skills.

ウ　His tutor didn't require him to write in complete sentences at first.

エ　After seven years of hard work learning to read, he felt literate.

5　Which is the most suitable phrase to put into (　A　)?

ア　learn to read at home

イ　get the support they need

ウ　call up their courage to confess the truth

エ　think they are winners

(☆☆☆○○○)

【４】次の英文を読んで，あとの1～5の問いに答えなさい。

　Proxemics is the study of physical space between people. Proxemics send important messages to your clients, co-workers, and supervisors in the workplace. We will discuss how managers should use personal space and distances in their interactions with others. Managers should be aware of the twofold value of proxemics. To others, the managers' relationship to the environment says much about the manager. To a manager, another's use of the environment can say a great deal about the person.

　(　1　) But, as we shall see, the concept of proxemics encompasses far more than just that. Edward Hall studied our use of personal distances and determined that we have four arbitrarily established proxemic zones in which we interact (1966). Managers should be aware of these zones both to understand their own reactions to others when their spaces are invaded, and to use the proxemic zones of others to the best advantage.

That all are aware of personal space to some degree is readily apparent in some of the verbal phrases in language. We talk about someone "keeping his or her distance," or complain when we perceive others "invading our territory," or say "they are crowding me on this issue" when in fact what they are doing has little to do with territory. When someone is pressing another on an issue, the other may (impolitely) respond, "Keep out of my face," or (certainly more politely), "Give me breathing room."

In North American culture, businesspersons generally operate within four zones: intimate, personal, social, and public. In the discussion that follows, keep in mind that the figures are averages. They reflect the culture in general as well as the relationship between the parties. (2) These can include personal appearance, physical attractiveness, gender, and age, not to mention pathology and deviance. Thus, we may react differently to a tall rather than short person, and may draw nearer to an attractive rather than an ugly individual (Malandro & Barker, 1983).

The intimate zone ranges from physical contact out to roughly eighteen inches to two feet. It is reserved for those closest to us. If it is invaded by others, especially for more than a moment, we usually (A), although often without knowing why. We either attempt to put more space between us, or we put up some kind of barrier between us. To test the almost tangible nature of this zone, stand close to someone you don't know too well.
If they are from a North American culture, the person will likely react as suggested above to achieve a more comfortable distance.

The personal zone goes from the edge of the intimate zone out to roughly four feet. It is reserved for our close friends only, although during introductions we may permit others to enter it, albeit temporarily. Even then, watch as two strangers draw together for an introduction. As they shake hands, they will often stand with one leg forward and the other ready to back up. Then, when the handshake is completed, both will often quickly (　B　) into the next zone.

This is the social zone. It extends from about four feet to about twelve feet and is the space in which we would like to conduct much of our daily business. Relationships between managers and their employees might begin in this area and continue for a time, but will often move into the personal zone from the social once trust has developed (Hunsaker, 1981).

Our public zone extends beyond twelve feet. It reflects the distance at which most would like to keep strangers. (　3　) Perhaps the only spoken communication that occurs would be the public speech. For example, photographs taken from above the recent dedication of a public building showed a sizeable, empty gap between the speaker's podium and the audience. This formal occasion dictated the distance people felt was appropriate, yet no formal demarcation was made to set people back at that distance. We can see a permanent institutionalized reflection of this distance in the arrangement of public auditoriums or even in the layout of many political rallies. Even if the latter is not too crowded the audience will often "keep its distance."

For managers, the value of understanding proxemics is clear. An observant communicator can gauge the warmth (or lack of warmth) that exists in a relationship by the distances that the individuals keep during interactions. As trust grows, distances should predictably diminish. If they do not, they must consider some other factors may be entering into the equation.

Keep in mind that proxemic zones vary from culture to culture (and even between the genders). Thus, for example, South Americans and Arabs typically interact with people at far closer ranges than do North Americans. Often when people from North America interact with individuals from either of these two cultures, the varying proxemic zones expected by the two groups create confusion unless one of the participants is aware of the need to adapt to the needs of the other. That is, either the North Americans give up some of

232

their ground, or the others keep their distance. Frequently, when two people from such varying cultures interact, a curious backwards "dance" develops as the one invades and the other evades.

1 本文中の(1)〜(3)に入れるのに最も適切なものをア〜エの中から一つずつ選び，その記号を書きなさい。

ア A number of other factors enter into any interpersonal relationship to change the details.

イ Very little communication of a business nature takes place here.

ウ Hearing the word "proxemics," most people probably think only of the personal "bubble" surrounding a person, and that is a good place to start.

エ Personal distance is the most important thing in business situations.

2 本文中の(A)に入れるのに最も適切なものをア〜エの中から一つ選び，その記号を書きなさい。

ア feel uncomfortable and are likely to react

イ judge them from their appearance

ウ redeem our reputation by working hard

エ welcome them as a stakeholder

3 本文中の(B)に入れるのに最も適切なものをア〜エの中から一つ選び，その記号を書きなさい。

ア concede　イ invade　ウ isolate　エ retreat

4 本文の内容と一致するものをア〜カの中から二つ選び，その記号を書きなさい。

ア It is obvious that we are scarcely conscious of personal space in our daily lives, and we can see it in conversational expressions related to it.

イ According to the passage, the least suitable zone for business is the social zone because it meets cultural expectations.

ウ If you go to a political speech, you can see a big gap between the presenter and audience regardless of how crowded it is.

エ A handshake is one example of dancing between zones as people try to avoid awkwardness.

　オ　A curious backwards "dance" always happens when people from different cultures have interactions.

　カ　Managers can check their client's credibility by entering into the intimate zone.

5　経営者や管理職が"Proxemics"を理解することでどのような恩恵を受けられるか。また，異文化間のやりとりで，"Proxemics"を理解しないことによって起こり得る問題は何か。本文に即して日本語で書きなさい。なお，解答で"Proxemics"に言及する際は英単語のまま用いなさい。

(☆☆☆☆◎◎◎◎)

【5】2020年には，東京オリンピックの開催に伴い，さらに多くの外国人観光客が日本を訪れることが予想されます。この2年のうちに日本が為すべきことは何か。具体的な例を含めて150語程度の英語で書きなさい。

(☆☆☆☆◎◎◎◎)

【6】次の1と2の問いに日本語で答えなさい。

1　次の文章は，高等学校学習指導要領解説(外国語編)からの抜粋である。空欄(　A　)〜(　E　)に適する語句を書きなさい。

第2節　外国語科の目標

　外国語科の目標は，コミュニケーション能力を養うことであり，次の三つの柱から成り立っている。
①　外国語を通じて，言語や文化に対する理解を深めること。
②　外国語を通じて，積極的にコミュニケーションを図ろうとする態度を育成すること。
③　外国語を通じて，情報や考えなどを的確に理解したり適切に伝えたりする能力を養うこと。

(中略)

---

②は，外国語の学習や外国語の使用を通して，（　A　）や考えなどを的確に理解したり適切に伝えたりすることに積極的に取り組む態度を育成することを意味している。具体的には，理解できないことがあっても，（　B　）するなどして聞き続けたり読み続けたりしようとする態度や確認したり（　C　）や説明を求めたりする態度，自分の考えなどを積極的に話したり書いたりしようとする態度などを育成することを意味している。このようなコミュニケーションへの積極的な態度は，（　D　）が進展する中にあって，異なる文化をもつ人々を理解し，自分を表現することを通して，異なる文化をもつ人々と（　E　）して生きていく態度に発展していくものである。したがって，外国語の学習や実際の使用を通してこの目標を達成しようとすることは，極めて重要な意味をもつ。

2　学習指導要領には「英語の授業は英語で行うことを基本とする」と示されている。その上で文法はどのように指導すべきとされているか。次の語を使用し，説明しなさい。

「文法」「説明」「日本語」

(☆☆☆◎◎◎◎)

解答・解説

【中高共通】

【1】1　ウ　　2　イ　　3　ウ　　4　イ　　5　イ
〈解説〉スクリプトは非公表だが，選択肢から推測できることを挙げるので参考にされたい。会話を聞いて質問に解答する形式で，放送は1回

のみである。1は女性がこれからバイクをどうするかという質問であると推測できる。2は男性がいつ到着するかという質問であると推測できる。3はClaireがどこに移動するかという質問であると推測できる。動詞と場所の両方を注意して聞く必要があるだろう。4はブースに訪れた人数の質問であると推測できる。5は女性が何をしたいと思っているかという質問であると推測できる。イのlive by herselfは「自力で生活する」という意味である。

【2】1　ウ　　2　イ　　3　エ　　4　ア

〈解説〉スクリプトは非公表だが，選択肢から推測できることを挙げるので参考にされたい。まとまりのある英文を聞き，内容についての質問に解答する形式で，放送は1回のみである。放送前に聞き取るべきポイントを予測することが必要である。本問では，選択肢全体からロボットが人間の仕事にもたらす影響であることが予測できる。1は「挨拶を誰が誰にするのか」という質問であると推測できる。2はItが何を指すのかが不明だが，おそらくロボットでありその行動の質問であると推測できる。3はTo不定詞で始まっていることからロボットの働きの目的を問う質問であると推測できる。4は動詞で始まっていることから2及び3と同じようにロボットの行動を問う質問であると推測できる。選択肢アとイ，ウとエで目的語が異なるため目的語も聞き逃さないように注意したい。

【3】1　イ　　2　エ　　3　ア　　4　ウ

〈解説〉注意点は【1】及び【2】と同様だが，この問題は，選択肢の英文からテーマが日本の世界におけるランキングやgender equality「男女の平等」についての内容だと推測できる。1は2017年の男女の平等ランキングで日本の順位が前年からどのくらい落ちてしまったかという設問である。2は2017年のランキングで日本の順位が落ちた主要因が何かを答える設問である。3は2017年においてグローバルに男女格差が広がった主要因が何かを答える設問である。2と選択肢の内容が全く

一緒なので混同しないよう注意する必要があるだろう。4は本文で正しい内容を答える設問なのでいち早く設問に目を通して正しい答えがどれかを判断する必要がある。

【中学校】

【1】1　ウ　　2　イ　　3　エ　　4　エ　　5　ア　　6　ア　　7　エ
8　イ

〈解説〉1　beneficial to ～で「～にとって有益である」の意味。
2　designate A as Bで「AをBに指名する」の意味。　　3　be acquainted with ～で「～に精通している」の意味。　　4　permission to doで「～する許可」という意味。permit「許可する」の名詞形である。

5　honesty「正直さ」というプラスの性質の意味を持つ語が補語になっているのでattribute「性質，特質」が文意に最も合致する。

6　make provision for ～で「～に備える」の意味。　　7　consecutiveは「連続した」の意味でthree consecutive winsで「3連勝」となる。他にthree wins in a rowという言い方もある。スポーツの放送などで頻出の表現。　　8　be complacent aboutで「～の現状に満足した，～に甘んじる」の意味。

【2】1　エ　　2　ア　　3　ウ　　4　エ　　5　エ

〈解説〉1　Aの1回目の発言「ちょっと(お時間)いいですか」に対して応答として適切なのはエ「どうしました？」のみ。　　2　待ち合わせの時間と場所を決めている場面である。アの「時間通りに着けるようにします」が適切。イのa quarter to fiveは4時45分を指しているので不適切。　　3　Aの2回目の怒っている発言「人の物に触らないで」に着目。Bが実際に触ってしまった発言はウとエであるが，エはAの1回目の発言「テーブルの上の私の携帯電話見なかった？」に合わない。

4　Aの2回目の発言「I am」に着目。このI amの後には前の会話が省略されており，直前のBの発言としてはエの「君は急いでいると思っていたよ」が適切。省略されているのはin a hurryであり，Aの2回目の発

言はI am in a hurry.「私は(実際に)急いでいるの」という意味。

5　Aの今週末の予定を尋ねている発言に対し，エの「大した予定はないです」が適切。それを受けてAはパーティに誘っている。

【3】1　イ　　2　ア　　3　ウ

〈解説〉1　good at -ingで「〜することが得意である」の意味。よってmaking friendsとする。　2　for hoursで「数時間」の意味。hourは可算名詞なので単数なら冠詞anが必要。イはcome up with「(解決策などを)思いつく」という表現なので正しい。　3　文末にnowがあるのでカンマ以下は仮定法過去になり，we wouldn't be criticizedとしなければならない。

【4】1　イ　　2　エ　　3　ウ

〈解説〉1　第1段落でSarahが生まれた頃は女の子は野球をするより観戦する時代であったこと，その中でSarahは父親と一緒に公園で野球をしていたことが述べられている。よってイが適切。　2　第7段落の半ばでI believe that experience gave me the desire to walk again.とあり，このthat experienceは設問文にある子供時代の経験を指すのでエが適切。　3　第7段落でSarahとその父親に野球に誘ってもらったことを感謝している内容が何度も述べられておりウが適切。

【5】1　ウ　　2　ウ　　3　ア

〈解説〉1　それまでの会話から雨がまだ降っていてNickは全身濡れていることがわかる。また空欄の後のthe rainにつながるのはウでget out of the rainで「雨宿りをする」という意味になる。　2　直後のKateの発言I gave up eating meat five years ago.からKateはベジタリアンであることがわかり，またYes, I am.ともうまくつながるためウが適切と判断できる。　3　アは本文に記述がない。Kateは「ベジタリアンの食事を楽しんでいるからコーヒーショップによく来る」とは述べていない。Kateの4回目の発言で「静かだから勉強しに来ている」という発言がある

のみである。イはKateの8及び9回目の発言と一致する。ウはNickの5回目の発言と一致する。エはNickの最後の発言と一致する。ベジタリアンのKateとは対照的なハンバーガーショップで働いているので少し気後れしたのである。

【6】1 ア 2 イ 3 オ

〈解説〉アは第1段落3文目の内容と一致する。イは第6段落2文目の内容と一致する。ウは設問文の中のblowing bubblesとrepeating a new wordは正しいが，running fastについては第3段落の内容に反する。走ることと言語能力には関係がない。エは第5段落の内容に反する。パズルを解くのと言語が得意なのには関係がない。オは最終段落の最終文の内容に一致する。

【7】The positive effect using English in classes can have on confidence, fluency, and real world communication. Interaction is communicative, natural and authentic. Successful interaction in English builds students' confidence in their English. And it gives the students lots of opportunities to use English. So teachers should encourage students to use English. In order to encourage students, teachers need to use English consistently in every lesson. And also, teachers should use gestures and any other easy words to support the meaning of the instructions they are giving in English. (88 words)

〈解説〉この問題では，「生徒が英語に触れる機会を充実させる」と「授業を実際のコミュニケーションの場面とする」というのが目的として挙げられているため，その目的に沿ったねらいと留意事項を記載するのがポイントとなるだろう。解答例では，一文一文を短くやさしい英語を用いて簡潔に表現しており，まず最初の3文でねらいを，その後に留意事項を述べている。また，表現上の語彙としては，confidence「自信」，fluency「流暢さ」，interaction「相互のやり取り」，communicative「コミュニケーションに関する」，authentic「本物の」，encourage O to do「Oに〜することを奨励する」，consistently「一貫して」

などがポイントになる。

【8】1　①　資質・能力　　②　活用　　③　伝え合ったり　　④　配慮　　2　単に授業等において積極的に外国語を使ってコミュニケーションを図ろうとする態度のみならず，学校教育外においても，生涯にわたって継続して外国語習得に取り組もうとするといった態度。

〈解説〉1　学習指導要領の「目標」は出題されやすいので空欄問題でも解答できるよう正確に暗記しておいたほうがよいだろう。　2「主体的に」という点がポイントである。学校内の授業で受け身のまま学ぶのではなく積極的に外国語を使ってコミュニケーションを取ろうとする姿勢と，さらに授業外でも自主的に外国語学習に励み外国語を用いたコミュニケーションを積極的に行う態度を書けばよい。

【9】①　他者　　②　再構築

〈解説〉①は空欄の後の「との関わり」がヒントになるだろう。②はやや難しい。「再構築」の意味として学習指導要領解説では「多様な人々との対話の中で，目的や場面，状況等に応じて，既習のものも含めて習得した概念(知識)を相互に関連付けてより深く理解したり，情報を精査して考えを形成したり，課題を見いだして解決策を考えたり，身に付けた思考力を発揮させたりすることであり」と述べている。

【10】①　エ　　②　オ　　③　イ

〈解説〉学習指導要領の「目標」からの出題である。「書くこと」に関しては「聞いたり読んだり」してインプットした内容を「正確さ」「まとまりのある(文章)」でアウトプットする大切さが目標として掲げられている。

【11】1　これまで，特に「話すこと」及び「書くこと」などの言語活動が適切に行われていなかったり，「やり取り」・「即興性」を意識した言語活動が十分ではなかったりしたため。　　2　小学校での経験

を生かし，内容を伝え合うことに重点を置いた指導を心掛ける必要がある。

〈解説〉1 「話すこと」は，これまであまり適切に活動が行われていなかったからこそ設定されたという点に着目する。さらに，「目標」にある「その場で適切に応答」「互いに会話を継続する」という部分から，実際の会話らしい言語活動が重要であるという趣旨を書けばよい。2 問題文にある通り，小学校では自分のことを話したり，相手に対して質問したりするという短く一方的な会話に終始していた。そこから発展させ，中学校では会話のやり取りをして内容をお互いに伝えるということに重点を置くことが心掛けとして考えられる。

【高等学校】

【1】1 ア 2 エ 3 エ 4 ア 5 ウ

〈解説〉1 another ＝ an otherなのでa few days「数日」にotherが加わった形になる。よってanother few daysで「もう数日」という意味になる。2 2文目で「彼は自分が高い金利を払っていることに気づいた」と書かれているので1文目のwithout以下は「しっかり読まずに」という内容になると考えられ，エが適切。 3 take turns -ingは「交代で～する」の意味。 4 Green Search Associatesは複数形のsがついているように見えるが一つの企業名である。よって3人称単数のアが適切。one of our important clientsやitsもヒントになる。 5 oppositeは「正反対の」という意味。on opposite sides of the river で「川を挟んだ両側にある」という意味になる。

【2】1 Rapid concrete development has. または(Large-scale)Hard pavements have. 2 The large-scale flooding in Beijing in 2012 did. 3 They have the capacity to hold more water (during heavy rain). 4 It wants them because they offer a natural escape route for runoff flood water. またはIt wants them because it is difficult to create room for new green space. 5 It implies that the city can absorb runoff flood water like a sponge.　またはIt means the city is a sponge to absorb water.

〈解説〉1　第4段落1文目に答えが書かれている。別解として，第5段落の large-scale hard pavementsも地面に水が吸収されるのを阻害する原因として挙げられている。　2　第7段落1文目に答えが書かれている。 3　第8段落3文目に答えが書かれている。　4　最終段落2文目にrunoff floodwater「流出水」の処理のためと書かれている。別解として1文目の「新しい緑地のための余地を生み出すのが難しい」を挙げてもよい。 5　本文全体の内容を踏まえると，"Sponge City"とはスポンジのように水を吸収する機能を有する都市であることは明らかであろう。absorb「吸収する」という動詞が使えるかどうかが鍵となる。

【3】1　ウ　　2　エ　　3　ア　　4　イ　　5　イ

〈解説〉1　アははっきりとした根拠と言えるかどうかはやや疑わしいが，第1段落1文目と一致すると考えられる。イは第2段落1文目から正しい。ウが明らかに第3段落3文目に反するので正解と判断する。エは第3段落全体の内容と一致する。　2　教師をしていた際，自信のなさゆえに自分の行動が気になっていたことが第6段落5文目と6文目に書かれているためエが適切。　3　第7段落で妻のCathyに自分の秘密を初めて打ち明けることが書かれているためアが適切。　4　アは第9段落1文目と一致する。イは本文に記述がない。筆者の家庭教師が筆者の助けになってくれたことは第10・11段落に書かれているが，筆者以外の生徒への対応については書かれていない。ウは第10段落3文目と一致する。エは第10段落4文目と一致する。　5　筆者は読み書きができなかったことを長年誰にも打ち明けられずにいたが，自分に必要なサポートを受けることで最終的に読み書きができるようになった。その経験から空欄のある第12段落の1文目で「希望はあり，遅すぎるということはない」と述べていることを読み取る。自分のように必要なサポートを受ければ悪循環に陥ることはないというのが筆者の主張だと考えられ，イが適切だと判断する。

【4】 1 (1) ウ   (2) ア   (3) イ   2 A ア   3 B エ
4 ウ，エ   5 経営者や管理職にとって，"Proxemics"を理解するこ
とで得られる明白な恩恵は，顧客や同僚，上司といったような相手と
の関係が良好であるかどうかが，やりとりをしている両者の距離の取
り方によって正確に判断できるということである。一方で，
"Proxemics"を理解しないと，文化的な違いによる衝突が起こり得る。
〈解説〉 1 (1) 空欄(1)の後のButから始まる文では「proxemicsの概
  念はそれよりはるかに多くのことを含んでいる」と述べられている。
  よって空欄にはproxemicsの基本的な定義が入ると考えられ，ウが適切
  だと考えられる。   (2) 空欄(2)の後のThese can include 〜 「これ
  らは〜を含んでいる」に着目する。このTheseは空欄内の複数形の単語
  を指していることを表し，複数形の単語のないイは除外される。エの
  business situationsだとするとpersonal appearance「容姿」やphysical
  attractiveness「身体的魅力」がbusiness situationsに含まれることになる
  のでエも不適切と判断でき，残ったアが正解である。   (3) 空欄
  (3)の段落では他者との距離が最も離れているpublic zoneについて
  書かれている。この領域はコミュニケーションも非常に少なくなって
  しまうと考えられ，イが適切だと判断できる。   2 空欄(A)があ
  るこの段落では最も親密な者同士の距離感について述べられている。
  私たちは親密な間柄だと18インチから2フィートの距離を保っていて，
  それが侵害されるとどうなるかというのが空欄に入る。適切な距離感
  が侵害されるとマイナスの感情を持つということになり，アが適切。
  3 握手の時だけは相手との距離が縮まるが，握手が終わると相手と
  の距離を空ける状態に移行すると述べられている。よって，エretreat
  into 〜「〜に引っ込む」が適切。   4 アは第3段落1文目の内容と反す
  る。イは第7段落2文目の内容と一致しない。ウは第8段落最終文の内
  容と一致する。エは第6段落4文目の内容と一致する。オは最終段落の
  最終文の内容に反する。本文にはFrequentlyと書かれておりalwaysでは
  ない。カは該当する記述が本文にない。   5 「恩恵」と「起こり得る
  問題」を本文に即してそれぞれ順に記述する。「恩恵」は第1段落と第

243

9段落に書かれている，相手との関係を相手との距離から正確に判断することである。「起こり得る問題」は最終段落の文化的差異について記述すればよい。

【5】In order to prepare for the 2020 Tokyo Olympics, I think we should focus on improving communication services and language education. I think there are two main things that we should do.

First, I think Japan should gather volunteers who can speak to foreigners in their native languages. It is important for visitors to be able to communicate with local people to quickly get the information they need. If there are enough such volunteers at the Olympic events, visitors will be able to enjoy themselves with less stress.

Second, we should offer language education to the locals. This would be best for people who are working at shops, tourist spots, restaurants and hotels around the event sites. They can prepare themselves for foreign guests by practicing role plays, and receiving "point and communicate"lists of common phrases, which could also be available online.

I believe these two measures would greatly improve the Tokyo Olympics in 2020. (156 word)

〈解説〉解答例では，第1段落で「意思伝達のサービスや言語教育を向上させる」という成すべき2つの目標を述べている。いわゆる結論を最初に述べる書き方である。第2段落では「意思伝達のサービス」，第3段落では「言語教育」について何をすべきか具体的な例について詳細に説明されている。第4段落は「この2つのことを成し遂げることで東京オリンピックは良い方向に向かうと信じている」という締めの内容となっている。

【6】1　A　情報　　B　推測　　C　繰り返し　　D　国際化　　E　協調　　2　教師は授業を英語で行うとともに，生徒が授業の中でできるだけ多くの英語を使用し，文法を活用する力をつけるように，文法

を実際に用いた言語活動を授業の中心とすべきである。実際の指導では，当該文法を用いた多様な文を聞いたり読んだりする活動や，話したり書いたりする活動の中で，新しい文法事項を積極的に用いることを奨励したり，生徒が文法をコミュニケーションに活用できるように配慮しなければならない。このように，文法を言語活動と効果的に関連付けて，言語活動を行うことを授業の中心とすれば，必要に応じて文法の説明などは日本語を交えて行うことも考えられる。

〈解説〉1　学習指導要領解説の目標は出題の可能性が高いため，どのような出題形式でも解答できるようにできる限り暗記しておくとよいだろう。しかし前後の文脈を頼りに正解を導くことは十分可能なのでわからなくても諦めずに考えることが大切である。　2　重要なポイントとしては，「文法を実際に用いた言語活動を授業の中心とする」「必要に応じて文法の説明は日本語を交えて」の2点であろう。文法はあくまでツールでありそれを用いた実際の言語活動が授業の中心であるというのが要点である。また文法の説明は生徒に正確に理解してもらう必要があるため，日本語を適宜用いる必要性も現実問題として挙げるとよいだろう。

2018年度　実施問題

【中高共通】

【1】これから，会話と質問が5つ放送されます。質問に対する答えとして最も適切なものをア～エの中から一つずつ選び，その記号を書きなさい。なお，会話と質問は一度だけ放送されます。

1
　ア　They will go to a theater.
　イ　They will meet friends.
　ウ　They will stay home.
　エ　They will stop by the rental shop.

2
　ア　She doesn't have any brushes.
　イ　She doesn't paint anymore.
　ウ　She has no idea about painting.
　エ　She is a better painter now.

3
　ア　She will admit her mistake.
　イ　She will have to pay extra money.
　ウ　She will pay the correct amount of money.
　エ　She will send a new bill.

4
　ア　She wants the man not to give up smoking.
　イ　She wants the man not to mind her smoking.
　ウ　She wants the man to give a cigarette to her.
　エ　She wants the man to stop smoking.

5
　ア　Buy a vase.

イ　Get a clock.

ウ　Show a present.

エ　Talk to John and Mary.

(☆☆☆◎◎◎)

【2】これから，まとまりのある英文が放送されます。英文の後に，その内容について質問が四つ出されます。その質問に対する答えとして最も適切なものをア～エの中から一つずつ選び，その記号を書きなさい。なお，英文と質問は一度だけ放送されます。

1

ア　It increases musicality in infants.

イ　It makes them smarter.

ウ　It doesn't make them smarter.

エ　It promotes improvements in brain function.

2

ア　They took an arithmetic test then listened to classical music in a quiet room.

イ　They took an arithmetic test then listened to different genres of music in a quiet room.

ウ　They took an arithmetic test while listening to classical music in a quiet room.

エ　They took an arithmetic test while listening to different genres of music in a quiet room.

3

ア　Harp.

イ　Harp and piano.

ウ　Harp and piano with orchestra.

エ　Piano.

4

ア　Classical music enhances subjects' abilities to perform tasks rapidly and accurately.

イ　Classical music helps to lower levels of stress, anxiety and cholesterol.

ウ　Classical music is more effective than pop music in promoting creativity.

エ　Classical music is not proven to be helpful in promoting productivity and efficiency.

(☆☆☆☆○○○○)

【３】これから，まとまりのある英文が一度だけ放送されます。質問に対する答えとして最も適切なものをア～エの中から一つずつ選び，その記号を書きなさい。

1　According to the article, why do many families use credit cards?

ア　To buy essentials.

イ　To make contracts.

ウ　To pay for luxuries.

エ　To solve the recession.

2　According to the article, how do credit cards make people spend more money?

ア　They allow people to write cheques slowly.

イ　They enable people to meet a lot of people online.

ウ　They give people a large cash bonus at first.

エ　They offer people long periods of no interest to start.

3　According to the article, what problem do young people have regarding debt?

ア　It is difficult to rent accommodations.

イ　There are not enough houses they can buy.

ウ　They refuse to live with their parents.

エ　They tend to escape from their houses.

4　According to the article, which of the following is the best solution to credit card debt?

ア　Financial education for young adults.

イ　Government support for young people.

ウ　Harder controls on credit.

エ　Investment from baby boomers.

(☆☆☆☆◎◎◎)

【中学校】

【1】次の1～8の英文の(　　)にあてはまる最も適切な英語を，それぞれ
ア～エから一つずつ選び，その記号を書きなさい。

1　What color tie do you think would (　　) with this suit?

　　ア　go　　イ　come　　ウ　get　　エ　look

2　The banking industry has to (　　) the problem of bad loans.

　　ア　impose　　イ　try　　ウ　tackle　　エ　summon

3　Some people find spicy Thai food very (　　). But I don't like spicy food
very much.

　　ア　enthusiastic　　イ　capable　　ウ　glamorous　　エ　appetizing

4　My manager has told me that I'm to be (　　) from the accounting section
to the postal section.

　　ア　transacted　　イ　transferred　　ウ　resumed　　エ　restrained

5　The (　　) of drivers often causes traffic accidents.

　　ア　absence　　イ　negligence　　ウ　concern　　エ　objectivity

6　Japanese people learning English are often bewildered by the frequent
lack of (　　) bettween spelling and pronunciation.

　　ア　correlation　　イ　correction　　ウ　collaboration

　　エ　cooperation

7　Although no certificate is required, applicants for the job are expected to
be (　　) in French.

　　ア　chronic　　イ　fragile　　ウ　eternal　　エ　proficient

8　It took two hours to (　　) the sacks of sand onto the truck, and another
hour to unload them at the construction site.

249

　　ア　snub　　イ　thread　　ウ　heave　　エ　accomplish

　　　　　　　　　　　　　　　　　　(☆☆☆☆○○○○)

【2】次の1〜5の会話文中の(　　)にあてはまる最も適切な英語を，それ
ぞれア〜エから一つずつ選び，その記号を書きなさい。

　1　A:　How long have you been staying in Japan, Tom?

　　　B:　I've been here for about nine months.

　　　A:　(　　　)

　　　B:　It's fascinating. There are so many things to do and see.

　　　　ア　What did you do during those nine months?

　　　　イ　When will you go back to your country?

　　　　ウ　Where will you stay in this country?

　　　　エ　How do you like Japan, so far?

　2　A:　I wonder if I might ask you a favor.

　　　B:　(　　　) What do you want?

　　　A:　Sammy's birthday is next month, isn't it?

　　　B:　Yes?

　　　　ア　I don't think I can help you.

　　　　イ　Sure, go ahead.

　　　　ウ　I'm too busy to help you.

　　　　エ　Why don't you go and ask Tom?

　3　A:　I'm looking for a biography of Hellen Keller, but I can't remember
　　　　the title.

　　　B:　There are many books about her in this library. Do you know the
　　　　author's name?

　　　A:　No, I don't. But it was a best-seller.

　　　B:　(　　　)

　　　　ア　Well, could you at least tell me the focus of the book?

　　　　イ　What's the title of the book?

　　　　ウ　Someone else has it.

エ　When did you begin to read it ?

4　A:　You don't think Dave heard what we were saying, do you?

　　B:　(　　) We were only whispering.

　　A:　What we are going to give him will be a surprise.

　　ア　No, I'm sure he did.

　　イ　No, I'm sure he didn't.

　　ウ　No, I'm not sure he did.

　　エ　No, I'm afraid so.

5　A:　I want to make chocolate chip cookies but I don't have an oven in my apartment.

　　B:　Well then, let's use my place.

　　A:　Are you sure you don't mind? (　　)

　　B:　Don't worry about it.

　　ア　Nothing really.

　　イ　What is it?

　　ウ　It's wonderful news.

　　エ　I'm a pretty messy cook.

(☆☆☆◎◎◎)

【3】次の1〜3の各文の下線部で，英語の文法上または表現上適切ではない語句があります。それぞれア〜エから一つずつ選び，その記号を書きなさい。

1　ア Every players イ may practice in the gym ウ whenever they desire エ to do so.

2　We ア looked at the pictures イ on the museum for three hours before ウ deciding エ to have dinner.

3　Computers ア are used イ primarily to ウ calculate answers and エ processing data around the world.

(☆☆☆◎◎◎)

251

【４】次の英文を読んで，後の質問に対する最も適切な答えを，それぞれ
　　ア～エから一つずつ選び，その記号を書きなさい。

Do you know the Japanese word, *"Mottainai"* ? A woman heard about this
word when she visited Japan and was impressed. Then this word became
famous around the world as the theme of the Economy Campaign held about
ten years ago. The woman's name was Wangari Maathai. She was born in
Kenya in 1940. She was interested in all living things when she was a girl.
She studied biology in the U.S. when she was young. When she went back to
Kenya, she got a shock. In those days, the forests in Kenya were becoming
smaller and smaller. One of the causes was the number of people there. It was
increasing every year. More people were cutting down the trees to make their
lives convenient; for example using them as firewood when they cooked food.
So the forests in Kenya became much smaller while she was abroad.

Why are forests so important to the people in Kenya? Forests can hold a lot
of water. If the trees in forests are cut down, the land becomes bare. The bare
land cannot hold water, and cannot produce enough food for the people. The
people cannot get the firewood they need either. Forests also provide food for
many kinds of animals. They save the lives of people and animals, so forests
are very important.

Maathai wanted to protect the forests in Kenya. She had the idea to make a
group of people to plant trees. She founded the Green Belt Movement in
Kenya in 1977. She began to plant trees to protect the forests. There were
many women working on the farms in villages in Kenya. They were very
poor, and their children were always hungry. They couldn't take good care of
their children. Some of the children couldn't go to school. So Maathai wanted
to help these women by having them join the Green Belt Movement. She
began to work with the women. She paid them money for their work. The
money given to them helped to make their lives better. And their children
became happier than before. At the same time, Maathai taught the women
many things, such as how to read and write. They also learned that they could

do something good for their society. They noticed that they were working together for a better world. Maathai succeeded in saving not only the forests in Kenya but also the poor people there.

In 2004, Maathai received the Nobel Peace Prize. She was the seventh person, and the first woman, from Africa to receive it. The next year, she visited Japan and saw the special Japanese word, *"Mottainai"*. She was impressed with this word, and spread the MOTTAINAI Campaign around the world.

In 2011, she died of cancer at the age of 71 in Kenya. Her last request was that her coffin not be made of wood. She loved the forests and wanted to protect them until the end.

1　Why did the forests in Kenya became smaller while Wangari Maathai was studying biology in the U.S.?

　ア　The number of people who cut down trees and used them for many kind of animals increased.

　イ　The number of people who cut down trees to move from Kenya to other countries increased.

　ウ　The number of people who cut down trees to use them for firewood when they cooked increased.

　エ　The number of people who cut down trees for bare land to produce food increased.

2　Why did Wangari Maathai want the women who worked on the farms in Kenya to join the Green Belt Movement?

　ア　So they could go to school.

　イ　So she could pay them money and make their lives better.

　ウ　So she could take care of their children.

　エ　So they could leave their homes.

3　According to the passage, which of the following is true?

　ア　Maathai studied biology to join the Green Belt Movement.

　イ　There were many rich forests in Kenya when Maathai went back home.

ウ　The Green Belt Movement started about forty years ago.

エ　No one from Africa received the Nobel Peace Prize until 2004.

（☆☆☆◎◎◎）

【5】次の対話文を読んで，後の質問に答えなさい。

Kyoko:　What do you think about the coming consumption tax raise?

Takeshi:　I am totally against it. I think I won't be able to afford to buy things that are not absolutely necessary. This country is putting more pressure on all of its citizens.

Kyoko:　Maybe so. But I support it. The government debt is getting out of control, and raising tax is necessary to keep the country from going bankrupt. Higher taxes are certainly better than turning into a financial disaster.

Takeshi:　I was thinking of buying a new motorcycle, so I have to buy it before the tax rate goes up. I will also have to cut back on travelling after the tax raise.

Kyoko:　Well, maybe you won't feel as rich because you won't be able to buy everything you want. (　①　), you may feel more secure if the tax raise helps the national health insurance system and social welfare.

Takeshi:　Yes, but I hardly ever get sick, and I plan to take care of myself when I'm old. Anyway, I think they should set up a system where everyday necessities are tax-free.

Kyoko:　Like what?

Takeshi:　For example, food and children's clothing.

Kyoko:　I think all goods should be taxed, and the money used to help the socially deprived such as the elderly.

Takeshi:　Well, I support my parents, who are retired. The government will not support them further, (　②　) I pay more tax.

Kyoko:　I am sorry to hear that. Perhaps the increase in tax will enable the

254

government to help you support your family.

Takeshi: I certainly hope so. Otherwise, I won't be able to save enough money for retirement. As I said before, the rise in consumption tax will definitely discourage me from buying anything. It will cost me a lot to buy anything. That is a problem for a healthy economy.

Kyoko: This new law will certainly be an opportunity for all of us to think about our lifestyles. Don't you think modern lifestyles have become quite wasteful and even thoughtless?

Takeshi: You are right. Perhaps our generation will find a new meaning for happiness. Looking on the bright side, we may have something to gain from this seemingly negative change.

Kyoko: That's a good point. It's food for thought.

1 文の内容から考え，文中の(①)に適する語句を，次のア～エから一つ選び，その記号を書きなさい。

ア Because of that　イ As a result　ウ On the other hand
エ Generally

2 文の内容から考え，文中の(②)に適する語句を，次のア～エから一つ選び，その記号を書きなさい。

ア as if　イ even if　ウ just in case　エ by no means

3 次のア～エから，本文の内容と一致しないものを一つ選び，その記号を書きなさい。

ア Takeshi thinks the coming rise in consumption tax will put more pressure on all citizens.

イ Takeshi thinks the government should set up a system where everyday necessities are tax-free.

ウ Kyoko thinks all goods should be taxed, and the tax money be used to help children all over the world.

エ Kyoko thinks this new law will certainly be an opportunity for all of us to think about our lifestyles.

(☆☆☆◎◎◎)

【６】次の英文を読んで，本文の内容と一致するものを，後のア～オから三つ選び，その記号を書きなさい。

A serious issue in our modern society is the noise that has accompanied technological advancement. The noise has reached the level of pollution － an urban problem in which unwanted and intense sound upsets daily living, causing stress and fatigue. Jet aircraft taking off produce the most widely recognized noise problem. The situation in the area of Heathrow Airport, on the edge of London, where 453,000 airplanes take off and land annually, has not only disturbed the sleep of residents but interfered with schooling. A similar result has been found for the areas surrounding O'Hare Airport in Chicago, where one teacher claimed that children just stop listening every time a plane takes off, or about every three minutes.

Schools and houses near Heathrow and O'Hare － along with houses in the flight pattern of San Francisco International Airport － are now being sound-proofed, usually with two layers of glass.

Consequently, reducing the noise leads to the environmentally problematic need for air-conditioning.

Whether along the once quiet banks of the Seine in Paris or on the streets of Rome, the automobile has polluted the world's urban environment. Its spread seems to be never-ending: the tremendous number of automobiles produces harmful exhaust gas, as well as noise. In the United States, the steady stream of automobile noise on major roadways on the edge of residential districts has led to the introduction of sound walls, usually conspicuous and unattractive reinforced-concrete structures, found in almost all large American cities. Ohio and New Jersey have been experimenting with "vegetative walls," high mounds of dirt covered by tightly planted trees and flowers.

Car stereo systems and "boom boxes" (portables stereos) force noise on everyone within range. Of lesser volume, but no less noticeable, is the harmful effects of the cell phone. Its intensive use in cars has raised concern about road safety, both because of the motorist's hand being off the steering wheel to hold the phone and the possibility of the motorist paying less attention to the road while using the phone. Ireland, Great Britain and Israel have already banned using phones while driving, as has the state of New York. Moreover, because it is used in almost every social environment, it has frequently changed private speech to a form of public display. The sudden sound of someone speaking to an unseen and unheard party has an unpleasant effect and seems impolite.

Thus, the use of cell phones has been banned in certain places, like theaters and libraries, where it would be very troublesome. Wired News reported in its online issue from February 5th, 2003, that the actor Kevin Spacey interrupted a stage performance to yell at a member of the audience whose cell phone was ringing: "Tell them you're busy." The Sacrament Bee, a California newspaper, carried an article on the subject in its online edition from April 6th, 2003, in which a moviegoer complained that a person arriving late at the theater phoned the friends he was to have met as he walked among the audience in order to determine where they were sitting.

(注) the Seine「セーヌ川」   reinforced-concrete「鉄筋コンクリート」

ア Jet aircraft taking off prevented pupils from concentrating on lessons in the area of Heathrow Airport, on the edge of London.

イ The intensive use of cell phones has caused concerns about road safety, for example, the motorist's hand being off the steering wheel to hold a phone.

ウ The actor Kevin Spacey was arrested for threatening a member of the audience whose cell phone was ringing.

エ The banks of the Seine in Paris are still quiet and unpolluted, despite the tremendous number of automobiles around.

オ The steady stream of automobile noise on major roadways on the edge of residential districts has led to the introduction of sound walls that are found in almost all large American cities.

(☆☆☆☆◎◎◎)

【7】 中学校学習指導要領解説外国語編(平成20年9月)の「第2章　外国科の目標及び内容」における「2　内容」の「(4)　言語材料の取扱い」に，次のような内容が記載されています。

> イ　文法については，コミュニケーションを支えるものであることを踏まえ，言語活動と効果的に関連付けて指導すること。

　　コミュニケーションの中で，基本的な語彙や文法事項を活用する力を十分身に付けさせるために，具体的にどのような指導が考えられるか，あなたの考えを80語以上の英語で書きなさい。

　　なお，最後に語数を記入すること。語数については，同じ語を2回使用した場合，2語と数えること(のべ数)とします。

(☆☆☆☆◎◎◎◎)

【8】 次の文章は，中学校学習指導要領解説外国語編(平成20年9月)の「第2章　外国語科の目標及び内容」における「2　内容」の「(2)　言語活動の取扱い」からの抜粋です。文中の(①)〜(③)にあてはまる語句として，最も適切なものを，それぞれア〜ウから選び，その記号を書きなさい。

> ア　3学年間を通じ指導に当たっては，次のような点に配慮するものとする。

> (ア)　実際に言語を使用して互いの考えや気持ちを伝え合うなどの活動を行うとともに，(3)に示す言語材料について(①)活動を行うようにすること。

　ア　理解したり練習したりする
　イ　聞いたり読んだりする
　ウ　用語を解説したり用法を区別したりする

> (イ)　実際に言語を使用して互いの考えや気持ちを伝え合うなど
> の活動においては，(　②　)ができるようにすること。

　ア　生徒全員が習った表現を使いこなせるような言語活動
　イ　4技能を統合的に活用させられる言語活動
　ウ　具体的な場面や状況に合った適切な表現を自ら考えて言語活動

> (ウ)　言語活動を行うに当たり，主として次に示すような
> (　③　)を取り上げるようにすること。

　ア　特有の表現がよく使われる場面や考えや意図を伝える場面
　イ　言語の使用場面や言語の働き
　ウ　生徒の発達段階や興味・関心に即した場面

(☆☆☆☆◎◎◎◎)

【9】中学校学習指導要領(平成20年3月)の「第2章　第9節　外国語」で
は，「書くこと」の言語活動について，次のように述べられています。
文中の(　①　)～(　④　)にあてはまる適切な語句を書きなさい。

> 第2　各言語の目標及び内容等
> 　英語
> 　　2　内容
> 　　(1)　言語活動
> 　　　エ　書くこと
> 　　　　主として次の事項について指導する。
> 　　(ア)　文字や符号を識別し，語と語の区切りなどに注
> 　　　　意して正しく書くこと。
> 　　(イ)　語と語の(　①　)などに注意して正しく文を書く
> 　　　　こと。
> 　　(ウ)　聞いたり読んだりしたことについてメモをとっ
> 　　　　たり，感想，賛否やその理由を書いたりなどする
> 　　　　こと。

259

　　　　(エ)　(　②　)における出来事や体験したことなどについて，自分の(　③　)や気持ちなどを書くこと。

　　　　(オ)　自分の考えや気持ちなどが(　④　)に正しく伝わるように，文と文の(　①　)などに注意して文章を書くこと。

(☆☆☆☆◎◎◎◎)

【10】外国語科の指導について，中学校学習指導要領解説外国語編(平成20年9月)の「第1章　総説」における「2　外国語科改訂の趣旨」の中で，次のように述べられています。下線①，②について，実際の授業の中で，どのような指導が考えられるでしょうか。それぞれ日本語で簡潔に書きなさい。

○　自らの考えなどを相手に伝えるための「発信力」やコミュニケーションの中で基本的な語彙や文構造を活用する力，内容的にまとまりのある一貫した文章を書く力などの育成を重視する観点から，①「聞くこと」や「読むこと」を通じて得た知識等について，自らの体験や考えなどと結び付けながら活用し，「話すこと」や「書くこと」を通じて発信することが可能となるよう，4技能を総合的に育成する指導を充実する。

○　中学校における「聞くこと」，「話すこと」という音声面での指導については，②小学校段階での外国語活動を通じて，音声面を中心としたコミュニケーションに対する積極的な態度等の一定の素地が育成されることを踏まえ，指導内容の改善を図る。併せて，「読むこと」，「書くこと」の指導の充実を図ることにより，「聞くこと」，「話すこと」，「読むこと」及び「書くこと」の四つの領域をバランスよく指導し，高等学校やその後の生涯にわたる外国語学習の基礎を培う。

(☆☆☆☆◎◎◎◎)

【11】次の文は，中学校学習指導要領(平成20年3月)の「第2章　第9節
外国語」で，「話すこと」の言語活動の中の(エ)について示されたもの
です。これを読んで，下の問いに答えなさい。

> (エ)　つなぎ言葉を用いるなどのいろいろな工夫をして話を続け
> ること。

1　この指導事項は，生徒のどのような能力を育成するための活動か，
日本語で書きなさい。

2　「いろいろな工夫」とは，どのようなことが考えられるか，具体例
を一つ日本語で書きなさい。

(☆☆☆☆◎◎◎)

【高等学校】

【1】次の1〜5の各文の(　　)に入る最も適切なものをア〜エの中から一
つずつ選び，その記号を書きなさい。

1　"Hey, we've got to hurry! We're going to miss the plane."
　　"If we take a taxi, we can make (　　)."
　　　ア　for
　　　イ　it
　　　ウ　out
　　　エ　up

2　Is this the bag of (　　) you have been looking for?
　　　ア　her
　　　イ　hers
　　　ウ　that
　　　エ　which

3　There (　　) no available information on transportation, I asked the
station staff.
　　　ア　being
　　　イ　having

ウ seemed

エ were

4 As fuel prices rose, bus companies raised their fares and (　　).

ア neither did the airlines

イ neither the airlines did

ウ so did the airlines

エ so the airlines have done

5 John was rushing around madly trying to (　　) out the fire.

ア extinguish

イ put

ウ take

エ vanish

(☆☆☆○○○)

【2】次の英文を読んで，1〜5の問いに対する答えを英語で書きなさい。

In the morning of life came a good fairy with her basket, who said:

"Here are gifts. Take one, leave the others. And be wary, chose wisely; oh, choose wisely! for only one of them is valuable.

The gifts were five: Fame, Love, Riches, Pleasure, Death. The youth said, eagerly:

"There is no need to consider; and he chose Pleasure.

He went out into the world and sought out the pleasures that youth delights in. But each in its turn was short-lived and disappointing, vain and empty; and each, departing, mocked him. In the end he said: "These years I have wasted. If I could but choose again, I would choose wisely."

The fairy appeared, and said:

"Four of the gifts remain. Choose once more; and oh, remember — time is flying, and only one of them is precious."

The man considered long, then chose Love; and did not mark the tears that rose in the fairy's eyes.

After many, many years the man sat by a coffin, in an empty home. And he communed with himself, saying: "One by one they have gone away and left me; and now she lies here, the dearest and the last. Desolation after desolation has swept over me; for each hour of happiness the treacherous trader, Love, has sold me I have paid a thousand hours of grief. Out of my heart of hearts I curse him."

"Choose again." It was the fairy speaking.

"The years have taught you wisdom — surely it must be so. Three gifts remain. Only one of them has any worth — remember it, and choose warily."

The man reflected long, then chose Fame; and the fairy, sighing, went on her way.

Years went by and she came again, and stood behind the man where he sat solitary in the fading day, thinking. And she knew his thoughts:

"My name filled the world, and its praises were on every tongue, and it seemed well with me for a little while. How little a while it was! Then came envy; then detraction; then calumny; then hate; then persecution. Then derision, which is the beginning of the end. And last of all came pity, which is the funeral of fame. Oh, the bitterness and misery of renown! Target for mud in its prime, for contempt and compassion in its decay."

"Choose yet again."It was the fairy's voice.

"Two gifts remain. And do not despair. In the beginning there was but one that was precious, and it is still here."

"Wealth — which is power! How blind I was!" said the man. "Now, at last, life will be worth the living. I will spend, squander, dazzle. These mockers and despisers will crawl in the dirt before me, and I will feed my hungry heart with their envy. I will have all luxuries, all joys, all enchantments of the spirit, all contentments of the body that man holds dear. I will buy, buy, buy! deference, respect, esteem, worship — every pinchbeck grace of life the market of a trivial world can furnish forth. I have lost much time, and chosen badly heretofore, but let that pass; I was ignorant then, and could but take for best what seemed so."

Three short years went by, and a day came when the man sat shivering in a mean garret; and he was gaunt and wan and hollow-eyed, and clothed in rags; and he was gnawing a dry crust and mumbling:

"Curse all the world's gifts, for mockeries and gilded lies! And miscalled, every one. They are not gifts, but merely lendings. Pleasure, Love, Fame, Riches: they are but temporary disguises for lasting realities — Pain, Grief, Shame, Poverty. The fairy said true; in all her store there was but one gift which was precious, only one that was not valueless. How poor and cheap and mean I know those others now to be, compared with that inestimable one, that dear and sweet and kindly one, that steeps in dreamless and enduring sleep the pains that persecute the body, and the shames and griefs that eat the mind and heart. Bring it! I am weary, I would rest."

The fairy came, bringing again four of the gifts, but Death was wanting. She said:

"I gave it to a mother's pet, a little child. It was ignorant, but trusted me, asking me to choose for it. You did not ask me to choose."

"Oh, miserable me! What is left for me?"

"What not even you have deserved: the wanton insult of Old Age."

1　List the fairy's gifts in order of the man's choice.

2　What happened to the people the man loved?

3　Why did the fairy sigh after the man chose Fame?

4　What did the man name Fame in the end?

5　To whom did the fairy present the most valuable gift?

(☆☆☆☆◎◎◎◎)

【３】次の英文を読んで，1〜5の問いに対する答えとして最も適切なものをア〜エの中から一つずつ選び，その記号を書きなさい。

It's been claimed that Finland's baby boxes, given to every newborn in the country, help reduce sudden infant death syndrome(SIDS); the unexpected and unexplained death of an apparently healthy baby. But what evidence is there that they actually lower infant mortality rates?

Finland has one of the lowest infant mortality rates in the world — 2 deaths per 1,000 live births, compared with a global rate of 32 per 1,000. In Finland, every pregnant mother is given a cardboard box filled with baby products, such as clothes, nappies, bedding and a mattress — even the box can be used as a bed. But how does this reduce the infant mortality rate? In theory, these boxes provide babies a safe place to sleep.

In the early 90s, many Western countries introduced Back to Sleep campaigns, when it was discovered that babies who sleep on their fronts are more vulnerable to SIDS. This led to a significant reduction of SIDS in countries like the US and UK. However, "the remaining SIDS is much harder to try to alleviate," says Professor Helen Ball, director of the Parent-Infant Sleep Lab in the UK. "And so people are looking for new ways to specifically help some of the more vulnerable families."

Baby boxes have been available in Finland since 1938. Infant mortality rates had been falling across Europe, but Finland's was still higher than that of neighbouring countries. The government decided to offer baby boxes to low income women. But they received more than just the box. They were introduced along with pre-natal care. Women had to attend clinics early on in their pregnancy to qualify for them. Their health could then be monitored throughout and after pregnancy. Hospital births also became more popular after legislation in 1944 made it a legal obligation for municipalities to provide maternity and child health clinics.

Baby boxes have received a lot of attention in the United States where they are struggling with a poor infant mortality rate. Its rate is 6 per 1,000 births, similar to Poland and Hungary, despite their income differences. Professor Emily Oster, an economist at Brown University, compared data from the US with various European countries. She says the US does fairly well in the first month of life, but from a month to a year, the mortality rate in the US accelerates at a faster rate. When looking at women with a college degree — a marker for relatively (　A　) income — infant mortality rates were (　B　) and similar to the same groups in Finland. "What we see is that well-off women in Finland and the US, are very, very similar," she says. "The difference is well-off women in Finland and less-educated women in Finland have very similar infant mortality profiles. Whereas that is not true in the US."

But it's not clear from their research what specifically causes these deaths — because there are many things which make the US different, such as its health care system. Also, unlike the US, most countries in Europe have a pretty robust home visiting programme after birth. "What often comes along with the boxes is some additional contact with somebody," says Oster. "The box alone doesn't seem likely to matter."

While baby boxes are hugely popular in Finland, they are emblematic of a wider health care system. After all, there are countries with the same infant mortality rate as Finland, such as Iceland, Estonia and Japan, which do not have baby box programmes. It seems the apparent benefits of baby boxes are actually from the improved education for parents and care that come with them.

1　According to the passage, which of the following is true?

ア　Finland's baby boxes have been thought to help prevent babies from dying.

イ　The baby boxes in Finland are offered at the lowest price in the world.

ウ　The infant mortality rate in Finland is lower than any other country in the world.

エ　The items in Finland's baby boxes are the key to a lower infant mortality rate.

2　Which of the following is NOT mentioned in the passage?

ア　Back to Sleep campaigns led to the decline of SIDS in many countries.

イ　In 1938, the government of Finland started a new social programme for low income women.

ウ　Professor Helen Ball invented the baby box social programme.

エ　Since 1944, all pregnant women in Finland have had access to health clinics.

3　Choose the proper words for the blanks (　A　) and (　B　).

ア　A: high　　　B: high

イ　A: high　　　B: low

ウ　A: low　　　B: high

エ　A: low　　　B: low

4　According to the passage, which of the following is true?

ア　A wider health care system matters more than baby boxes.

イ　Education for parents is solely effective to reduce the infant mortality rate.

ウ　European countries have several emblems for their baby boxes.

エ　The US government should start giving baby boxes to poor families.

5　Which of the following titles is the most suitable for the passage?

ア　Can the "Back to Sleep Campaign" reduce SIDS?

イ　Do baby boxes really save lives?

ウ　Is Finland the best country for pregnant mothers?

エ　Will baby boxes become available in Japan?

(☆☆☆☆◎◎◎◎)

【4】次の英文を読んで，1～5の問いに答えなさい。

The OECD, which runs tests in math, reading and science, is considering adding another test which would look at how well pupils can navigate an increasingly diverse world, with an awareness of different cultures and beliefs. The OECD's education director Andreas Schleicher explains why there is such a need for new rankings to show young people's competence in a world where globalization is a powerful economic, political and cultural force.

Education leaders around the world are increasingly talking about the need to teach "global competence" as a way of addressing the challenges of globalization. It was one of the key topics at the meeting of education ministers from the G7 group of leading industrial countries, held in Japan, on May 14th, 2016. Globalization can mean different things to different people. It can mean innovation and higher living standards for some — but it can also contribute to social division and economic inequality. (1) For some "cross border migration" means being able to travel for work between different countries, while for others it means escaping from poverty and war. Educators have been struggling with how to prepare students for the culturally diverse and digitally-connected communities in which they work and socialize.

In the past, education was about teaching people something. Now, it is also about making sure that children develop a reliable compass, the navigation skills and the character qualities that will help them find their own way through an uncertain, volatile and ambiguous world. Schools need to prepare students for a world where many will need to collaborate with people of diverse cultural origins. They will need to appreciate different ideas, perspectives and values. It's a world in which people need to decide how to trust and collaborate despite differences. Schools can provide opportunities for young people to learn about global development, equip them with the means of accessing and analyzing different cultures, help students engage in international and intercultural relations, and foster the value of the diversity of people. Some of these objectives already feature in many countries' curriculums. But nowhere do policymakers or educators have ready answers about how to embed global competence in schools and learning. (2)

The OECD's Programme for International Student Assessment (PISA) has now put that on its agenda. The definition of global competence proposed by the OECD for PISA is new and challenging:

Global competence is the capacity to analyze global and intercultural issues critically and from multiple perspectives, to understand how differences affect perceptions, judgments, and ideas of self and others, and to engage in open, appropriate and effective interactions with others from different backgrounds on the basis of a shared respect for human dignity.

The idea is to provide an internationally comparative PISA assessment that would offer the first comprehensive overview of education systems' (　A　) in preparing young people to have such global competence. It could assess 15-year-olds' knowledge and understanding of global issues and interactions with other cultures. This new measurement of global skills could be included in the next round of PISA tests in 2018.

The proposal also includes asking students questions about communicating appropriately and effectively with people from other cultures or countries. How well can they comprehend other people's thoughts, beliefs and feelings, and see the world from their perspectives? How can they adjust their own thoughts, feelings or behaviors to fit new contexts and situations? Can they analyze and think critically in order to scrutinize information given to them? There is also a discussion about looking at more general attitudes, such as the openness of students towards people from other cultures. What is their sensitivity towards, curiosity about, and willingness to engage with other people and other perspectives on the world?

(　3　) But comparative evidence from tests could help countries to study how well their students are prepared for life and employment in a globalized world. It could find out how much their students are exposed to global news and how they understand and critically analyze global issues. What are the different approaches to multicultural and global education used in different countries? How are culturally diverse groups of students being taught? How well are schools challenging cultural and gender biases and stereotypes?

The OECD sees global competence as being shaped by three (　B　) : "equity", "cohesion" and "sustainability".

Equity: The increased inequality of income and opportunities, along with the fact that poor children receive poor education, puts the issue of equity and inclusive growth high on the global agenda. The digital economy is hollowing out jobs consisting of routine tasks and radically altering the nature of employment. For many, this is liberating and exciting. It's a great moment to be a twenty something entrepreneur with a disruptive internet business model. But for others, it means the end of a livelihood.

Cohesion: In all parts of the world, we are seeing unprecedented movements of people, with the most dramatic flows coming from countries mired in poverty and war. How can receiving countries integrate diverse groups of people and avoid rising extremism and fundamentalism?

Sustainability: Delivering on the UN Sustainable Development Goals is a priority in the international community. Development that meets the needs of the present, without compromising the ability of future generations to meet their own needs, is more relevant than ever before, in the face of environmental degradation, climate change, over-consumption and population growth.

　Today, all three are at risk. But the OECD sees global competence as the centerpiece of a broader vision for 21st-century education.

1　本文中の(　1　)～(　3　)に入れるのに最も適切なものをア～ウの中から一つずつ選び，その記号を書きなさい。

　　ア　A big part of the problem is that there is no clear definition of what global competence should embrace, and how to make it measurable for educational policy and practice.

　　イ　PISA is just in the first stages of exploring how to measure these dimensions.

　　ウ　Automation and the digital economy could be seen as an entrepreneurial opportunity ― or a weakening of job security.

2　本文中の(　A　)に入れるのに最も適切なものをア～エの中から一

つ選び，その記号を書きなさい。

ア collapse　　イ control　　ウ disability　　エ success

3　本文中の(B)に入れるのに最も適切なものをア〜エの中から一つ選び，その記号を書きなさい。

ア ambiguities　　イ firmness　　ウ practices　　エ principles

4　本文の内容と一致しないものをア〜オの中から二つ選び，その記号を書きなさい。

ア　Educators are already successfully equipping pupils with the skills to interact and integrate with other cultures.

イ　People need to leave school equipped with knowledge, skills, and attitudes that will enable them to learn, work and live in a globalized world.

ウ　The digital economy will need workers who can work in different cultures.

エ　The next round of international PISA tests could examine the skills needed to live and work alongside people of different cultures.

オ　Young people who do not develop global competence are equally equipped to build more just, peaceful, inclusive and sustainable societies.

5　Global Competenceとは何か，本文に即して日本語で説明しなさい。

(☆☆☆☆○○○○)

【5】高校生がSNS(ソーシャル・ネットワーキング・サービス)を利用することについて，良い面と悪い面の両方を挙げながら，あなたの考える改善策を150語程度の英語で書きなさい。

(☆☆☆☆○○○○)

【6】次の1と2の問いに日本語で答えなさい。

1　次の文章は，高等学校学習指導要領解説(平成22年5月告示)第1章第2節　外国語の目標の一部である。空欄(A)〜(E)に適する

271

語句を書きなさい。

第2節　外国語科の目標

　　外国語科の目標は，（　A　）を養うことであり，次の三つの柱から成り立っている。

①　外国語を通じて，言語や（　B　）に対する理解を深めること。

②　外国語を通じて，積極的にコミュニケーションを図ろうとする（　C　）を育成すること。

③　外国語を通じて，情報や（　D　）などを的確に理解したり（　E　）に伝えたりする能力を養うこと。

2　岩手県がこれから国際化を進める上で，課題となるのはどのようなことだと考えますか。また，その課題を解決するためにはどのような取り組みが必要だと考えますか。課題と取り組みを明らかにして，あなたの考えを述べなさい。

(☆☆☆◎◎◎◎)

解答・解説

【中高共通】

【 1 】1　ウ　　2　イ　　3　ウ　　4　エ　　5　エ

〈解説〉スクリプトが公表されていないので詳細は不明だが，放送は1回のみである。また，各小問ともに会話を聞いて質問に解答する形式である。1はこれから2人がどうするのかという質問であると推測できる。2は彼女がもう一人の人物と絵画に関する会話をした後の質問であると推測できる。エについては，放送ではShe paints well.と言っていた可能性もある。3のイとウは同じような内容だが，エのbillは請求書なので意味合いが異なる。4のアとエは正反対の意味，イは彼女自身がタ

バコを吸いたい，ウは彼からタバコを1本もらいたいという意味である。5は，質問文はWhat does the man(or woman) want to do? だと推測できる。

【2】1　ウ　　2　イ　　3　イ　　4　ア
〈解説〉スクリプトが公表されていないので詳細は不明だが，放送は1回のみである。問題用紙に選択肢が印刷されているので，放送前に聞き取るべきポイントを予測することが必要である。1は「音楽を聴いて成績は上がるか」という質問が予想される。2は「静かな室内でどういうことを行ったのか」という質問が予想される。3は「どんな楽器が使われたか」などの質問が予想される。4は「クラシック音楽はどんな効果があるか」という質問が予想される。

【3】1　ア　　2　エ　　3　イ　　4　ウ
〈解説〉注意点は【1】及び【2】と同様だが，この問題は，テーマがクレジットカードに関する内容だと推測できるので，常識的な判断を働かせることが重要である。1は「クレジットカードを使う理由」を聞かれているので，常識的に考えてもアが正解である。エのrecessionは「不況，景気後退」の意味である。2はクレジットカードの趣旨から考えてア，イ，ウのいずれも正解とは言い難い。3の正解は，家が高すぎて借金しないと買えないというイが適切である。4の正解は，アまたはウが妥当である。アについては，最近の消費者教育の流れでもあるので注意する必要がある。

【中学校】
【1】1　ア　　2　ウ　　3　エ　　4　イ　　5　イ　　6　ア　　7　エ
　8　ウ
〈解説〉1　go with〜で「〜に合う，合致する」の意味。　2　tackle「〜と向き合う，取り組む」の意味。　3　第5文型である点に注意。spicy Thai foodが目的語，very以下が補語である。　4　transferは「配置転換

する，乗り換える」の意味である。　5　negligenceは「怠慢」の意味。「運転手の怠慢が交通事故の原因」の意味である。　6　correlationは「相関」の意味。英語のスペリングと発音にはしばしば相関関係がないことを述べている。　7　「フランス語に堪能な」の意味である。8　heaveは「持ち上げる」の意味。荷物の積み下ろしのことを言っている。

【2】1　エ　　2　イ　　3　ア　　4　イ　　5　エ
〈解説〉1　Bの2回目の発言のIt's fascinating.に注目する。この応答になる質問はエのみである。　2　ask a favor of youで「お願いがある」の意味。What do you want? と返答しているので，その前の発言はOKの意味になる。　3　Aは最初に本の書名がわからないと言っているので，イは誤り。the focus of the bookは「本の主な内容」の意味である。4　「Daveに話を聞かれていないよね」という問いに対して，「ささやいただけだから」と答えているので，「聞かれていないのは確かだ」と考えればよい。　5　Bの家で料理をすることになったが，Aが「本当に平気か」と聞いたのに対して，Bが「それは心配ない」と答えていることから，エの「料理をするとひどく散らかす」が適切。

【3】1　ア　　2　イ　　3　エ
〈解説〉1　everyは単数扱いなので，playerが正しい。　2　「美術館の中で」の意味なので，inが正しい。　3　to calculateとセットになる表現なのでprocessが正しい。

【4】1　ウ　　2　イ　　3　ウ
〈解説〉1　第1段落12文目の最初からconvenientまでに注目する。なお，for example以下でその具体例が述べられている。　2　第3段落12文目に注目する。労働の対価として報酬を支払ったのである。　3　アはto join以下が誤り。第1段落7文目biology以下，「若い頃にアメリカで学んだ」と述べている。イはThereからKenyaまでが誤り。第1段落9文目the

forests以下，「当時は森林が減少し続けていた」と述べている。ウは正しい。第3段落3文目で「1977年に創設した」と述べているので，約40年前である。エは誤り。第4段落1文目及び2文目に，「2004年にMaathaiがアフリカ人として7人目のノーベル賞受賞者になった」と述べている。

【5】1　ウ　　2　イ　　3　ウ

〈解説〉1　Kyokoの3回目の発言1文目のmaybeからrichまでに注目する。この部分に対して，同2文目のyouからsecureまでが対比的に述べられているのである。　2　Takeshiは1回目の発言1文目にあるように増税には反対である。したがって，空欄直後の部分は，「仮にもっと税金を支払うとしても」の意味になるのである。　3　アは正しい。Takeshiの1回目の発言3文目のputting以下にこの意味のことが述べられている。イは正しい。Takeshiの3回目の発言2文目they should以下にこの意味のことが述べられている。ウはthe tax以下が誤りである。Kyokoの5回目の発言the money以下で「高齢者のような社会的弱者を助けるために税金を使う」と述べている。エは正しい。Kyokoの7回目の発言1文目にこの意味のことが述べられている。

【6】ア，イ，オ

〈解説〉アは，第1段落4文目のthe area以下の内容と一致する。イは，第5段落3文目の最初からhold the phoneまでの内容と一致する。ウはwasからthreateningまでが誤り。第6段落2文目のthe actorからringingまでと一致しない。エはareからunpollutedまでが誤り。第4段落1文目のonceから最後までと一致しない。オは，第4段落3文目のthe steadyからsound wallsまでの内容と一致する。

【7】In order to be able to communicate in English, it is necessary not only to have a knowledge of grammar and vocabulary, but also the ability to use English for the purpose of actual communication. Thus, teachers should give students goals for the required skills of listening, speaking, reading and writing, each term and each grade clearly. Through the repetition of activities in which English is used to express their thoughts, feelings or ideas, students will master grammar and vocabulary. (80 words)

〈解説〉問題文に正対することが重要である。そのためには，指示文を注意して読むことが必要である。この問題では，「基本的な語彙や文法事項を活用する力」と「具体的にどのような指導が考えられるか」の2点がポイントである。解答例では，It…to 〜の形式主語の構文を使ってわかりやすく表現している。また，表現上の語彙としては，the ability to〜「〜する能力」，for the purpose of〜「〜のために」，each term and each grade「各学期，学年ごとに」，repetition「繰り返し」などがポイントになる。

【8】①　ア　　②　ウ　　③　イ

〈解説〉①　言語を使用する活動を重視するあまり，発音の基本，語句や文の構造についての指導を軽視してはならない。また，逆に，言語材料について理解したり練習したりする活動を重視して，言語を使用する活動自体を軽視してはならない。　②　実際に言語を使用して互いの考えや気持ちを伝え合うなどの活動の中では，表現しようとすることを個々の生徒が自ら考え，ふさわしい表現を選択できるように配慮することが大切である。実際の指導では，具体的でわかりやすい場面や状況を設定するとともに，その場面や状況にふさわしいものを示すことが必要である。　③　「言語の使用場面」や「言語の働き」について特に具体例を示している。これは，日常の授業において実際的な指導の手掛かりとなるように考慮されたものである。なお，第1学年では，小学校の外国語活動の内容を取り上げることで，中学校の外国語学習の円滑導入を図ることが重要である。

【9】①　つながり　　②　身近な場面　　③　考え　　④　読み手

〈解説〉①　この指導事項は，文構造や語法の理解が十分でなく正しい文

が書けないという課題に対応したものであり，語順の重要性を強調し
たのは，英語では語順が意味の伝達において重要な役割を持っている
からである。　②・③　ここでは，実際に自分が体験したことなどに
ついて自分の考えや気持ちなどを自由に書く活動のことを述べてい
る。これは，家庭や学校などの日常生活，旅行や行事の体験などにつ
いては，積極的に自分の考えや気持ちを書いて表現することが比較的
容易であると考えられるからである。　④　このためには，一文一文
を正しく書くだけでなく，接続詞や副詞を使って，文と文の順序や相
互の関連性にも注意をはらい，全体として一貫性のある文章を書くよ
うにすることが大切である。

【10】①　英語で書かれた短い物語文の内容を読み取り，その要旨と自分
の感想を，友達に英語で話す活動に取り組むよう指導する。
②　中1初期の英語学習において，小学校外国語活動で子ども達が慣
れ親しんだ，身の回りのものや身近なことを表す表現を用いた，音声
による言語活動を設定し，取り組ませる。
〈解説〉①　解答例では，ペアワークの活動内容について述べている。
「読み取り」の部分で「読むこと」，「その要旨」の部分で「書くこと」，
「英語で話す」の部分で「話すこと」及び「聞くこと」の活動が含ま
れている。このような活動は，4技能を総合的に育成する指導と言え
る。　②　解答例の全文は，小学校での外国語活動による一定の素地
を踏まえて，その内容を取り上げることにより，中学校第1学年での
外国語の指導が円滑に行われるように配慮したことを示す内容となっ
ている。

【11】1　・積極的に会話を継続し発展させていく態度や能力を育成する
ための活動である。　　・紋切り型の応答や一往復だけのことばのや
りとりで終わってしまうのでなく，必要な表現や技法を用いて会話を
継続発展することができる。　　2　・会話を始めたり発展させたり
するために，相手に質問をする。　　・知らない表現については，身

振り手振りや既習の表現などを使い，何とかして自分の考えを伝える。
・相手が話しやすいように，I see.やSure.など，相づちを打つ表現を適
宜用いる。　　から1つ

〈解説〉1　「つなぎ言葉」とは，Let me seeやWellなど，言葉や会話を続
けるために使われる表現である。Really? やAre you sure? なども同様に
考えてよい。　　2　解答例の2つ目に「身振り手振り」とあるが，これ
はいわゆる「ボディー・ランゲージ」と考えてよい。また，「何とか
して自分の考えを伝える」とあるが，このことは異文化理解には必要
な行動である。そのためには，習慣や考え方の違いなどについて学ぶ
姿勢が大切である。

【高等学校】

【1】1　イ　　2　イ　　3　ア　　4　ウ　　5　イ

〈解説〉1　make itで「うまく行く，やり遂げる，切り抜ける」などの意
味である。　　2　hersで「彼女の物」の意味である。　　3　beingは現在
分詞の分詞構文の用法で「理由」を表している。Because there was no
～transportation,の意味である。　　4　副詞が強調された倒置構文であ
る。so the airlines raised their faresの意味である。　　5　put outで「消化
する」の意味で，extinguishと同意である。

【2】1　Pleasure, Love, Fame, Riches(Wealth) and Death.　　2　One by one,
they went away and left him. They all died.　　3　She sighed because the
man didn't choose the valuable gift. She sighed because she knew that it
wasn't the correct choice.　　4　The man named it "Shame."　　5　She
gave it to a mother's little child.

〈解説〉1　Pleasureが第2，Loveが第5，Fameが第9，Wealthが第13段落に
出てくる。Deathは第17段落のOld Ageと考えればよい。　　2　第6段落
のOne by oneからthe lastまでをまとめる。　　3　第10段落4文目の最初
Howから同5文目の最後persecutionまでに，嫉妬や毀損，冤罪，憎悪，
迫害などが羅列されている。これらはvaluable giftを想起するものでは

ない。　4　第14段落4文目のダッシュ以下のPain, Grief, Shame, Povertyの部分に注目する。　5　第15段落2文目のI gaveからchildまでに答えがある。

【3】1　ア　2　ウ　3　イ　4　ア　5　イ
〈解説〉1　アは正しい。第1段落1文目のIt's beenから(SIDS)までの内容と一致する。イはat the以下が誤り。論旨にはない。ウはlower than以下が誤り。第2段落1文目のone ofからthe worldまでと一致しない。エはthe key以下が誤り。第4段落2文目のbut以下と一致しない。　2　アは正しい。第3段落2文目のreduction以下と一致する。イは正しい。第4段落3文目のdecided以下と一致する。ウは誤り。論旨にはない。エは正しい。第4段落8文目のafter以下と一致する。　3　大卒なので収入が高く，その分健康保持のための支出も可能になるからである。
4　アは正しい。第7段落1文目のthey以下と一致する。イはEducationからeffectiveまでが誤り。第7段落3文目のthe improved以下と一致しない。ウは誤り。論旨にはない。エはshould以下が誤り。第6段落3文目及び4文目で「baby boxesを導入するだけでは問題解決に至らない」と述べている。　5　アは死亡率の説明の一側面である。イは，全ての段落でbaby boxesに言及しているので，タイトルとして適切である。ウはフィンランドの政策の一部を説明している。エは日本が比較対象として引用されているだけである。

【4】1　(1)　ウ　(2)　ア　(3)　イ　2　エ　3　エ　4　ア，オ　5　グローバルコンピテンスとは，異文化間で生じる問題を批判的に，かつ多面的な視点から分析する能力，違いがどのように自分や他者の認識・判断・アイディアに影響するかを理解する能力，人間の尊厳の尊重という考えに基づいた上で，異なる背景を持つ人々と率直で適切かつ効果的なやりとりを行う能力のこと。
〈解説〉1　(1)　第2段落4文目のダッシュの前後では正反対の意味のことが述べられている。　(2)　第3段落8文目のnowhere以下が，アのthere

is以下に続いている。　(3)　第6段落6文目のsensitivityからwithまでの内容が，イのthese dimensionsに該当する。　2　空欄Aの直後の前置詞がinであることに注意。ここからsucceed in「…に成功する」を想起できれば，エが適切とわかる。　3　OECDがglobal competenceをどのように見なしているかを考える。第4段落2文目のコロン(：)に続くGlobal competence is以下の説明と，空欄B直後の3つの内容を併せて考えると，エのprinciples「原理，原則」が適切である。　4　アはare already以下が誤り。第3段落8文目のnowhere以下の内容と一致しない。イは正しい。第3段落6文目のequip以下の内容と一致する。ウは正しい。第2段落7文目のprepare students以下の内容と一致する。エは正しい。第5段落3文目全体の内容と一致する。オはwhoからcompetenceまでが誤り。論旨にはない。　5　第4段落2文目のコロン(：)に続くGlobal competence is以下に明確に定義されている。同文中のto analyzeからperspectivesまで，to understandからothersまで，及びto engageから最後までをまとめればよい。

【5】 These days, social networking services called SNS are becoming the main means of communication for high school students. There are both advantages and disadvantages to them using SNS.

One of the advantages is that SNS make it possible to communicate with all kinds of people easily. For example, some Japanese students exchange messages with foreign students through Facebook. They can learn about different cultures, and learn new opinions on common social issues.

On the other hand, there have been a lot of troubles caused by SNS. Some students get bullied on LINE, because it allows people to post terrible comments in a closed community. What's worse, others may get involved in illegal activities with adults through SNS.

Therefore, I believe that it is important for high school students to learn how to use SNS properly. Parents can discuss the rules and manners of using it with their children and schools can offer classes to teach them its risks. (158 words)

〈解説〉第1段落では高校生とSNSの現状について述べていて，導入となっている。第2段落では良い面(advantages)について述べている。ここでは，For example以下で具体例を示している。第3段落では悪い面(disadvantages)について述べているが，disadvantageという単語は使わず，thereからSNSまでの文章で「悪い面」という意味を表している点に注意。また，Some以下で第2段落と同様に具体例を述べている。第4段落では，I believeからproperlyまでで結論を述べ，さらにParents以下でその具体策を記述している。非常に読みやすく説得力のある英文である。

【6】1　A　コミュニケーション能力　　B　文化　　C　態度
D　考え　　E　適切　　2　近年のグローバル化により，本県においても国際化が進み，外国人観光客の数は増加している。また留学生やALT，プロのスポーツ選手，技能実習生として本県に住む外国人や，日本人と結婚している人たちも多くいる。しかし，言葉や文化の問題により，地域社会において十分なつながりを持つことができない傾向にある。また，福祉や教育問題等も無視できない状況である。このような現状を踏まえ，課題となるのは多様な文化的背景を持つ人々を受け入れる素地を作ることだ。

　この課題を解決するために，学校教育において，特に英語の授業を通して，多様な文化を受け入れ，協働していくことの重要性を子どもたちに理解させる必要がある。そうすることで，違いを理解し受け入れる人材を育成することとなり，本県の国際化および活性化に貢献しうると私は考える。

〈解説〉1　現行の高等学校学習指導要領では，外国語科の目標として，「外国語を通じて，言語や文化に対する理解を深め，積極的にコミュニケーションを図ろうとする態度の育成を図り，情報や考えなどを的確に理解したり適切に伝えたりするコミュニケーション能力を養う」と定めている。また，③に示す能力は，コミュニケーション能力の中

281

核をなすものであり，高等学校においては，4技能を総合的に育成するための統合的な指導を行う必要がある。　2　指示文をよく読み，指示に正対することが重要である。解答例では，第1段落で課題を明確にして，第2段落でその具体的な解決策と自分の考えを述べている。この論述方法が一般的であり，論旨も一貫することができる。

2017年度 　 実施問題

【中高共通】

【 1 】これから，会話と質問が5つ放送されます。質問に対する答えとし
て最も適切なものをア～エの中から一つずつ選び，その記号を書きな
さい。なお，会話と質問は一度だけ放送されます。

1

　　ア　$20

　　イ　$80

　　ウ　$100

　　エ　$120

2

　　ア　http://adams.blog.ab2.com/

　　イ　http://adam-smith.blog.ab2.com/

　　ウ　http://adam.smith.blog.ab2.com/

　　エ　http://adamsmith.blog.ab2.com/

3

　　ア　He is a teacher.

　　イ　He is a school counselor.

　　ウ　He is an architect.

　　エ　He is an office worker.

4

　　ア　It was a little too long.

　　イ　It was a success to some extent.

　　ウ　She shouldn't have gone fishing.

　　エ　She should have gone farther away.

5

　　ア　Meg's job performance.

イ　Meg's new manager.

ウ　The new evaluation system.

エ　The responsibilities of managers.

(☆☆☆◎◎◎)

【2】これから，英文Aと英文Bが放送されます。それぞれの英文の後に，その内容について質問が二つずつ出されます。その質問に対する答えとして最も適切なものをア～エの中から一つずつ選び，その記号を書きなさい。なお，英文と質問は一度だけ放送されます。

A

1

ア　A group of people traveling in Amsterdam.

イ　A pilot for a new work style project.

ウ　The name of a car company.

エ　The website of a research center.

2

ア　Citizens will get used to traffic jams in Amsterdam.

イ　Companies in Amsterdam will be able to easily hire employees.

ウ　It will be easy for people to exit the island.

エ　It will save people time commuting.

B

3

ア　Avoid correcting the other person.

イ　Avoid expressing our emotions.

ウ　Enter into conversations more positively.

エ　Try to prove ourselves right.

4

ア　Exclusive pronouns cause us instant feelings of positivity and familiarity.

イ　If you expect to be liked when meeting people, you will project cold

284

negativity.

ウ　It's not about what you say, but how and when you say it.

エ　Talking about yourself will make you a good conversationalist.

(☆☆☆○○)

【3】 これから，まとまりのある英文が一度だけ放送されます。質問に対する答えとして最も適切なものをア〜エの中から一つずつ選び，その記号を書きなさい。

1　According to the article, what features do bike-sharing bicycles have?

　　ア　They are built for speed, rather than stability.

　　イ　They have greater visibility.

　　ウ　The rider sits higher.

　　エ　They tend to be lighter.

2　According to the article, what kind of people are a factor in increasing bike-sharing safety?

　　ア　Bike-sharing users who try to save money and keep themselves healthy.

　　イ　Cyclists who try to treat the things that they are renting more carefully.

　　ウ　Less experienced riders who exhibit more considerate cycling behavior.

　　エ　Recreational riders as opposed to commuters.

3　According to the article, what is a big factor in bike-sharing safety?

　　ア　Helmets

　　イ　Infrastructure

　　ウ　Programs

　　エ　Short trips

4　Which of the following statements is mentioned in the article?

　　ア　Bike-sharing brings a flood of inexperienced cyclists onto dangerous roads.

イ　No bike-sharing user has been seriosly injured or killed in a traffic accident.

ウ　People drive more slowly when they are used to seeing cyclists.

エ　There is no relation between bike-sharing and increased safety.

(☆☆☆◎◎◎)

【中学校】

【１】次の1〜10の英文の(　　)にあてはまる最も適切な英語を，それぞれア〜エから一つずつ選び，その記号を書きなさい。

1　I'm going to use e-mail to keep in (　　) with my sister in Australia.

ア　exchange　　イ　mind　　ウ　touch　　エ　relation

2　I've heard that in the U.S. smoking is (　　) in public places such as stations or cafes.

ア　excluded　　イ　banded　　ウ　relapsed　　エ　withdrawn

3　Lydia is a really (　　) person, so she cleans her apartment every day.

ア　nutritious　　イ　vague　　ウ　temporary　　エ　neat

4　The number of CD stores has been (　　) over the last 20 years. One reason is that more and more people are buying music through the Internet.

ア　expanding　　イ　declining　　ウ　curving　　エ　settling

5　Jim had never been to New York. He had a few (　　) there but no close friends who could help him start a new life.

ア　acquaintances　　イ　passengers　　ウ　representatives

エ　specialists

6　It is (　　) that about 40% of the total population of Japan will be 65 years old or older in the year 2050.

ア　provided　　イ　dedicated　　ウ　estimated　　エ　achieved

7　The (　　) of the test was questioned since no actual surveys were done in the class.

ア　agility　　イ　relativity　　ウ　facility　　エ　validity

8　Fifty years ago, no one (　　) a worldwide network of instant communication, but today, it is a reality.

ア　endeavored　　イ　enlisted　　ウ　envisioned　　エ　endured

9　The waiter was very attentive and (　　), so we gave him a big tip.

ア　courteous　　イ　anxious　　ウ　tolerable　　エ　stable

10　The mayor (　　) a return to traditional community values in her speech.

ア　regulated　　イ　advocated　　ウ　imitated　　エ　originated

(☆☆◎◎)

【2】次のそれぞれの会話文中の(　　)にあてはまる最も適切な英語を，下のア～エから一つずつ選び，その記号を書きなさい。

1　A: I think I need to start exercising again. I didn't do much all winter.

B: I thought you said you go for a jog every day.

A: I try to. (　　).

B: Well, now that the weather is better, you have no excuse not to jog.

ア　In fact, I really like jogging in the snow.

イ　But when it's cold and snowy, I get lazy.

ウ　Actually, I don't usually jog in the spring.

エ　Exercising in the winter keeps me warm.

2　A: Excuse me, do you know where the city library is?

B: It's over there, but I don't think it's open now.

A: That's OK. (　　) I moved here recently.

B: Oh, I see. Welcome to the area.

ア　I'm just trying to get familiar with the facilities around here.

イ　It's urgent for me to talk with the librarian about some books.

ウ　I wouldn't mind if you opened the door for me.

エ　It's costly, but the quality is exceptional.

3　A: I'm having difficulty deciding what to buy Melanie for her birthday.

B: (　　)

A: Then that's something I should avoid getting.

ア　Don't you have any ideas?

イ　That's your opinion.

ウ　I bought her a CD.

エ　When is her birthday?

4　A: Well, Joe, we're finally here in Tokyo! Where do you think we should go first?

B: (　　　) I'm up for anything.

A: If it's all right with you, I'd like to see Senso-ji Temple first.

B: That's a good idea. It's supposed to be one of the most famous sights in Tokyo.

ア　It doesn't really matter to me.

イ　It seems like the right thing to do.

ウ　How long will we stay here?

エ　I hope I can go someday.

5　A: Do you think we'll be able to go to the mountains tomorrow?

B: Why do you ask? (　　　)

A: No. I'm worried that it might rain, though.

ア　Will we be able to finish our homework?

イ　Will the weather be OK?

ウ　You want to go?

エ　Has there been a change of plan?

(☆☆◎◎)

【3】次の1～4の各文の下線部で，英語の文法上または表現上適切でない語句があります。それぞれア～エから一つずつ選び，その記号を書きなさい。

1　Let's ask ₇that woman if she ₄could ₉teach us where the station ₌is located.

2　₇The place I visited last month is ₄considered to be one of ₉the top ten ₌tourist spot in Japan.

3　If you ₇go abroad, you will realize how inconvenient ₄is it ₉not to be able to have yourself _エunderstood in English.

4   The prime minister promised in 1997 that he would _アbe led a humble country, _イbe a uniter not a divider, and _ウthat he would make conservatism _エcompassionate.

(☆☆◎◎)

【4】次の英文を読んで，後の質問に対する最も適切な答えを，ア～エか らそれぞれ一つずつ選び，その記号を書きなさい。

Nowadays, there is a multimillion dollar industry around skateboarding. There are magazines and television programs about skateboarding, as well as clothing, accessory and sporting gear companies which depend on the popularity of skateboarding. However, skateboarding was originally created by ordinary kids living in parts of California, who practiced it every day simply because they loved it. Skateboarding's growth as both a sport and an industry may be characterized as a 'horizontal' to 'vertical' transformation. Let us see how this is so.

It is said that the first skateboarders were Californian teenagers in the late 1950s. These kids were heavily into surfing. However, wave conditions varied according to the time of year and day, and they were not able to surf 24 hours every day. Therefore, in order to do something similar to surfing when there were no suitable waves, they nailed roller skate wheels to pieces of wood, and rode on them. This was how the first skateboards came into existence.

Soon, skateboarding began to emerge as an after-school activity of young boys, leading to the first skateboarding contest held in 1963. Some companies began to manufacture and sell skateboards, and within a three-year period, over fifty million skateboards had been sold.

One of the characteristics of the skateboards manufactured in the 1960s was that the wheels were made out of clay. This affected skateboarding in two ways. First, because clay wheels could easily break, the style of skateboarding was necessarily horizontal. Kids would demonstrate difficult balancing acts

289

such as headstands, and slow, graceful turns on their skateboards. Second, because clay wheels do not grip the road very well, a lot of skateboarders would fall and hurt themselves. Soon, there was a public controversy over skateboarding, and in the fall of 1965, skateboarding suddenly died. Manufacturers stopped making skateboards.

After this, some dedicated skateboarders continued to skateboard, resorting to hand making their own skateboards. Then, in 1972, a surfer by the name of Frank Nasworthy thought of making skateboard wheels made out of plastic. Unlike clay wheels, plastic wheels would not break under impact. As you would expect, this resulted in the revival of skateboarding, and it became popular again. This meant that kids could skateboard faster and harder than ever before.

During this time, skateboarders started practicing in empty swimming pools, and this was when they began to skate vertically. At first, they skated from the bottom of the pool to the rim of the pool. Finally, they were skating out of the pool and jumping back in! Skateboarders were now truly flying.

Since the 1970s, skateboarding has taken off. First, it has grown into a multimillion dollar industry. Secondly, the trend to skate vertically has continued; nowadays, skateboarders regularly perform complicated tricks while they are in the air. Who knows how skateboarding will change in the future?

1　What prevented the earliest skateboarders from jumping into the air?

　ア　They could not buy skateboards with plastic wheels.

　イ　They did not spend enough time practicing.

　ウ　They did not know how to grip the road very well.

　エ　They could not depend on ocean waves.

2　According to the passage, which of the following is true?

　ア　The popularity of skateboarding has grown accidentally.

　イ　The popularity of skateboarding has grown significantly.

ウ　The popularity of skateboarding has grown desperately.

エ　The popularity of skateboarding has grown openly.

3　Which of the following is the most suitable title for the passage?

ア　Historical Surfing

イ　The Evolution of Skateboarding

ウ　Clay versus Plastic Wheels

エ　Industry's Effect on Sports

(☆☆☆◎◎)

【5】次の英文を読んで，後の質問に答えなさい。

According to Dan Buettner, the author of *Blue Zones*, a book about the areas of the world where people are most likely to live long and healthy lives, there are four factors that seem to contribute to the likelihood that someone will celebrate a triple-digit birthday.

The first two are physical: a healthy diet and regular exercise. People who garden, for example, increase their chances of living longer. For one thing, they are out in the sunshine getting plenty of vitamin D, which is good for their bones. Also if they are growing fresh vegetables, it is likely that they are eating them, too, and fresh vegetables are full of life-preserving antioxidants and vitamins. According to Buettner, tomatoes, green leafy vegetables, squashes, and beans are all part of the longevity diet. Another benefit to cultivating food at home is that home gardeners get regular, yet not overly strenuous exercise. There is a lot of scientific (　①　) to support the importance of regular activity for maintaining body strength and flexibility as one ages.

The third and fourth factors are associated with the psyche. One important psychological factor is having strong personal relationships. The research is clear. People who are lucky enough to live among a community of close friends and family simply live (　②　) than people who don't live in such a community. For example, a great-grandfather who still lives with his family,

291

jokes with his great-grandchildren, and carves the turkey at Thanksgiving enjoys better mental health than a man of the same age living (③   ) or in a rest home among strangers. We can see another example in a small town of 1,700 people on the island of Sardinia, Italy, where five of the world's forty oldest people live and 6 people per 3000 live to see their 100th birthday. There it is not uncommon for a ninety-year-old man to chop wood in the morning, eat lunch with his family in the afternoon, and then visit with friends at a café in the evening.

The fourth factor that contributes to a long life is having a strong sense of purpose. For some, that sense of purpose might be helping with the grandchildren; for others, it might also include volunteer work at a hospital. When people know that someone is counting on them, they have a reason to get up in the morning. They report having energy all day and doing their work with ease, whereas those without a similar sense of purpose say they feel drained at the end of a busy day.

In sum, it seems that the lifestyle that leads to a long life is one that is full of pleasure and meaning. If people follow these guidelines they can anticipate two or three bonus decades, free from the stresses of raising children and paying the bills, and will find themselves with time to pursue activities that feed the soul. Whether continuing to make breakthroughs in nuclear physics or just playing the role of a nuclear physicist on television, older people are already changing the rules of aging.

(注)　Dan Buettner「ダン・ベットナー(*Blue Zones*の著者)」　*Blue Zones*「ブルーゾーン(書籍名)」　triple-digit「3桁の」　antioxidant「抗酸化物」　squash「ウリ類(カボチャなども含む)」

1　文中の(　①　)に適する語をア～エから一つ選び，その記号を書きなさい。

ア　substance　　イ　workforce　　ウ　evidence　　エ　utterance

2　文の内容から考え，文中の(　②　), (　③　)に適する語を1語書き

なさい。

3　次のア～エから，本文の内容と一致しないものを一つ選び，その記号を書きなさい。

ア　Vitamin D, which is good for our bones, can be gotten by staying in the sun.

イ　Strong relationships are one of the factors that contribute to living a longer life.

ウ　If people know that they are counted on by someone, they are likely to live longer.

エ　The fourth factor that contributes to a long life is having a strong sense of humor.

(☆☆○○○)

【6】次の英文を読んで，本文の内容と一致するものを後のア～キから四つ選び，その記号を書きなさい。

　The oceans have traditionally been taken for granted as a source of wealth, opportunity and abundance. The vastness of ocean space that fueled our inspiration and curiosity, suggested that there could be few if any limits to its use or abuse. Our growing understanding of the oceans has fundamentally changed this perception. It has led to a growing appreciation of not only the importance of the oceans to social and economic progress but also of their vulnerability.

　We now know that abundance is giving way to scarcity, in some cases at an alarming rate, and conflicts are arising over the use of oceans.

　Life on our planet is dependent upon the oceans. They provide us with food, energy, and water, they sustain the lives of hundreds of millions of people, and they are the main highway for international trade as well as the main regulator of the world's climate. However, in the space of only a few decades the oceans have become the setting for an expanding list of problems. Territorial disputes that threaten peace and security, global climate change, overfishing, species extinction, pollution, terrorism, and the destruction of coastal communities are among the problems that today form part of the drama of oceans.

The challenge posed by the oceans is one of truly historical dimensions, since the extent to which it is met will have a major bearing on the well-being not only of almost everyone alive today but also of future generations.

Our findings provide cause for hope as well as concern. It is not exaggerating to say there is crisis in the oceans. This crisis cannot be seen in isolation from the many problems that affect both land and air. Indeed, together they form part of the major problem of our biosphere in which issues at sea are connected to those on land through rivers, the atmosphere and the coastal zone. All form part of a larger picture that links the abuse of resources to the well-being of future generations and, ultimately, to prospects of human survival.

The problem has many dimensions, including moral and ethical ones. These find clear expression in the inequalities of opportunities existing between rich and poor nations, which do not benefit equally from the use of oceans. They are also manifest in the failure to safeguard the interests of future generations, not only of those who will be born into poverty and underdevelopment but also of the descendants of today's privileged minority. There are issues of fairness that must be addressed in relation to the oceans. To do so calls for solidarity with present and future generations.

 (注) vulnerability「脆弱(ぜいじゃく)さ」 scarcity「不足」
  bioshere「生物圏」

ア There is only one side to the problem in our oceans.

イ Our growing understanding of the oceans has fundamentally changed how we perceive it.

ウ In the space of only a few decades the tropics have become the setting for an expanding list of problems.

エ　What happens to the oceans today will not affect future generations.

オ　The oceans have a major effect on the world's climate.

カ　The oceans benefit life on our planet.

キ　The problems in the oceans are manifest in the failure to protect the interest of future generations.

(☆☆☆◎◎)

【7】中学校学習指導要領解説外国語編(平成20年9月)の「第1章　総説」における「2　外国語科改訂の趣旨」に，次のような項目があります。

> ○　「聞くこと」，「話すこと」，「読むこと」及び「書くこと」の4技能の総合的な指導を通して，これらの4技能を<u>統合的に活用</u>できるコミュニケーション能力を育成するとともに，その基礎となる文法をコミュニケーションを支えるものとしてとらえ，文法指導を言語活動と一体的に行うよう改善を図る。また，コミュニケーションを内容的に充実したものとすることができるよう，指導すべき語数を充実する。

　上記の項目で求められている，複数の技能を<u>統合的に活用</u>させる指導の具体例を80語以上の英語で書きなさい。なお，最後に語数を記入すること。語数については，同じ語を2回使用した場合，2語と数えること(のべ数)とします。

(☆☆☆◎◎)

【8】次の文章は，中学校学習指導要領外国語編(平成20年9月)の「第2章　外国語科の目標及び内容」における「2　内容」の「(2)　言語活動の取扱い」からの抜粋です。文中の(　①　)～(　③　)に当てはまることばとして，最も適切なものを後のア～オから一つずつ選び，記号を書きなさい。

> イ　生徒の学習段階を考慮して各学年の指導に当たっては，次のような点に配慮するものとする。
>
> (ア)　第1学年における言語活動
>
> 　　小学校における外国語活動を通じて音声面を中心としたコミュニケーションに対する積極的な態度などの一定の素地が育成されることを踏まえ，身近な言語の使用場面や言語の働きに配慮した言語活動を行わせること。その際，(　①　)。
>
> (イ)　第2学年における言語活動
>
> 　　第1学年の学習を基礎として，言語の使用場面や言語の働きを更に広げた言語活動を行わせること。その際，第1学年における学習内容を繰り返して指導し定着を図るとともに，(　②　)。
>
> (ウ)　第3学年における言語活動
>
> 　　第2学年までの学習を基礎として，言語の使用場面や言語の働きを一層広げた言語活動を行わせること。その際，第1学年及び第2学年における学習内容を繰り返して指導し定着を図るとともに，(　③　)。

ア　様々な考えや意見などの中からコミュニケーションが図れるような話題を取り上げること

イ　自分の気持ちや身の回りの出来事などの中から簡単な表現を用いてコミュニケーションを図れるような話題を取り上げること

ウ　慣れ親しんだ表現を用いてコミュニケーションが図れるような話題を取り上げること

エ　事実関係を伝えたり，物事について判断したりした内容などの中からコミュニケーションを図れるような話題を取り上げること

オ　生徒のスキーマを活用してコミュニケーションを図れるような話題を取り上げること

(☆☆○○○○)

【9】 次の文章は，中学校学習指導要領(平成20年3月)の「第2章　第9節　外国語」における「3　指導計画の作成と内容の取扱い」からの抜粋です。文中の(①)～(④)にあてまはる適切な語句を書きなさい。

> (2)　教材は，聞くこと，話すこと，読むこと，書くことなどのコミュニケーション能力を総合的に育成するため，実際の言語の使用場面や言語の働きに十分配慮したものを取り上げるものとする。その際，英語を使用している人々を中心とする世界の人々及び日本人の日常生活，風俗習慣，物語，地理，歴史，伝統文化や自然科学などに関するものの中から，生徒の発達の段階及び(①)に即して適切な題材を変化をもたせて取り上げるものとし，次の観点に配慮する必要がある。
> ア　(②)なものの見方や考え方を理解し，公正な判断力を養い豊かな心情を育てるのに役立つこと。
> イ　外国や我が国の生活や文化についての理解を深めるとともに，言語や文化に対する関心を高め，これらを(③)する態度を育てるのに役立つこと。
> ウ　広い視野から国際理解を深め，国際社会に生きる日本人としての自覚を高めるとともに，(④)の精神を養うのに役立つこと。

(☆☆◎◎◎◎)

【10】 次の(1)，(2)を読み，後の問いに答なさい。

(1)　小学校学習指導要領(平成20年3月)

> 「第4章　外国語活動　第1　目標」
> 　外国語を通じて，言語や文化について体験的に理解を深め，積極的にコミュニケーションを図ろうとする態度の育成を図り，外国語の音声や基本的な表現に慣れ親しませながら，コ

ミュニケーション能力の素地を養う。

(2)　中学校学習指導要領(平成20年3月)

「第2章　第9節　外国語　第1　目標」
　　外国語を通じて，言語や文化に対する理解を深め，積極的にコミュニケーションを図ろうとする態度の育成を図り，聞くこと，話すこと，読むこと，書くことなどのコミュニケーション能力の基礎を養う。

【問い】　これらの目標を踏まえ，小学校において外国語活動を経験した中学1年生に対して，中学校外国語科教員は，授業中，どのようなことに配慮して指導すべきか日本語で2つ答えなさい。

(☆☆☆◎◎◎)

【11】次の文は中学校学習指導要領(平成20年3月)で，「読むこと」の言語活動の中の(イ)について，示されたものです。これを読んで，下の問いに答えなさい。

（イ)　書かれた内容を考えながら黙読したり，その内容が表現されるように音読すること。

【問い】　この指導事項では，黙読と音読の二つの読み方について示されていますが，生徒に黙読や音読を行わせる際，具体的にどのような指導が必要でしょうか。黙読と音読に分け，それぞれ日本語で書きなさい。

(☆☆☆◎◎◎)

【高等学校】

【１】次の1～5の各文の(　　　)に入る最も適切なものを，ア～エの中から一つずつ選び，その記号を書きなさい。

1　If Kevin doesn't stop smoking, he will (　　　) the risk of developing lung cancer.

ア　get

イ　make

ウ　put

エ　run

2　"Everything you cook tastes really good."

"Thanks, but I don't think I'm (　　) cook as you."

ア　a good as

イ　as a good

ウ　as good a

エ　good as a

3　His condition (　　) that he should stay in bed for a few more days.

ア　decides

イ　inquires

ウ　requests

エ　requires

4　Nobody knows that Nancy has been ill for a few months, (　　)?

ア　do they

イ　don't they

ウ　has she

エ　hasn't she

5　When my co-workers get into arguments, I try to avoid taking (　　). It's safer to stay neutral.

ア　angles

イ　places

ウ　sides

エ　turns

(☆☆☆○○○)

【2】次の英文を読んで，1～5の問いに対する答えを英語で書きなさい。

At 53 years old, Makoto Murase is a man on a mission. His objective—and life-passion—is to solve urban water shortages by providing water to millions of people and changing the way city planners view rainfall. In most cities, rainwater is something to quickly dispose of, lest it cause flooding and clog sewage systems. To Murase, it is a resource we can no longer afford to waste.

As a longtime employee of Sumida Ward in Tokyo, Murase sprang to prominence by convincing the city government and Japan's Sumo Wrestling Federation to include a rainwater recycling system in a new arena. The success of this system, which uses rainwater collected and stored on the roof for flushing toilets and as an emergency reservoir, set a new standard for construction in Tokyo.

Now Murase is the head of the Rainwater Utilization Promotion Section of Sumida City, an organization created for him. He has sketched out a plan that he claims could reduce household water consumption by one quarter and make most big buildings virtually self-sufficient in terms of water supply.

One of his many projects is the creation of mini-dams—basins that already dot Tokyo neighborhoods. The water is used mainly for gardening and other non-drinking applications. However, Murase sees them becoming part of water-utility infrastructure. He says, "Rainwater is ideal for drinking, and that should be its primary use, especially in places where ground water is contaminated." While using rainwater for drinking is complicated—it can need treating, and the first rainwater collected from roofs after a dry spell contains dirt—the problems can be overcome. At the same time, untreated rainwater is perfectly suited for many other household uses, such as watering plants, flushing toilets and washing clothes.

"Sky water" —Murase's term for rain—can have many household uses for millions of city-dwellers worldwide. "What we need now is to make people more aware of the potential and train a new generation of application engineers who understand the how and why of recycling urban rainwater." At the moment, society is "simply throwing this incredibly valuable resource away." It is a luxury the world can no longer afford.

By the middle of this century, a greater proportion of the world's population will be living in cities. Murase says, "Without using urban rainwater, there is no way to support the people without destroying the rural environments that provide food."

Murase has few illusions about the task ahead. "We must change a lot of preconceptions before we can really start moving forward." He has proved he can push his ideas through local government with imagination and courage. The millions of mini-dams he envisions may someday dwarf the giant reservoirs that are symbolic of modern man's quest to conquer nature instead of cooperating with it.

1　What is Murase's main goal?

2　How is the rainwater which is collected on buildings with Murase's system used?

3　What does Murase think the chief use of rainwater collected in mini-dams should be?

4　What are the problems with using rainwater for drinking?

5　According to Murase, why will rainwater be needed, especially in big cities, in the future?

(☆☆☆◎◎)

【3】次の英文を読んで，1〜5の問いに対する答えとして最も適切なものをア〜エの中から一つずつ選び，その記号を書きなさい。

Students who take handwritten notes generally outperform students who type their notes via laptop, according to studies from Princeton and UCLA. "The written notes capture my thinking better than typing," says educational psychologist Kenneth Kiewra at the University of Nebraska in Lincoln, who studies differences in how we take notes and organize information.

Ever since ancient scribes first took reed pens to papyrus, taking notes has been a catalyst for the alchemy of learning, by turning what we hear and see into a reliable record for later study and recollection. Indeed, something about writing things down excites the brain, brain imaging studies show. "Note-taking is a pretty dynamic process," says cognitive psychologist Michael Friedman of Harvard University who studies note-taking systems. "You are transforming what you hear in your mind."

Researchers have been studying note-taking strategies for almost a century. Not until recently, though, did they focus on the differences caused by the tools we use to capture information. Note-taking with a lead pencil (first mass-produced in the 17th century,) just isn't that different from using a fountain pen (1827); a ballpoint pen (1888); or a felt-tipped marker (1910). Today, however, virtually all college students have laptops; the keyboard clatter of note-taking is the soundtrack of higher education.

Generally, researchers have found that people who take notes on a laptop do take more notes and can more easily keep up with the pace of a lecture than people scribbling with a pen or pencil. College students typically type lecture notes at a rate of about 33 words a minute. People trying to write them down manage just 22 words a minute.

In the short run, typing pays off. Researchers at Washington University in St. Louis found in 2012 that typists could recall more of a lecture and performed slightly better than their pen-pushing classmates when tested immediately after class. Any advantage, though, is temporary. After just 24 hours, the typists typically forgot the material they had transcribed. Nor were their copious notes much help in refreshing their memory because they were so superficial.

In contrast, those who took notes by hand could remember the lecture material longer and had a better grip on the concepts presented in class, even a week later. Experts say the process of writing notes down encodes the information more deeply in people's memories. Longhand notes are also better for review because they are more organized.

In three experiments conducted during 2014, psychologists Pam A. Mueller of Princeton and Daniel Oppenheimer of UCLA arranged for students to listen to talks on a variety of topics, including algorithms and bats, while taking notes either via laptop or pen and paper. The 67 students were tested immediately afterward and then again a week later, after being given an opportunity to review their notes.

Those who wrote out their notes took down fewer words, but appeared to think more intensely about the material as they wrote, and digested what they heard more thoroughly, the researchers reported in Psychological Science. "All of that effort helps you learn," says Dr. Oppenheimer.

Laptop users instead took notes by rote, taking down what they heard almost word for word. When tested, "the longhand note takers did significantly better than laptop note-takers despite the fact that laptop note takers had more notes to look at," Dr. Mueller says. "Having all these notes did not help refresh their recollection." Ironically, the problem is a typist's tendency to take verbatim notes: more faithful notes do not result in better understanding or retention.

However, because it requires such concentration, the process of taking notes itself can be distracting. At the University of Nebraska, Dr. Kiewra conducted 16 experiments to gauge the completeness of handwritten notes and found that people usually took down only a third or so of the information presented. Moreover, in their haste to keep up with the spoken word, people omitted important qualifiers, failed to record context, and skipped key details.

Dr. Kiewra recalled that when he was still a student, one of his professors banned note-taking in class because he wanted students to pay full attention to the lesson. The teacher instead supplied prepared notes for the entire class. Nonetheless, Dr. Kiewra continued taking his own notes, cradling his head in his arms to shield his notebook as he wrote. One day, however, the professor caught him in the act.

"Mr. Kiewra, are you taking notes in my classroom?" he demanded. The flustered student lied, "I'm only writing a letter to a friend back home."

"Oh, (A)," the professor said. "I thought you were taking notes."

1　According to the passage, which of the following is true?

　ア　Both typing and handwriting notes are good for long-term memories.

　イ　Both typing and handwriting notes are good for short-term memories.

　ウ　Typing notes is better for short-term memories than handwriting.

　エ　Typing notes is better for long-term memories than handwriting.

2　Which of the following problems is NOT mentioned in the passage?

　ア　Typing notes does not balance taking notes and thinking.

　イ　Typing notes does not help commit the contents to long term memory.

　ウ　Typing notes is expensive because it requires a laptop.

　エ　Typing notes results in a superficial understanding of the contents.

3　Replace (　A　) with the most suitable phrase.

　ア　God knows,

　イ　thank goodness,

　ウ　why are you lying to me?

　エ　words fail me,

4　Which of the following is mentioned in the passage?

　ア　American college students handwrite more class notes than they type.

　イ　In a survey conducted in 2014, college students were asked questions three times.

　ウ　It's not until recently that note-taking strategies have been studied.

　エ　Trying to keep up at lectures by taking notes can cause students to miss key points.

5　Which of the following titles is the most suitable for the passage?

　ア　Can handwriting make you smarter?

　イ　Can note-taking speed affect your academic record?

　ウ　Will laptop computers dominate the classroom in near future?

　エ　Will teachers ban note-taking in their classes?

(☆☆☆◎◎)

【4】次の英文を読んで，1〜5の問いに答えなさい。

Education begins at birth, long before schooling begins. We learn how to function as human beings, physically and socially, from our family and our community. Education is largely conducted orally, without a written text. When parents convey critically important messages to their children, they encapsulate them in a story to make sure they are successfully delivered. These stories evolve into the various versions of folktales that are told over and over across regions and generations, in the same manner as myths. We can all agree, from experience, that the memory of a message lasts longer when taught through a story, since stories deliver messages more holistically. In addition, when stories are communicated effectively, we learn how to make ourselves understood to others using the same methods.

Various countries have adopted these stories, in the form of folktales, into their national education curricula for the purpose of learning life skills and "increasing cultural knowledge." Folktales can help students to obtain a clearer understanding of themselves within their community while supplying the wisdom and creativity to assist in overcoming the daily struggles of human life. (1   ). Just like individuals, all cultures exist in relation to, influence, and mutually define one another. Therefore, long-living stories like folktales are vessels of communication that cross generations and cultural boundaries, encouraging mutual understanding in pursuit of the common good for the larger global community. Education for International Understanding (EIU) has pursued the objective of "learning to live together" since 2000 when the Asia-Pacific Centre of Education for International Understanding (APCEIU) was established in Seoul under an agreement between UNESCO and the Republic of Korea.

With the purpose of broadening common understanding among students from different cultures, folktales from within the primary education curricula of twelve countries (eleven ASEAN member countries and the Republic of Korea) were collected into one volume in 2010, entitled *Telling Tales from Southeast Asia and Korea: Teachers' Guide.*

Twenty-seven folktales were chosen as the material with which to weave

305

mutual understanding and communication. (　2　). Apart from these stories, two guiding articles are introduced at the beginning of the book for teachers' use: one on the pedagogical significance of folktales in education and the other on how to tell the stories in the classroom as an amateur teacher-storyteller. (　3　). The English language level is also softened to the level of ESL primary school students. As a result, they can be adapted either for reading or telling, depending on the students and their level of fluency.

The stories in the collection are grouped into five categories: animals, food, nature, people, and places, along with an uncategorized story at the opening and another at the closing. Readers will be introduced to the importance of thinking of others and the effects our actions have on them through the opening story from Thailand, "A Drop of Honey." A ruler accidentally drops some honey, causing a chain reaction which he ignores as "not our problem." When the situation gets out of control, resulting in civil war, the careless ruler's eyes are opened to his mistake and leads him to declare that "the drop of honey was our problem." This teaches us that our tiny actions can have unexpected consequences and can negatively influence others, especially when we are in a position of leadership.

If we agree that love is a common value among humankind, we must also agree that the way of embodying that value is diverse, varying from one people to another. For example, in the story of "Shim Cheong" from Korea, the leading motif is that of a child serving her father. The devoted daughter goes through the well-known cycle of suffering, death, and salvation, sacrificing herself in order for her widowed father to regain his eyesight. Her devotion ends up doubling the blessings imparted upon her by both healing her father's eyes and allowing her to gain the status of queen.

In addition to theme of familial love, other common aspects are noticeable between these stories. In all the stories the natural enviromnent is closely influenced by the human community, changing as it changes, and vice versa. Shim Cheong's sacrifice for her father's eyesight calms the sea, benefits the sailors, and leads to her miraculous salvation. On the opposite side of the spectrum, the "ungrateful" son in the Indonesian story "Malin Kundang" is punished by the ocean for his misdeeds. Natural protection and disaster are presented not as isolated non-human monsters but as powers that somehow react to or intervene in human affairs for the sake of justice—as reward or punishment. This reflects the teachings of cosmic retribution, morality, and community.

Origin stories are another common theme. The tale "Crocodile Island" from Timor Leste depicts growing tension between a boy and a crocodile but concludes with reconciliation and the sacrificial transformation of the crocodile into the crocodile-shaped island which becomes Timor Leste. The volume also includes the origins of Cambodia and Vietnam. These tales tell about not only the glorious births of nations but also the hardships and hopes involved in the process of settling new territory until ☐ A ☐ is achieved between people, society and the natural environment.

Wisdom and humor in folktales also keep us connected to our traditions and help shape our culture. The protagonist in "The Old Wise Man," a story from Myanmar, plants mangos not for himself but for the generations to come: as he has eaten mangos planted by his grandfather, so will his children's children eat the mangos he is planting. If our sense of sharing is concerned only with this generation, we will fail to create a better world, so this story becomes ☐ B ☐ of the widespread resource sharing that our ancestors envisioned.

Folktales help to teach important values, for both the individual and the community, and comparative study of different folktales helps to illustrate that many of these values are shared values. The APCEIU believes that the best way of managing diversity and assuring a peaceful and sustainable dynamic is to learn about others through their folktales. Learning about folktales from various regions with shared themes will allow young people to grow with understanding and respect for both themselves and others.

1 本文中の(1)～(3)に入れるのに最も適切なものを，次のア
～ウのうちから一つずつ選び，その記号を書きなさい。

　ア　An equally meaningful reason for learning folktales is to help students
　　　to recognize commonalities that cross cultural boundaries

　イ　Of course, cultural explanations are given at the end of each story to
　　　avoid misunderstandings that may arise from cultural differences

　ウ　The folktales were chosen by teachers and scholars with the goal of
　　　cultivating cultural richness and shaping values

2 本文中の　A　に入れるのに最も適切なものを次のア～エのうち
から一つ選び，その記号を書きなさい。

　ア　harmony　　イ　progress　　ウ　serenity　　エ　sincerity

3 本文中の　B　に入れるのに最も適切なものを次のア～エのうち
から一つ選び，その記号を書きなさい。

　ア　a discovery　　イ　a judgment　　ウ　a reminder

　エ　a warning

4 本文の内容と一致しないものを次のア～カのうちから二つ選び，
その記号を書きなさい。

　ア　Folktales need to be collected because teachers are worried that fewer
　　　parents are delivering their messages by telling stories to their children
　　　at home.

　イ　Learning through stories enables us to keep lessons in mind for a long
　　　time and it leads to us expressing our thoughts and feelings more clearly.

　ウ　*Telling Tales from Southeast Asia and Korea: Teachers' Guide*,
　　　which has twenty-seven folktales from twelve different countries, was
　　　produced in 2010.

　エ　Folktales are vessels for critically important messages, but themes are
　　　vastly different depending on the region.

　オ　APCEIU, which was established in Seoul, thinks that folktales help
　　　young people acquire the values and wisdom necessary for living
　　　together, in both local and global communities.

カ　Folktales from Timor Leste, Cambodia and Vietnam tell us how these nations were born, including the difficulties they had in the course of settlement.

5　教育に民話を取り入れることについて，あなたはどう思いますか。あなた自身の考えを100語程度の英語で書きなさい。

(☆☆☆◎◎◎)

【5】日本における選挙権年齢が20歳から18歳に引き下げられたことに関して，期待される効果と心配な点を挙げながら，あなたの考えを150語程度の英語で書きなさい。

(☆☆☆◎◎◎)

【6】次の1と2の問いに日本語で答えなさい。

1　次の文章は，高等学校学習指導要領(平成21年3月告示)第2章　第8節　外国語のうち，英語表現Ⅰの抜粋である。空欄(A)～(E)に適する語句を書きなさい。

第5　英語表現Ⅰ

1　目標

　英語を通じて，積極的にコミュニケーションを図ろうとする態度を育成するとともに，事実や(A)などを多様な観点から考察し，(B)や表現の方法を工夫しながら伝える能力を養う。

2　内容

(1)　生徒が情報や考えなどを理解したり伝えたりすることを実践するように具体的な言語の使用場面を設定して，次のような言語活動を(C)行う。

ア　与えられた話題について，(D)で話す。また，聞き手や目的に応じて簡潔に話す。

イ　読み手や目的に応じて，簡潔に書く。

ウ　聞いたり読んだりしたこと，学んだことや経験した

　　　　ことに基づき，情報や考えなどをまとめ，（　E　）する。

2　グローバル人材の育成のために高等学校の英語教育が果たすべき
　役割にはどのようなものがあると思いますか。あなたの考えを述べ
　なさい。

　　　　　　　　　　　　　　　　　　　　　　（☆☆☆◎◎◎）

解答・解説

【中高共通】

【1】1　エ　　2　ウ　　3　ア　　4　イ　　5　ア
〈解説〉会話と質問は1度しか読まれないが，選択肢は先に目を通せるの
　で，キーワードだけに集中すればよい。問題数も少なく，会話も短い
　ものと予想されるため，集中力が途切れることもないだろう。

【2】1　イ　　2　エ　　3　ア　　4　ウ
〈解説〉2つの英文に対して2題ずつ出題されることから，やや長い文章で
　あることが予想できる。英文と質問は1度しか読まれないので，事前
　に各選択肢のポイントをおさえることが必須となるだろう。

【3】1　イ　　2　ウ　　3　イ　　4　イ
〈解説〉本問では質問と解答があらかじめ示されているので，本文の内容
　をあらかじめ予測することもできる。特に本問では文章の大意を把握
　することが求められる。対策としてはラジオやテレビの英語放送を聴
　き，英語に慣れると同時に聴きながらメモをとる習慣をつける等があ
　げられる。

【中学校】

【1】1 ウ　2 イ　3 エ　4 イ　5 ア　6 ウ　7 エ
8 ウ　9 ア　10 イ

〈解説〉1　keep in touch with ～で，「～(人)と連絡を取り続ける，消息を知らせあう」という意味のイディオムである。　2　banは「禁止する」という意味の動詞で，「喫煙は禁止されている」となる。prohibitedでも同義である。　3　後半に「自分のアパートを毎日清掃している」とあるので，「きちんとした，こぎれいな」という意味のneatが適切である。　4　後半に「一つの理由として，多くの人がインターネット経由で音楽を購入するようになってきていることがある」とあるので，CDストアは「減少してきている」，つまりdecliningが適切である。ここではdecreasingでもよい。　5　but no close friends (しかし親しい友人はいない)とあるので，「友人ほどではない」ということから「知人」のacquaintancesが適切である。　6　2050年の事であり，推測を述べていると考えられるので，「見積もられる」のestimatedが適切である。　7　「クラス内で実際の調査は行われなかった」場合，テストの何が疑問視されるか，という問題。エは妥当性・信頼性で「テストの信頼性は疑わしい」とする。　8　世界的なネットワークについて，50年前の人はどう捉えていたかを考える。「誰も予測しなかった」とするenvisionがあてはまる。　9　ウェイターについての文で「多額のチップをはずんだ」とあるので，選択肢の中では「丁寧な」のcourteousが適切である。　10　目的語がa return to traditional community values (伝統的な社会価値への回帰)であり，全文訳は「市長は伝統的な社会価値への回帰をスピーチで提唱した」となる。

【2】1 イ　2 ア　3 ウ　4 ア　5 エ

〈解説〉1　Bの最後のコメントに「もう気候がよくなったし…」とあるので，Aは「気候のせいでジョギングをさぼっていた」といったのだろうと判断できる。したがって，「寒くて雪が降っていると怠けてしまう」があてはまる。　2　「図書館は閉まっている」に対して「大丈

夫」と言っているので，図書館職員との話し合いが目的とするイは不適，ウとエは道を聞いたことにも図書館にも無関係である。アは「引っ越してきたばかりだ」から「この辺の施設に親しんでおこうと思って」といっている。　3　誕生日プレゼントについてAがBに相談を持ちかけている。Aが「じゃあそれは用意しないほうがいいね」と言っているので，Bは「私は彼女にCDを買った」と言ったと判断できる。4　be up for ～で「～をする気がある，～に乗り気である」の意。Bは「何でも乗り気」と言っており，「どこにでも行く気がある」という意味ととらえ，「(どこだって)私はかまわないよ」とするアが適切。ウの「ここにはどれくらい滞在する予定？」も，実際の会話ではあり得なくはないが，そうであれば「もし何日もいることになるなら，初日は…」と続くことが考えられ，「どこにでも行く気がある」の前置きとしては不自然である。　5　アは明日の行楽の予定と直接繋がらない。イは「天気，大丈夫かな？」だが，AがNoと返しつつ「雨が心配だ」といっているのは不自然である。ウも最初のAのコメントで「[私たちは]明日行けるだろうか？」と，すでに2人とも行くことになっているのに「行きたいの？」と聞いているので不自然である。

【3】1　ウ　　2　エ　　3　イ　　4　ア

〈解説〉1　動詞teachは学習環境において使われ，知識を伝達したり方法論を指導したりする場合の言葉である。「道を教える」の場合はtellを使う。　2　top tenと「10箇所」であるから，エはtourist spotsと複数でなければならない。　3　how inconvenient is itだと「どの程度不便ですか」という疑問文になってしまう。ここでは「どんなに不便か」という意味の文中の節なので，how inconvenient it isと主語－動詞の順序でなければならない。　4　「総理大臣の公約」であるから，he would leadと能動態にすべきである。

【4】1　ア　　2　イ　　3　イ

〈解説〉1　初期のスケートボーダーが空中に飛び上がらなかったのはな

ぜか，との質問。第4段落に「(初期の)クレーのホイールは壊れやすかったため，平面的な動きに限られた」とあるので，アの「樹脂のホイールのスケートボードが買えなかったため」があてはまる。　2　スケートボードの人気上昇がどのようであったかについてなので，「目覚ましく，著しく」人気が上がった，とするイが適切である。

3　Skateboardingの出現から現在に至るまでを書いているので，「スケートボードの進化」が適切である。中心テーマはskateboardなので，アはsurfingを中心にしているため不適切，ウの「クレーのホイールvs樹脂ホイール」およびエの「スポーツへの産業の影響」はともに文内容の一部でしかない。

【5】1　ウ　　2　② longer　　③ alone　　3　エ
〈解説〉1　空欄は「(regular以下の内容の)重要性を支持する[証拠]」と考えることができるのでevidenceが適切である。　2　②　文冒頭から「健康な長寿」について述べられているので，ここはlongerかshorterのどちらかしかない。同段落の第2文に「強い対人的絆が重要」とあり，「親しい友人や家族に囲まれて生活している人たち」は「長生き」と考えられるのでlongerが適切。　③　「大家族と共に生活する曽祖父」が「よりよい精神的健康を享受している」とあり，それは誰と比較してか，と考えれば「独居老人と」と判断できる。　3　ビタミンDについては第2段落に，人間関係については第3段落に，目的意識や「頼られること」については第4段落に，それぞれ言及がある。「ユーモアのセンス」については特に言及がない。

【6】イ，オ，カ，キ
〈解説〉イは第1段落第3文のOur growing understanding …と一致する。オは第3段落第2文後半の(they are the main highway for international trade) as well as the main regulator of the world's climate.と一致する。カは第3段落冒頭のLife on our planet is dependent upon the oceans.と一致する。キは最終段落第3文のThey are also manifest in the failure to safeguard the

interest of future generations, …と一致する。

【7】 The following is an idea to integrate reading and writing skills.

　　Teachers can add writing activities where students are required to express their thoughts or feelings with regard to what students have read.

　　Teachers should remind the students at the beginning of the lesson that they will be expected to write about their impressions concerning certain narrative stories. In addition, the writing activity should be based on the "CAN-DO List".

　　This will lead students to read the text carefully and motivate them to write. (84 words)

〈解説〉解答例では「読み」と「書き」の統合的活用がテーマとなっているが「話す・聞く」をとりあげても，また4技能をすべてとりあげてもかまわない。採点対象の「内容」については，選択したテーマについて自分の考えを具体的かつ明確な根拠を示して書けているかを確認しながら書くとよいだろう。構成はテーマ，考察，例示，結論の要素を盛り込むこと，文章は難解な語を使って間違えるよりは，間違いなく書けるレベルの語および文法を使って書くことを心がける。語数制限については日頃から実際に書いてみて練習することが必須である。

【8】① イ　　② エ　　③ ア

〈解説〉学習指導要領の内容なので，暗記していれば解ける問題である。暗記していなくとも，第1～3学年の記述に関する問題なので，発達に応じた学習内容，つまり学年が上がるにつれて学習レベルも向上することを念頭に選択肢を考えること。「言語活動の取り扱い」については特に出題頻度が高いので十分な学習が求められる。

【9】① 興味・関心　　② 多様　　③ 尊重　　④ 国際協調

〈解説〉外国語の学習では言語の習得だけでなく，その言語圏の文化などに関する理解も含まれていることに注意したい。特にウについて，学

習指導要領解説では「文化の多様性や価値の多様性に気付かせ，異文化を受容する態度を育てる。さらに，世界の国々の相互依存関係を正しく認識させる」など，国際社会の中の日本人としての位置づけを強調している。

【10】 ・「聞くこと」や「話すこと」に関しては，小学校で慣れ親しんだことのあるような身近な言語の使用場面や言語の働きを用いた言語活動を行わせること。　・「読むこと」や「書くこと」といった文字を使った言語活動については，生徒が過度の負担を感じないよう身近な言語の使用場面を設定したり，簡単な表現を用いてコミュニケーションを図ったりできるような話題を取り上げること。　・授業場面において，生徒が外国語活動で経験してきたチャンツやゲームを利用した活動を行う。　・新出の文法事項や対話文を学習する際，文字からではなく，音声から導入する。

〈解説〉解答作成にあたっては，まず小学校と中学校の学習の差違を明確にすることが必要になるだろう。小学校の目標では「コミュニケーション能力の素地を養う」とある。つまり，小学校ではコミュニケーション能力の育成というより，中学校からの学習で戸惑わないための準備段階とみてよい。そのため，小学校では音声面でのコミュニケーションを主体としており，文法はもちろん，単語やアルファベットも学習を補助するものとして，児童に学習負担を感じさせないようにする程度でしか扱わない。以上を踏まえ，小学校の学習を踏まえつつ，効果的な学習方法を考えるとよい。

【11】 ・黙読については，英文の内容理解を中心として行い，生徒が自分にあった速度で読むことができ，確認のために繰り返して読んだり，前に戻って読み返したりして柔軟な読み方ができるよう指導する。
　・音読については，語句や文，まとまりのある説明文，意見文，感想文，対話文，物語などの意味内容を正しく理解した上で，その意味内容にふさわしい音声化する必要がある。生徒が，登場人物の心情を表

現するために，強弱や速さにも変化をつけて感情豊かに表現できるよう指導する。

〈解説〉解答例は「学習指導要領解説」の説明を一部修正したものである。学習指導要領解説は学習指導要領の主旨の理解のためだけでなく，試験対策としても重要なので，学習の際，ぜひ読んでほしい。

【高等学校】

【1】1　エ　　2　ウ　　3　エ　　4　ア　　5　ウ

〈解説〉1　run the risk of ～ingで「～する危険をおかす」という意味のイディオムである。he以下は「彼は肺癌になる危険をおかすことになるだろう」という意味になる。　2　as ～ as …の原級比較構文で「…くらい～だ」という意味を表す場合，「～だ」に当たる箇所に「冠詞＋形容詞＋名詞」が入ると，「as－形容詞－冠詞－名詞－as」の形になる。これはasと形容詞が接した形を作るため，形容詞が前に出て行かざるを得ないためである。　3　"require＋人"の形の場合requireは「人に～を強要する」という意味になる。直訳すれば「彼の体調が彼にもう数日ベッドで過ごすことを強要している」であるが，無生物主語の場合，そのまま主語として訳すと日本語として奇妙な文になるので，問題文なら「体調のせいで，彼はもう数日ベッドで静養せざるを得ない」など，人を主語にして訳すことを心がけるとよい。　4　付加疑問では迷うケースも多いと思われるが，この文はその一例。まずNobodyはそれ自体否定形なので，付加疑問は肯定形となる。また「誰も知らない」に対し「いや，知っているのか？」とする対象は，単数形にすると「一人だけ知っている」ということになり，話者にとって曖昧な認識だからこそ付加疑問をつけたにもかかわらず情報を限定してしまうことになるため，複数形で受ける。　5　take sidesで「どちらか一方の側につく」という意味のイディオム。avoid taking sidesで「どちらかに味方することを避ける」という意味である。

【2】1　It is to solve urban water shortages.　　2　It is used for flushing toilets and as emergency reservoirs.　　3　It should be used for drinking. 4　Rainwater needs treating, and the first rainwater collected from roofs contains dirt.　　5　Without using urban rainwater, there is no way to support the people in growing cities without destroying the rural environments that provide food.

〈解説〉1　第1段落第2文のobjective—and life-passionは，質問中のmain goalと同義と考えられるので，is to solve以下を引く。　2　第2段落第2文に，国技館でのMurase's systemについて言及があるので，そこを引く。　3　第4段落第4文に，雨水を飲用にすべきというMurase氏の考えが書かれているので，そこをまとめる。　4　第4段落第5文に，雨水の飲用に関する問題点が書かれているので，そこをまとめる。 5　将来の都市部における水にかかわる問題については，第6段落にMurase氏自身の言葉が書かれているので，そこをまとめる。

【3】1　ウ　　2　ウ　　3　イ　　4　エ　　5　ア

〈解説〉1　第5段落冒頭に「短期的にはタイピングの方が効果をあげる」とあり，続いてテスト直後の内容記憶についての説明が述べられている。　2　第6段落，第9段落にメモと記憶の関連について記述されている。本文全体を通してラップトップの価格についての言及はない。 3　thank goodnessは「よかった，ほっとした」といった意味である。教授は「授業に集中し，すべてを記憶におさめるべく努力することが重要」と考え，「ノートをとることを禁止」していたとあり，この安堵の言葉は自分の方針について教授がいかに信念を持っていたかを示すエピソードとなっている。　4　第3段落第2文にエと同主旨の記述がある。　5　問題文は「手書きでのノート取り」と「コンピュータでのノート取り」の比較論であり，イの「ノート取りのスピード」，ウの「将来コンピュータがノート取りの主要な方法となるか」，エの「教師たちはクラスでのノート取りを禁ずるようになるか」については論じていない。第1段落冒頭に「手書きでノートを取る学生はラッ

プトップでノートを取る学生より高い成果をあげている」とあり，ア
の主旨に沿っている。

【4】1　1　ア　　2　ウ　　3　イ　　2　ア　　3　ウ　　4　ア，エ
5　The author says that, "the memory of a message lasts longer when taught
through a story, since stories deliver messages more holistically." I think this
is the advantage of students learning through folktales. Most children like to
read stories and sometimes they read the same stories again and again. When I
was a child, I liked to read a book called "Kasa Jizo". It is the story of a poor
but warm-hearted old man who gives Jizo, stone statues, bamboo hats he and
his wife made to sell. This story tells us that treating others well and making
sacrifices might make you happy, as well as others. The story is very
impressive, so it has remained in my memory. I think folktales might be good
materials for teaching children how to behave. (133words)

〈解説〉1　1　空欄の前は「民話は，生徒が自分の属する社会における自
　　分自身について明確な認識を持つことを容易にする」，後は「個々に
　　おいてと同様，すべての文化も…」と続いている。適切な肢であるア
　　は「民話を学ぶことの有意義な理由は，文化的な境界を越える場合に
　　も，(個人の場合との)共通性があることを生徒が理解するのを容易に
　　する点である」。　　2　空欄前に「27編の民話が選定された」とあるの
　　で，空欄には，民話に関する内容が入ると考えられる。適切な肢であ
　　るウは「これらの民話は，教師と学者により，文化的な豊かさを育て，
　　価値観を形成するという目的のもとに選定された」という意味である。
　　3　空欄前に「教師用のガイド」が添付されていることが書かれてい
　　るので，空欄にはその説明が記述されていると判断できる。適切な肢
　　であるイは「文化的な違いから誤解を生じる可能性を避けるため，当
　　然，文化背景の説明がなされる」といった意味である。　　2　until以
　　下は「人々相互，社会，そして自然環境の…が達成されるまでの」と
　　いう意味であり，ここでは調和(harmony)が適切である。　　3　空欄前
　　に「共有についての感覚が今の世代だけに関わるならば，よりよい世

界を作ることはかなわないだろう」とあるので，「この物語は，先祖が思い描いた広範囲に及ぶ資源共有の感覚を[思い出させるもの]となるのである」とするa reminderがあてはまる。　4　ア　生徒の父兄の民話についての考え方や，それについての教師の憂慮については，本文に言及がない。　エ　本文第2段落に「(民話のような長く語り継がれている話は)世代や文化の境界を越えるもの」とあり，「地域により大幅に内容が異なる」とするエと一致しない。　5　解答例では民話を読んだ体験を通じて，民話の教育的側面について，問題文と関連づけながら述べている。「自分の考え」であるから，例えば実際の授業での取り扱い方や，教授法について述べるなど，他のアプローチも考えられるだろう。

【5】 Recently, there has been a lot of news regarding lowering the voting age in Japan to 18 from 20. It has been in the news a lot because the voting age changed this June. I think there are many advantages and disadvantages to lowering the legal voting age to 18 from 20.

One of the advantages is that more young people will become interested in politics. This means that politicians will have to listen to young people's opinions and young people will care more about the future.

One of the disadvantages is that 18-19 year-olds are not prepared for voting. They are not mentally mature enough and don't know very much about political issues.

Since the law has already changed, I think we need to help prepare young people for the responsibility of voting. Perhaps schools and local communities can offer classes or seminars on how Japan's political system works, and on various important issues. (155words)

〈解説〉自由英作文ではとにかくアプローチ方法を素早く決め，文法的な誤りのないよう，またテーマ，説明，例示，結論，という形式を守りながらわかりやすく書くことが大事である。本問では社会問題についての意見を求められているが，まったく知識がない，あるいは関心が

ないテーマなので書きようがない，といった事態にならぬよう，社会問題，特に教育や子供など若年層に関連の深い問題については関心を持つことが大事である。新聞やニュースなどで日頃から情報を収集しておこう。

【6】1　A　意見　　B　論理の展開　　C　英語で　　D　即興
E　発表　　2　社会の急速なグローバル化の中で，グローバル社会で活躍できる人材のニーズはますます高まっており，より幅広い能力を持った，より幅広い層の，より早期からのグローバル人材育成が求められている。異文化理解や異文化コミュニケーションがますます重要になる中で，国際共通語である英語力の一層の充実はもちろんであるが，単に英語力だけではなく，異なる価値観を持つ人とコミュニケーションがとれる力や，チャレンジ精神・主体性といった幅広い能力が必要とされている。

　高校の英語教育においては，その基礎的・基本的な知識・技能とそれらを活用して主体的に課題を解決するために必要な思考力・判断力・表現力等を育成することが，生徒の将来的な可能性の広がりのために欠かせない。英語を用いた多様な言語活動を行うことで，「聞く」「話す」「読む」「書く」の4技能をバランスよく鍛えるとともに，異なる価値観に対する理解を深めた上で，臆せず積極的にコミュニケーションを図ろうとする態度を育成することができると考える。

　今後日本が世界の中で重要な役割を担っていくためにも，高校の英語教育が果たすべき役割を十分に理解し，高い英語力と課題解決能力を持った人材の育成に当たるべきである。
〈解説〉1　このような空欄補充問題は暗記事項と思われがちだが，全文暗記することは難しいので，各科目については，まず目標を前提にどのような学習をするのか，その位置づけを把握するとよい。　2　英語にせよ日本語にせよ，このような作文問題ではまず与えられたテーマにきちんと沿って自分の考えを明確に述べているかどうかを意識すること。そのため，英語教育や教育全般に関する知識を中心に，児童

生徒や若年層の問題などのテーマについて自分なりの考えを構築しておくことが大事である。字数制限は特に設けられていないが，解答例から見て400〜500字前後が適切と考えられるので，その範囲で自分の考えをまとめられるよう練習をしておきたい。

2016年度　実施問題

【中高共通】

【１】これから，会話と質問が5つ放送されます。質問に対する答えとして最も適切なものをア～エの中から一つずつ選び，その記号を書きなさい。なお，会話と質問はそれぞれ一度だけ放送されます。

1

　　ア　At 9:00 a.m.
　　イ　At 12:00 midnight.
　　ウ　Before lunch.
　　エ　This evening.

2

　　ア　Where the bus stop is.
　　イ　When the train leaves.
　　ウ　Which bus goes to Second Avenue.
　　エ　Whether the bus goes to the train station.

3

　　ア　Chicago is not expensive.
　　イ　Going by airplane is better.
　　ウ　The man should leave quickly.
　　エ　The man doesn't need to hurry.

4

　　ア　He should work without a tie.
　　イ　He should find a flashy tie.
　　ウ　He should wear a white shirt.
　　エ　He should put on a colorful shirt.

5

　　ア　She is unwilling to be back at work.

イ　She often complains about her work.

ウ　She had to take sick leave from work.

エ　She had a stomachache and didn't feel well.

(☆☆☆◎◎◎)

【2】これから，英文Aと英文Bが放送されます。それぞれの英文の後に，その内容について質問が二つずつ出されます。その質問に対する答えとして最も適切なものをア～エの中から一つずつ選び，その記号を書きなさい。なお，英文と質問は一度だけ放送されます。

A

1

ア　The sugars in fresh fruits.

イ　The sugars in soft drinks.

ウ　The sugars in vegetables.

エ　The sugars naturally found in milk.

2

ア　5%.

イ　10%.

ウ　50%.

エ　65%.

B

3

ア　Because the country's name in the Japanese language has Russian origins.

イ　Because the country of Georgia likes the US state of Georgia.

ウ　Because Georgia has stopped having good relations with Japan.

エ　Because Georgia and Japan established their diplomacy in 1992.

4

ア　Because Japan wanted to have better relations with Russia.

イ　Because Georgia and Japan expanded bilateral cooperation.

ウ　Because people would confuse it with the US state of Georgia.

エ　Because the number of coffee plantations in Georgia is decreasing.

(☆☆☆☆◎◎◎)

【3】これから，まとまりのある英文が放送されます。英文の後に，その内容について質問が四つ出されます。その質問に対する答えとして最も適切なものをア～エの中から一つずつ選び，その記号を書きなさい。なお，英文と質問は一度だけ放送されます。

1

ア　Older people.

イ　Middle-aged people.

ウ　Younger people.

エ　Children.

2

ア　They remember nothing at all.

イ　They remember only negative images.

ウ　They remember more positive images than negative ones.

エ　They remember more negative images than positive ones.

3

ア　They take more notice of trivial matters.

イ　They invest more in the emotionally important parts of life.

ウ　They believe that they will live forever.

エ　They lose sight of their priorities.

4

ア　"Facial Recognition Among Older People"

イ　"Life Doesn't Get Better with Age"

ウ　"Negative Emotions in Younger People"

エ　"Society Thrives with the Elderly"

(☆☆☆☆◎◎◎)

【中学校】

【1】次の1〜10の英文の(　　)にあてはまる最も適切な英語を，それぞれア〜エから一つずつ選び，その記号を書きなさい。

1　Hitoshi is so stubborn that it will be hard to (　　) him to change his mind.

　　ア　permit　　イ　suggest　　ウ　argue　　エ　persuade

2　Mary (　　) me many times while I was talking on the phone.

　　ア　interpreted　　イ　interrupted　　ウ　encountered
　　エ　promoted

3　Since everyone gave me different data, I could not (　　) who was right.

　　ア　speak　　イ　inform　　ウ　tell　　エ　talk

4　John was delighted at the news that his proposal had been (　　) by the student council.

　　ア　adopted　　イ　adjusted　　ウ　adverted　　エ　adapted

5　I had to have my son drive me to the office today because I realized that my driver's license had (　　).

　　ア　exhausted　　イ　expired　　ウ　excluded　　エ　extended

6　Only people under the age of 18 are (　　) to join the contest.

　　ア　appropriate　　イ　eligible　　ウ　possible　　エ　applicable

7　I apologize for the delay in responding to your invitation, but I have been (　　) recently.

　　ア　determined　　イ　anticipated　　ウ　preoccupied
　　エ　concentrated

8　We need a good engineer, but it's not easy to find a (　　) person in such a limited time frame.

　　ア　conceited　　イ　competent　　ウ　deficient　　エ　timid

9　Our baseball coach (　　) our team to its fifth consecutive championship.

　　ア　sailed　　イ　aimed　　ウ　steered　　エ　handed

10　About thirty percent of high school graduates quit their first job within three years, according to a survey (　　) last year.

　　ア　relapsed　　イ　resolved　　ウ　related　　エ　released

(☆☆☆◎◎◎)

【２】次のそれぞれの会話文中の(　　)にあてはまる最も適切な英語を，下のア～エから一つずつ選び，その記号を書きなさい。

1　A: I heard you plan to study French overseas.

　　B: Yes, from September to February.

　　A: (　　)

　　B: Maybe not, but even six months will help.

　　　ア　How much time do you need?

　　　イ　Is that enough time to really improve?

　　　ウ　Did you study there for a long time?

　　　エ　Can you get back in time?

2　A: Are you still accepting applications for the job?

　　B: (　　)

　　A: Oh, that's unfortunate.

　　　ア　Our company has many jobs on offer.

　　　イ　Applications are being accepted until tomorrow.

　　　ウ　I'm afraid the position was filled this morning.

　　　エ　Yes. Please fill in this form.

3　A: Did you know that company officials are closing the employee lounge to save money?

　　B: Yes, but it's not worth getting upset about.

　　A: Why not?

　　B: Because (　　).

　　　ア　coffee breaks are important to us.

　　　イ　we have no say in the matter.

　　　ウ　our company cares about its employees.

　　　エ　we shouldn't try to hide our feelings.

4　A: This assignment my biology professor gave is very difficult.

326

B: Yes, it looks that way (　　).

A: I still have one month before I have to hand it in.

B: Well, at least you still have plenty of time. I can help you with the research if you like.

　　ア　What is the professor's name?

　　イ　When is it due?

　　ウ　When was it assigned?

　　エ　What are you writing about?

5　A: I noticed that you only had a salad for lunch today. Are you feeling all right?

　B: Oh, yes. It's just that I'm going to this great restaurant tonight and I don't want to be too full before I go.

　A: It sounds like you're really going to enjoy it there. (　　)

　B: Italian, but they add some really interesting ingredients.

　　ア　What do they serve?

　　イ　Where is the cook from?

　　ウ　What's it called?

　　エ　Who are you going with?

(☆☆☆◎◎◎)

【3】次の1～4の各文の下線部で，英語の文法上または表現上適切ではない語句があります。それぞれア～エから一つずつ選び，その記号を書きなさい。

1　The number ア of people who イ was injured ウ was much higher than they エ had originally expected.

2　ア Considered her イ lack of experience, it is unbelievable that she has achieved ウ so エ much.

3　ア Before the spread of the Internet, it was difficult to communicate ideas to large イ audiences, but now ウ informations can be エ shared easily and quickly.

4 Although we are mainly ア<u>concerned with</u> the problem of energy イ<u>resources</u>, we ウ<u>must not</u> fail エ<u>recognizing</u> the necessity of environmental protection.

(☆☆☆◎◎◎)

【4】次の英文を読んで，後の1～3の英文の(　　)にあてはまる最も適切な英語を，本文の内容に合うように，それぞれア～エから一つずつ選び，その記号を書きなさい。

It was a cold winter night in 1801. The city of Vienna, Austria, lay sleeping under a bright full moon.

A young man was hurrying home through a strange section of the city. He was Ludwig van Beethoven, the famous writer of music.

Suddenly Beethoven stopped walking. He heard the sound of a piano from a nearby cottage. In fact, Beethoven recognized one of his own works. But it was not being played very well.

After a moment the music stopped. Then he heard the sound of crying. "I can't get it right," sobbed a girl's voice. "I'll never get it right."

Beethoven knocked at the cottage door. A young man opened it. Inside, the room was lit by only a few candles. Beethoven could barely make out an old piano and a girl sitting in front of it.

"I heard music and then crying," said Beethoven. "Can I help in any way?"

The girl gave a sigh. "I have been trying all night to play this piece of music. But I'm afraid I'll never get it right."

The girl was embarrassed. She told Beethoven that she and her brother had little money for music lessons. But she had gone to a piano concert and had heard this music. She and her brother knew that she would never play well unless she could hear good musicians play again. Beethoven smiled. "Would you like to hear a concert now?" he asked. "I'm a musician too."

"That is very good of you," replied the girl. "But the piano is old and we have no sheet music."

Beethoven was surprised. "No sheet music?" he asked. "But you were playing..." Then he was silent. He suddenly understood why the piano was in the dark. The girl was blind. She couldn't read any sheet music. She was playing his music from memory. Beethoven's eyes were filled with tears. He sat down at the piano and began to play. He played all the pieces of music that he knew. He played with all the feeling and skill that he had.

Finally the candles burned out. Beethoven went to the window and swept back the curtains. Moonlight flooded the room. It covered the bare floor and furniture with silver light. The scene inspired him. Beethoven started to play something new. He tried to describe for the girl what the moonlight was like. The notes filled the room with flowing sound. He had never played so well. The music grew softer. When it finally stopped, the girl whispered, "You must be Beethoven. No one else could play so well." Her brother added, "We will never forget this kindness."

That night Beethoven went home and finished the music he had played. It came to be called the Moonlight Sonata and is still played today. A few years later Beethoven started to grow deaf. Soon he could hardly hear. Sounds seemed to be coming through a blanket that got thicker and thicker.

Finally, Beethoven could not hear a single note. But still he kept on writing music. He heard the notes in his head. Some of his greatest works were written after he became deaf. It may be that the blind girl's struggle to play the piano that night encouraged him not to give up.

1　When Beethoven was on his way home, he heard(　).

　　ア　the sounds of strong wind

　　イ　someone playing the flute very well

　　ウ　someone playing one of his works badly

　　エ　some noise from the church

2　Beethoven's eyes were filled with tears because (　).

　　ア　he thought the girl had ignored Beethoven's words

　　イ　the girl's brother could play his music very well

　ウ　the girl refused to play the piano with him

　エ　he found that the girl was playing his music by memory

3　Beethoven wrote some pieces of music (　　　).

　ア　while he was playing with the girl and her brother

　イ　after he encouraged the girl's brother to play the piano

　ウ　even after he became unable to hear

　エ　when he saw a full moon that winter night

(☆☆☆◎◎◎)

【5】次の英文を読んで，各問いに答えなさい。

　　Many years ago when a person who owed money could be thrown into jail, a merchant in London had the misfortune of owing a huge sum to a money-lender. The money-lender, who was old and ugly, fancied the merchant's beautiful teenage daughter. He proposed a bargain. He said he would cancel the merchant's debt if he could have the girl instead.

　　Both the merchant and his daughter were horrified at the proposal. So the cunning money-lender proposed that they let *Providence decide the matter. He told them that he would put a black pebble and a white pebble into an empty money-bag and then the girl would have to pick out one of the pebbles. If she chose the black pebble, she would become his wife and her father's debt would be cancelled. If she chose the white pebble, she would stay with her father and the debt would still be cancelled. But if she refused to pick out a pebble, her father would be thrown into jail and she would starve.

　　(　①　) the girl agreed. They were standing on a pebble-strewn path to the merchant's garden as they talked and the money-lender stooped down to pick up the two pebbles. As he picked up the pebbles the girl, sharp-eyed with fright, noticed that he picked up two black pebbles and put them into the money-bag. He then asked the girl to pick out the pebble that was to decide her fate and that of her father.

Imagine that you were standing on that path in the merchant's garden. What would you have done if you had been the unfortunate girl? If you had had to advise her, what would you have advised her to do?

What type of thinking would you use to solve the problem? You may believe that careful logical analysis would find the solution to the problem. This type of thinking is straightforward vertical thinking.

Vertical thinkers are not usually of much help to the girl in this situation. The way they analyze it, there are three possibilities:

1. The girl should refuse take a pebble.
2. The girl should show that there are two black pebbles in the bag and expose the money-lender as a cheat.
3. The girl should take a black pebble and sacrifice herself in order to save her father from prison.

None of the suggestions are very helpful, for if the girl does not take a pebble, her father goes to prison, and if she does take a pebble, then she has to marry the money-lender. Exposing him as a cheat may not help her either.

This story shows the difference between vertical thinking and lateral thinking. Vertical thinkers are concerned with the fact that the girl has to take a pebble. But lateral thinkers are concerned with the pebble that is left behind. Vertical thinkers take the most reasonable view of a situation and then proceed logically and carefully to work it out. Lateral thinkers tend to explore all the (　②　) ways of looking at something, rather than accepting the most promising and proceeding from there. Luckily, the girl in the pebble story is a lateral thinker.

She put her hand into the money-bag and drew out a pebble. Without looking at it she fumbled and let it fall to the path where it was immediately lost among all the others. "Oh, how clumsy of me," she said, "but never mind — if you look into the bag, ③you will ＿＿＿＿＿＿＿＿＿＿＿＿＿＿＿ ＿＿＿＿＿＿＿＿＿＿ that is left."

(注) Providence 神意

331

1　文中の(　①　)に適する語をア〜エから一つ選び，その記号を書きなさい。

　　ア　Occasionally　　イ　Favorably　　ウ　Diligently

　　エ　Reluctantly

2　本文の内容から考え，文中の(　②　)に適する語を書きなさい。

3　下線部③の空欄を満たし，最もよく意味の通る文になるよう，次のア〜カを並びかえ，記号で答えなさい。

　　ア　of the one　　　イ　which pebble　　ウ　be able to

　　エ　by the color　　オ　I took　　　　　カ　tell

4　次のア〜オから，本文の内容と一致しないものを一つ選び，その記号を書きなさい。

　　ア　注意深い論理的思考こそ，問題を解決する決定的要因である。

　　イ　水平思考は問題を解決する場合，論理で考えられる以外の可能性にも目をむける。

　　ウ　娘が小石を選ばなければならないという前提にこだわるのは垂直思考である。

　　エ　与えられた条件にこだわらずに好ましい抜け道をさがすのは，水平思考のやり方である。

　　オ　金貸しが小細工をしなかった場合には，娘が窮地を脱する可能性は50％であった。

(☆☆☆◎◎◎)

【6】次の英文を読んで，本文の内容と一致するものを後のア〜キから四つ選び，その記号を書きなさい。

　　Biologically, there is only one quality which distinguishes us from animals: the ability to laugh. In a universe which appears to be utterly devoid of humor, we enjoy this supreme luxury. And it is a luxury, for unlike any other bodily process, laughter does not seem to serve a biologically useful purpose. In a divided world, laughter is a unifying force. Human beings oppose one another on a great many issues. Nations may disagree about system of government and human relations may be tormented by ideological factions and political camps, but we all share the ability to laugh. And laughter, in turn, depends on that most complex and subtle of all human qualities: a sense of humor. Certain comic stereotypes have a universal appeal. This can best be seen from the world-wide popularity of Charlie Chaplin's early work. The little man at odds with society never fails amuse no matter which country we come from. A great commentator on human affairs, Dr. Samuel Johnson, once remarked, 'Men have been wise in very different modes; but they have always laughed in the same way.'

A sense of humor may take various forms and laughter may be anything from a refined tinkle to an earthquaking roar, but the effect is always the same. Humor helps us to maintain a correct sense of values. It is the one quality which political fanatics appear to lack. If we can see the funny side, we never make the mistake of taking ourselves too seriously. We are always reminded that tragedy is not really that far removed from comedy, so we never get a one-sided view of things.

A sense of humor must be singled out as man's most important quality because it is associated with laughter. And laughter in turn, is associated with happiness. Courage, determination, initiative —these are qualities we share with other forms of life. But humor is uniquely human. If happiness is one of the great goals of life, then it is a sense of humor that provides the key.

ア The most important of all human qualities is a sense of humor.

イ Humor does not solve any problems, but merely blinds us to them.

ウ The ability to laugh is universal, but humor differs from country to country.

エ We are biologically different from animals in that we laugh.

オ Humor emphasizes the serious aspects of human life.

カ A sense of humor prevents us from taking ourselves too seriously.

キ Charlie Chaplin amused many people from many different countries.

(☆☆☆◎◎◎)

【7】 中学校学習指導要領(平成20年3月)外国語科の言語活動の取扱いにおいて，3学年間を通して配慮すべき事項の一つに次のような項目がある。

　　(ア)　実際に言語を使用して互いの考えや気持ちを伝え合うなどの活動を行うとともに，(3)に示す言語材料について理解したり練習したりする活動を行うようにすること。

　上記の項目では，どのようなことに留意した指導が求められているか80語以上の英語で書きなさい。なお，最後に語数を記入すること。語数については，同じ語を2回使用した場合，2語と数えること(のべ数)とします。

(☆☆☆◎◎◎◎◎)

【8】 次の文章は，中学校学習指導要領解説外国語編(平成20年9月)の「第1章　総説」における，「2　外国語科改訂の趣旨」からの抜粋です。文中の(　①　)～(　⑥　)にあてはまる語句として，最も適切なものを後のア～シから一つずつ選び，記号を書きなさい。

　今回の外国語科の改訂に当たっては，中央教育審議会の答申を踏まえ，次の四つの基本方針に基づいて改善を図った。

○　自らの考えなどを相手に伝えるための「(　①　)」やコミュニケーションの中で基本的な語彙や(　②　)を活用する力，内容的にまとまりのある一貫した文章を書く力などの育成を重視する観点から，「聞くこと」や「読むこと」を通じて得た知識等について，自らの(　③　)や考えなどと結び付けながら活用し，「話すこと」や「書くこと」を通じて発信することが可能となるよう，4技能を総合的に育成する指導を充実する。

○　指導に用いられる教材の題材や内容については，外国語学習に対する関心や意欲を高め，外国語で発信しうる内容の充実を図る等の観点を踏まえ，4技能を総合的に育成するための活動に資するものとなるよう改善を図る。

○　「聞くこと」，「話すこと」，「読むこと」及び「書くこと」の4技

能の総合的な指導を通して，これらの4技能を(　④　)に活用できる
コミュニケーション能力を育成するとともに，その基礎となる文法
をコミュニケーションを支えるものとしてとらえ，文法指導を
(　⑤　)と一体的に行うよう改善を図る。また，コミュニケーショ
ンを内容的に充実したものとすることができるよう，指導すべき
(　⑥　)を充実する。

ア	語数	イ	態度	ウ	統合的	エ	伝言
オ	文構造	カ	やりとり	キ	体験	ク	意見
ケ	言語活動	コ	識別	サ	発信力	シ	積極的

(☆☆☆◎◎◎◎)

【9】次の文章は，中学校学習指導要領(平成20年3月)の「第2章　第9節
　　外国語」における「第2　各言語の目標及び内容等」の「2　内容」の
　　「(2)　言語活動の取扱い」からの抜粋です。文中の(　①　)〜(　④　)
　　にあてはまる適切な語句を書きなさい。

　イ　生徒の学習段階を考慮して各学年の指導に当たっては，次のよう
　　な点に配慮するものとする。

　　(ア)　第1学年における言語活動
　　　　　小学校における外国語活動を通じて(　①　)を中心としたコミ
　　　ュニケーションに対する積極的な態度など一定の(　②　)が育成
　　　されることを踏まえ，身近な言語の使用場面や言語の(　③　)に
　　　配慮した言語活動を行わせること。その際，自分の気持ちや身の
　　　回りの出来事などの中から(　④　)な表現を用いてコミュニケー
　　　ションを図れるような話題を取り上げること。

(☆☆☆◎◎◎◎)

【10】中学校学習指導要領(平成20年3月)では，「書くこと」の言語活動の
　　中の(オ)について，次のように述べられています。このことについて，
　　どのような指導が求められているのか，中学校学習指導要領解説　外
　　国語編(平成20年9月)で述べられている内容を踏まえ，具体例を挙げて

日本語で書きなさい。

　(オ)　自分の考えや気持ちなどが読み手に正しく伝わるように，文と
　　　文のつながりなどに注意して文章を書くこと。

(☆☆☆◎◎◎◎)

【11】高等学校学習指導要領(平成21年3月)外国語科では，「授業は英語で
　行うことを基本とする」と明記されています。平成26年に開催された
　「英語教育の在り方に関する有識者会議」では，「グローバル化に対応
　した英語教育改革の五つの提言」において，今後の改革の方向性とし
　て「中学校においても，授業は英語で行うことを基本とする」とされ
　ています。
　　このことについて，以下のそれぞれについて日本語で答えなさい。
　(1)　英語科の授業を英語で行う目的
　(2)　授業を英語で行う際に配慮すべきこと

(☆☆☆☆☆◎◎◎◎)

【高等学校】

【１】次の1〜5の各文の(　　)に入る最も適切なものを，それぞれア〜エ
　の中から一つずつ選び，その記号を書きなさい。

　1　The flight to London leaves (　　) ten minutes.
　　ア　in
　　イ　on
　　ウ　for
　　エ　at

　2　"Could you (　　) me a few minutes?"
　　"Sorry, I'm busy now."
　　ア　save
　　イ　spare
　　ウ　spend
　　エ　take

3　Charles didn't know that the math assignment was (　　) next Monday.

　　ア　available

　　イ　due

　　ウ　liable

　　エ　valid

4　Okinawa's tropical climate and excellent hotels and beaches attract millions of tourists (　　).

　　ア　in the year

　　イ　for one year

　　ウ　the year

　　エ　yearly

5　Henry Wilson's new movie is different from his last one, (　　) it's based on a true story.

　　ア　for that

　　イ　in that

　　ウ　of which

　　エ　with which

(☆☆☆○○○)

【2】次の1〜5の各文において，(　　)内の語(句)を並べかえて最も適当な文を完成させなさい。解答は(　　)内の語(句)のみを書きなさい。

1　I (and / found / more / more atrractive / the job).

2　I saw my boss standing with (arms / at / folded / his / the window).

3　Those (about it / hold / know / little / should / who) their tongue.

4　Nowadays, hotels all over the world are (by / every effort / guests / cutting / making / the number of / to increase) rates and offering special services.

5　There (as to / caused / doubt / is / this problem / who / no).

(☆☆☆☆○○○○)

【３】次の英文を読んで，１～５の問いに対する答えを英語で書きなさい。

　　Helping others has always been important to Will and Chris Haughey. As kids, the brothers regularly volunteered to help communities in need. As adults, they expected to continue taking steps to make a difference. But they didn't know that giving back would become a major focus of their work.

　　Then in 2006, for the second time, Chris visited Honduras, a country where more than half the population lives in poverty. He returned home with a plan to go back and help. He and his brother, Will, came up with an idea. They would start a business in Honduras to create opportunities for people living there.

　　But what kind of business would they start?　They began by looking at the country's natural resources. The brothers chose to use wood from Honduras' lush forests. Next they had to decide what they would build with that wood. "Eventually, we found our way into the toy industry," says Will.

　　The brothers decided to make children's blocks, drawing inspiration from the traditional wooden toys they discovered on a trip to Germany. Then, they set about finding a way to put a modern twist on a classic favorite—by making the wooden blocks magnetic.

　　Will and Chris decided to call their company "Tegu," short for Tegucigalpa, the capital of Honduras. Then they staffed their factory with Honduran citizens. The employees more than approved of the company name. "We found that our workers in the factory are super proud that the name of their capital city is going out on their product and representing what they're able to do," says Will. In addition to giving Honduran citizens the opportunity to work and learn about running a business, Tegu is partnered with a school that helps educate the children of families that work at the Tegucigalpa trash dump.

　　But Will and Chris did not feel it was enough to simply help the people of Honduras—they wanted to make sure they took good care of the land, too. They felt it was important to make toys using a natural resource in a way that is sustainable.

"Choosing to work in a material that is basically self-replenishing is a big part of sustainability," Haughey said. "As we grow as a company, we use more and more trees and wood for our toys, but we don't necessarily have to be depleting the Earth's resources."

In order to do their part for the environment, Tegu works with woodcutting cooperatives and plantation-growers to select trees responsibly. The company also plants one, two, or three trees in place of every toy set that is produced. They've already planted more than half a million trees since Tegu was founded seven years ago.

Will thinks caring for the environment can start with an appreciation for the life forms that are in your backyard. If you take an interest in them and you have a natural sense of respect for them, then your sense of appreciation for nature will extend to include the world at large.

1   What is Honduras like?

2   How did Will and Chris find a way to put a modern twist on a classic favorite?

3   Why did the employees of "Tegu" approve of the company name?

4   Why didn't Will and Chris feel it was enough to simply help the people of Honduras?

5   What can caring for the environment start with?

(☆☆☆◎◎◎)

【4】次の英文を読んで，1～5の問いに対する答えとして最も適切なものをそれぞれア～エの中から一つずつ選び，その記号を書きなさい。

Surveys reveal that today's busy parents feel guilty about spending too little time with their children—but the actual numbers on American family life tell a different story. Since the mid-1970s, according to Pew Research, the time that fathers spend on child care (A   ). As for mothers, their time has gone up 57%—even though 71% of them are now working outside the home.

The real question is: Does all this extra time with our children do them any good?

A large-scale study, published this month in the Journal of Marriage and Family, is the latest effort to get some answers. Researchers used time diaries and survey data for 1,605 children, ages 3 to 11, and 778 adolescents, ages 12 to 18, at two points in time. They wanted to see, in particular, if the amount of time a mother spent with her children was associated with positive outcomes for them.

Lead researcher Melissa Milkie said that she was surprised by the results. She and her team found no significant relationship between a child's academic achievement, behavior or emotional well-being and the amount of either "engaged" time a mother spent with the child or "accessible" time (that is, time when she was available but not interacting directly). Some positive outcomes were linked instead to factors such as a mother's level of education, household income and family structure.

Dr. Milkie emphasizes that the study shouldn't be taken to mean that time with parents doesn't matter. Her research didn't focus on what families were actually doing—eating dinner together, for instance, or going to sports or music practice—but previous research has linked spending "quality time" with parents to positive childhood outcomes, like better academic performance and higher self-esteem.

Here are some suggestions for activities that can help parents spend more quality time with their children:

Listen to music. In a study of 760 young people published last year in the journal Frontiers in Psychology, researchers found that listening to music together as a family helps to create bonds, particularly in the teen years, when communication can be difficult. Music can also play an important part in building a family's identity, researchers note, and in shaping positive memories. Even just talking about music or a particular song is associated with greater well-being.

Drive the conversation. Car rides give you a captive audience—take advantage of it. As a conversation starter, Bruce Feiler, author of "The Secrets of Happy Families," suggests what he calls the "Bad & Good" game. Everyone, parents included, takes a turn talking about one bad thing and one good thing that happened during the day. It lets parents show that, when problems arise, there's a way to get through them.

Talk about homework. Homework has been called the new family dinner— and working on it together, if kept positive, can be a satisfying experience for both parents and children. Taking an interest in what they read and in the classes that engage them is a way to show they matter to you. It is also an opportunity, says Dr. Fernandez, to learn how a child feels about school and classmates.

Take a vacation. Research by Purdue University Professor Xinran Lehto, who studies tourism, has found that vacations help create enduring family ties. "You're in a new, unfamiliar setting, and there's a sense that you're all in it together," she says. On holiday, role reversals can happen, as when a child teaches a parent to ski, and these moments build greater intimacy and familiarity. "It's not only the trip itself that bonds," she says, "but after you come back, you now have shared memories that will continue to reinforce and even grow the bond over the years."

Be Facebook friends. In a study of 491 adolescents and their parents published last year in the journal Cyberpsychology, Behavior and Social Networking, researchers found that adolescents who engaged with their parents an social media felt more connected to them—and the connection grew stronger with more frequent interactions. Granted, social media may not exactly be a parent's idea of "quality time"—but even shared "likes" are no small thing in our busy, distracted modern families.

1　What is the most suitable to put into （　A　）?

　　ア　has almost passed

　　イ　has almost tripled

341

　　ウ　has been shortened by half

　　エ　has not changed significantly

2　What did researchers in the Journal of Marriage and Family want to see？

　　ア　They wanted to see if mothers don't need to worry about having a career as long as they spend "quality" time with their children.

　　イ　They wanted to see if many families are struggling just to survive with both parents working and spending less time with their children.

　　ウ　They wanted to see if mothers who spend more time with their children tend to have successful kids.

　　エ　They wanted to see if parents work to create family time for children.

3　Acording to the passage, which of the following is mentioned here？

　　ア　Research finds that quality, rather than quantity, counts most when it comes to spending time with your children.

　　イ　Family income and structure appear to play a large role, so men are statistically significant in raising well-adjusted and successful kids.

　　ウ　The passage appears to be offering an excuse to parents leaning more toward focusing on careers than raising their children.

　　エ　There is no way that mothers on average are spending more time with their kids, on top of having a job outside the house.

4　According to the suggestions, which of the following is NOT mentioned here？

　　ア　Listening to and talking about music together as a family is associated with positive outcomes for family bonding.

　　イ　Working on homework together is one way for parents to show their affection for their children.

　　ウ　On a family trip, role reversals between parents and their children may happen, and it can prevent greater intimacy and familiarity.

　　エ　Facebooking might not count as quality time, but parents can reinforce their family ties with frequent interactions.

5　Which of the following titles is the most suitable for the passage ?

　　ア　The Importance of Education and Household Income

　　イ　The Main Influence of Parents on Their Kids

　　ウ　The Problems Parents Face Raising Children

　　エ　The Right Way to Do Family Time

(☆☆☆☆◎◎◎◎)

【5】次の英文を読んで，1〜5の問いに答えなさい。

　　Artists open our eyes to the world in different ways. Once we have seen Van Gogh's paintings of sunflowers, wheat fields, and cypresses, we may forevermore see those things as he saw them. And the same is true of later artists who have their own way of forcing us to look at commonplace objects in new ways. With Marcel Duchamp's "Fountain," for instance, we look at an ordinary piece of plumbing equipment as a work of sculpture because he took it out of its usual setting in a men's restroom and mounted it on a pedestal as a work of art. The same happens to us when we see Roy Lichtenstein's comic strip paintings. The look almost identical to the real thing, but he has seen them in a way that opens our eyes to a new way of looking at these commonplace images—with his clean, sharp lines, with dots and other patterns covering large areas, with bright colors, all carefully composed and painted as if the subject was a vivid landscape. We may make similar discoveries with Chisto and Jeanne-Claude's umbrellas, running fences, and wrapped buildings, or Claes Oldenburg's giant shuttlecock, eraser, electric plug, and clothespin. All these are objects that we are so used to seeing that we may not bother to look at them with a sensitive eye until an artist jars our senses and shows us what we have been missing.

　　(　1　). My wife and I for years have spent Saturday mornings going to what are called in our part of the country "tag sales," sometimes called "estate sales." These are held in private homes near where we live in Now York. Couples may have retired and moved south, or they may have bought a new house, or may have died. Everything not wanted by the family is up for sale, and this can include hundreds of objects ranging from furniture, to works of art, clothing, jewelry, books, and often an amazing variety of objects that have been collected over the years.

What often amazes me in those tag sales is seeing what people have kept in their homes as mementos, often <u>things of no special monetary value, but which obviously meant something special to the owners</u>. I always feel that I can see something in those objects that is especially meaningful, although often I can't explain why.

In the course of my travels, many ordinary objects have caught my eye in the same way, and I have made a habit of making them part of my life. Once when I visited a cotton spinning plant owned by Springs Industries in South Carolina, I was dazzled to see hundreds of spools of cotton thread automatically rotated on holders as the cloth was made. Seeing several spools in a waste-bin, I took one to keep on my office desk. In Venice I bought an oarlock for a gondola that looks like a sculpture by Jean Arp. At another time in Lima, Peru, I saw some men making a large canoe out of reeds, so I picked up one of the reeds to add to my collection.

(　2　)—pointing to a beautiful curve here, a striking composition there, a powerful statement about life. They are just objects that appealed to me at a particular moment, and some instinct within me made me want to keep them. The images in my mind were formed by associations of which I was at best only vaguely conscious, and the intersection of these buried experiences with the objects I saw made me want to keep them.

(　3　) : something in me is touched by an object, and I am prompted to acquire it. There may or may not be a practical value in the object, but I know that just to have it in my possession adds something to my life. My wife, Laura, also has this instinct. She collects models of owls, and we have scores of them in our home. She would be hard put to explain why she loves them but her eyes light up when she finds a new one to add to her collection. I collect books, although I cannot explain why. I read as many as I can, but I could not possibly read the thousands of books I have bought over the years. Partly, I know, I buy them because I would like to read them someday; but even if I cannot find the time to do so, having them around me gives me an inexplicable pleasure.

Once when I was in Kenneth Clark's home in Saltwood, England, I asked him about one shelf in his library that contained very large books. He pulled one of them out and was clearly thrilled to show it to me. He probably hadn't looked at that book for years; but he knew that it was there, and occasionally, perhaps, glanced at its spine, along with those of all the other books on that and other shelves and just felt the pleasure of having it in his possession. That is how I feel about the books in my library. When I see them on the shelf, whether I have read them or not, they are part of my life, and I feel blessed by their (A).

Perhaps the most fabulous collector I have known of miscellaneous objects is Nathan Ancell, the founder of Ethan Allen stores. Walking into his house in New Rochelle, New York, is an unforgettable experience. There is practically no room to stand in the house, let alone sit down. There was never a plan in his head for what he would do with all these objects; just looking at something that fascinated him and deciding to add it to his collection gave him great joy. One time my wife and I admired a particularly lovely art nouveau sculpture on a shelf (along with dozens of others); Ancell picked it up and gave it to us. We have enjoyed displaying it in our dining room for years.

So how does one look at everything through the mind's eye? The shorthand answer is *with passion*. One can be passionate about anything one sees—*anything* and *everything*. All it takes is the willingness to open your eyes and your heart, and let feelings grow strong within you. What you look at could be a blade of grass, or a branch of a tree, or the shadow on a wall, or a fabulous diamond on display in a jewelry store.

The mind's eye is magical. Through it we can see loved ones who are no longer here, by looking at objects they owned that were precious to them. We can create works of art in our heads out of a special vision that we can nurture within us. One way that we can nurture this vision is by (　B　). There masterpieces can teach us how to transform what we look at with our naked eye, or what we imagine in our mind's eye. All we need is the will to do so.

1　本文中の(　1　)～(　3　)に入れるのに最も適切なものを，それぞれ次のア～ウのうちから一つずつ選び，その記号を書きなさい。

　　ア　I can't explain my attraction to these objects in traditional aesthetic terms

　　イ　Many people make such discoveries in different ways

　　ウ　This is the instinct that has led me to become a collector

2　本文中の(　A　)に入れるのに最も適切なものを次のア～エのうちから一つ選び，その記号を書きなさい。

　　ア　design　　　イ　distinctiveness　　　ウ　ingenuity　　　エ　presence

3　本文中の(　B　)に入れるのに最も適切なものを次のア～エのうちから一つ選び，その記号を書きなさい。

　　ア　creating works of art by ourselves

　　イ　focusing on the assessment of masters

　　ウ　informing masters of the importance of art

　　エ　looking at art created by masters

4　本文の内容と一致するものを次のア～オのうちから二つ選び，その記号を書きなさい。

　　ア　It is not until we look at works of art that we pay attention to the things which exist everywhere with more sensitivity.

　　イ　The author's hobby is making objects which caught his attention during his wife's travels.

　　ウ　The author became interested in collecting objects when he was a child.

　　エ　The author thinks Kenneth Clark and Nathan Ancell's love of

346

collecting things is different.

オ　If you are willing to open your eyes and your heart, you can be passionate about anything and everything.

5　本文中の下線部のことについて，あなた自身の体験に基づいて具体例を一つあげ，その理由を含めて100語程度の英語で書きなさい。

(☆☆☆☆◎◎)

【6】英語を通じて，情報や考えなどを話したり書いたりできる能力を育成するために，授業にどのような言語活動を取り入れますか。具体的な指導例を示しながら150語程度の英語で書きなさい。

(☆☆☆☆☆◎◎◎◎)

【7】次の1と2の問いに日本語で答えなさい。

1　次の文章は，高等学校学習指導要領(平成21年3月告示)　第2章　第8節　外国語のうち，コミュニケーション英語Ⅰの抜粋である。空欄(　A　)～(　E　)に適する語句を書きなさい。

第2　コミュニケーション英語Ⅰ

1　目標

　英語を通じて，積極的にコミュニケーションを図ろうとする態度を育成するとともに，情報や考えなどを的確に理解したり適切に伝えたりする基礎的な能力を養う。

2　内容

(1)　生徒が情報や考えなどを理解したり伝えたりすることを実践するように具体的な言語の(　A　)を設定して，次のような言語活動を英語で行う。

ア　事物に関する紹介や(　B　)などを聞いて，情報や考えなどを理解したり，概要や要点をとらえたりする。

イ　説明や物語などを読んで，情報や考えなどを理解したり，概要や要点をとらえたりする。また，聞き手に伝わるように(　C　)する。

　　ウ　聞いたり読んだりしたこと，学んだことや経験したことに
　　　基づき，情報や考えなどについて，話し合ったり（　D　）を
　　　したりする。
　　エ　聞いたり読んだりしたこと，学んだことや経験したことに
　　　基づき，情報や考えなどについて，（　E　）に書く。
　2　目標に準拠した学習評価により観点別学習状況の評価を行うこと
　は，高等学校の生徒にどのような効果を生み出すと考えられるか，
　あなたの考えを述べなさい。

（☆☆☆☆◎◎◎◎）

解答・解説

【中高共通】

【1】1　エ　　2　ア　　3　イ　　4　ウ　　5　ウ
〈解説〉スクリプトが非公表だが，選択肢から類推できることをあげるの
　で，参考されたい。　1　時間帯について聞かれているので，会話の
　流れをおさえること。　2　バスと列車が選択肢にある。「いつ」「ど
　ちら」などのポイントを取り違えないように注意したい。　3　選択
　肢からは，旅行者が急いでいるのでどの交通手段を使うべきかという
　質問であると類推できる。　4　選択肢からは，どのような服装が適
　切かという質問であると類推できる。flashy「派手な。けばけばしい」。
　5　事実関係がどうかを問う質問であろう。sick leaveで「病気休暇」
　という意味。

【2】1　イ　　2　エ　　3　ア　　4　ウ
〈解説〉スクリプトは非公表だが，選択肢から類推できることをあげるの
　で，参考されたい。　A　選択肢をみると，1が糖分の出どころについ
　ての質問，2が糖分の濃度の質問であることが予想できる。数値を表

す語の聴き取りに注意したい。　B　選択肢からは,「グルジア」の英語表記にかかわる設問であることが予想できる。なお,日本ではグルジアからの要請を受け,関係する法律の改正を行ったうえで,2015年4月からロシア語由来の「グルジア」を英語由来の「ジョージア」へ表記を変更している。

【3】1　ア　　2　ウ　　3　イ　　4　エ
〈解説〉スクリプトは非公表であるが,1からは年齢に関する内容,2からは記憶ないしは思い出に関すること,3からはその原因,4からは「この文章のタイトルは何か」が想像できる。放送は一度しか流れないので,放送が始まる前に選択肢にひととおり目を通し,聞き取るポイントを整理しておく必要がある。thrive「繁栄する。成長する」。

【中学校】

【1】1　エ　　2　イ　　3　ウ　　4　ア　　5　イ　　6　イ　　7　ウ
　　8　イ　　9　ウ　　10　エ
〈解説〉空欄補充問題では,日本語では同じような意味となる単語の使い分けができるかを含め,語彙力が大きく問われる。正答以外の語句についても辞書で確認しておくこと。　1　英文は「Hitoshiはとても頑固なので決心を変えさせるのは難しい」の意味。persuade「説得する」。2　英文は「Maryは私が電話中に何回も邪魔をした」の意味。interrupt「妨げる。さえぎる」。　3　英文は「誰もが私に異なるデータを出してきたので,私は誰が正しいのか区別できなかった」の意味。tellはcanやcouldを伴う場合,「わかる」という意味もある。　4　英文は「Johnは自分の提案が生徒会に採用されたと聞いて喜んだ」の意味。adopt「採用する」。スペルが似るadaptは「適合させる」の意味。
5　英文は「私は運転免許証が期限切れだとわかったので,息子に会社まで車で送ってもらった」の意味。have＋目的語＋動詞の原形の用法に注意。haveには使役の意味がある。expire「(期限などが切れて)無効になる」。　6　英文は「18歳未満の者だけがコンテストに参加する

資格がある」の意味。「以下」はor underである。eligible「資格のある。望ましい」。なお，possibleは人を主語にすることはできない。

7　英文は「あなたからの招待に対する返事が遅れてすみません，最近気をとられていたものですから」の意味。preoccupied「気をとられる。うわの空の」。　8　英文は「私たちは優秀なエンジニアを求めているが，そんなに期日が限られていては，能力ある人を探すのは簡単ではない」の意味。competent「能力のある。有能な」，time frame「期日」。　9　英文は「私たちの野球のコーチは，チームを5連覇に導いた」の意味。steer「操縦する。(進路などを)〜に進める」，consecutive「連続して」。　10　英文は「去年発表された調査によれば，高卒者の約3割が3年以内に離職している」の意味。release「公表する」。英文はA survey released last year says about thirty percent … within three years.としても同じ意味である。

【2】1　イ　　2　ウ　　3　イ　　4　イ　　5　ア
〈解説〉1　Bが最後にMaybe notと言っているので，これに対応する表現は，否定的な内容のものを選べばよい。イ「それは本当に上達するのに十分な期間ですか」。　2　Aが2回目に「まあ，それは不運な」と言っているので，これに対応する表現は，うまくいかない状況を述べているものである。ウ「その職種は今朝うまってしまったと思う」。

3　Bの最初の発言に対してAがなぜかと言っているので，これに対する理由を述べているものを選べばよい。イ「そのことに関して私たちには発言権がない」。get upset「腹を立てる」，have no say in …「…に対する発言権がない」。　4　Aが2回目で「1か月ある」と言っているので，これに対応するBの質問は期日に関するものと推測できる。イ「締め切りはいつですか」。　5　1回目のBの発言と2回目の発言のItalianを合わせれば，Aは料理の種類を聞いていることがわかる。ア「何の料理を出しますか」。

【3】1　イ　　2　ア　　3　ウ　　4　エ
〈解説〉1　英文は「けが人の数は当初の予想をはるかに上回った」の意味。whoの先行詞はpeopleなので，動詞は複数形となる。よって，wasではなくwereが正しい。　2　英文は「経験不足を考慮すれば，彼女がそんなに成果を上げたのは信じがたい」の意味。倒置表現を解消したIt is unbelievable that ～という文を考えれば，ConsideringまたはTo consideredが適当とわかる。　3　英文は「インターネットが広がる以前は，多数の聴衆に考えを伝えるのは困難だったが，現在では多くの情報が簡単に素早く共有できる」の意味。informationは不可算名詞なので複数形は不適。a lot ofまたはmuchをつけて表現する。　4　英文は「私たちはエネルギーの資源問題に主に関心があるが，環境保護の必要性を見落としてはならない」の意味。fail to ～で「～しない」という意味になるので，recognizingではなくto recognizeが正しい。

【4】1　ウ　　2　エ　　3　ウ
〈解説〉根拠となる箇所を特定し，その内容を適切に要約した選択肢を選べばよい。　1　ウは第3段落にその旨の記述がある。　2　エは第10段落8～9文目にその旨の記述がある。　3　ウは最後の段落3～4文目にその旨の記述がある。

【5】1　エ　　2　different　　3　ウ→カ→イ→オ→エ→ア　　4　ア
〈解説〉1　第2段落の内容と第3段落2文目のThey以下の内容から考える。reluctantly「不承不承に。しぶしぶ」。娘はしぶしぶ小石を引くことを承諾したのである。　2　空欄②を含む文は，lateral thinkers(水平思考をする者)について書かれており，その1文前ではvertical thinkers(垂直思考をする者)について書いていることから，この2文で両者を比較していることがわかる。したがって，all the (　②　) ways of looking at something はthe most reasonable view of a situationと対になる表現となる。空欄②には，「異なる」あるいは「様々な」などの意味を表す語を入れればよい。　3　「あなたは，私が取った小石の色がどちらなの

かわかるでしょう」という意味になればよい。この娘がいわゆる水平思考であることも注意しなければならない。　4　イは第8段落4〜5文目がヒントである。ウは第8段落2文目で述べていることである。エはイの別の日本語表現である。オの「小細工をしない」というのは，第2段落3文目で金貸しが出していた神託の条件「白と黒の小石を1つずつ」を指す。したがって確率は50％となるので，本文の内容と一致する。

【6】ア，エ，カ，キ

〈解説〉笑いとユーモアについての論述であり，チャップリンとジョンソン博士(英語辞書の編集で知られるイギリスの文学者)の例が引かれている。アは第3段落1文目と同じ内容である。イは本文中に記述がない。ウは第1段落6文目のwe all share the ability to laughと一致しない。エは第1段落1文目と一致する。オは第2段落3文目と逆の内容となっている。カはオと同じ部分がヒントである。we can see the funny sideをカではA sense of humorと言い換えている。キは第1段落10文目がヒントである。The little manとはChaplinのことである。

【7】In conducting language activities, it is essential for teachers to take into consideration the balance of the following:

・Activities to understand and practice the language elements

・Activities to share students' thoughts and feelings with each other

　Both kinds of activities mentioned above support each other, but the former activities are often focused on too much, giving students no chance to express themselves in English. Teachers should design a variety of suitable topics for the latter activities, setting a clear goal for the lesson. Moreover, the goal should be based on the CAN-DO list.　(95 words)

〈解説〉言語活動では，実際に言語を使用して互いの考えや気持ちを伝え合うなどの活動が重要である。そのためには，それを支える言語材料について理解したり練習したりする活動が必要である。その際には，

3学年間を通した言語活動の取扱いについて，理解と練習のバランスに配慮することが大切である。すなわち，言語活動を強調しすぎて，発音の基本，語句や文の構造についての指導がおろそかになってはならない。また，逆に，言語材料の理解や練習の活動を強調しすぎて，活動そのものが不十分にならないように配慮する必要がある。以上のような内容が述べられていればよい。以下に別解を示す。In language activities, it is important to communicate mutual thoughts and feelings with each other in the activities. For this purpose, students should do the activities for understanding and practice about underlying language material. At that time, the language activities through all the grades, it is required to consider that two types of activities should be done appropriately. That is, it mustn't be done to pay attention too much on activities and to be negligent to guide about how to pronounce basically, and construction of phrases and sentences, and vice versa.　(91 words)

【8】① サ　② オ　③ キ　④ ウ　⑤ ケ　⑥ ア
〈解説〉設問は，「聞くこと」「話すこと」「読むこと」「書くこと」の4技能の総合的な指導を通じて，生徒にこれらの4技能を統合的に活用できるコミュニケーション能力をつけさせるための配慮事項を示したものである。小学校における外国語活動にも触れていることに注意する必要がある。中学校学習指導要領(平成20年3月)外国語科では，従前より授業時数を増加させるとともに，指導する語数を増加させている。また，文法事項等の指導については各学校が創意工夫をして特色ある授業を実施できるように見直している。

【9】① 音声面　② 素地　③ 働き　④ 簡単
〈解説〉第1学年において重要なことは，「聞くこと」，「話すこと」について，小学校における外国語活動でも慣れ親しんだ身近な言語の使用場面や言語の働きを用いた言語活動を行わせることで，外国語の学習の円滑な導入を図ることである。小学校の外国語活動では，音声面を中

心としたコミュニケーションに対する積極的な態度や，言語や文化に対する体験的な理解などについて一定の素地が育成されていることに配慮する必要がある。

【10】一文一文を正しく書くだけでなく，例えば so や then などの接続詞や副詞も使って，文の順序や相互の関連にも注意をはらい，全体として一貫性のある文章を書くようにすることが大切である。また，「文と文とのつながり」は，接続詞や副詞によるほか，it などの代名詞を用いたり，Japanをthe countryと置き換えたりするなどの手法も適切に用いながら，一貫性の高い文章を作ることができるようにする指導が必要である。

〈解説〉「書くこと」の言語活動の中の(オ)は，2つの部分から成っている。前半は「自分の考えや気持ちなどが読み手に正しく伝わる」であり，後半は「文と文とのつながり」である。前者については，文自体が正しいことはもちろん，たとえばbutやalsoなどの接続詞や副詞も用いて，文相互の関連にも注意して，全体としてまとまりのある文章を書くことが大切である。後者については，接続詞や副詞以外にも，itなどの代名詞を用いたり，Australiaをthe countryと言い換えたりするなど，様々な手法を適切に用いて，一貫性のある文章を書くことが大切である。

【11】(1)　・授業を実際のコミュニケーションの場面とするため
・生徒が英語に触れる機会を充実するため　・中学校の学びを高等学校へ円滑につなげるため　　(2)　・生徒の理解の程度に応じた英語を用いること　・英語で指示した後に，すぐ和訳をつけないようにすること　・教師から指示など一方的な英語使用とせず，生徒から教師へ，生徒同士の対話の場を設定するなどして，生徒が英語を使用する場面を与えること

〈解説〉(1)　授業を実際のコミュニケーションの場面とする観点から，現在，高等学校では，授業を英語で行うことを基本としている。中学

校と高等学校の学びを円滑に接続する観点から，中学校においても，授業を英語で行うことを基本とすることが適当である。以上のような主旨でまとめればよい。 (2) 授業を英語で行う際に重要なことは，中学校・高等学校とも，授業を英語で行う主旨が，生徒が英語に触れる機会を充実するとともに，授業を実際のコミュニケーションの場面とするためであること，および，生徒の理解の程度に応じた英語を用いるよう十分配慮することを前提としていることを十分に理解することである。これを踏まえた記述である必要がある。

【高等学校】

【1】1 ア 2 イ 3 イ 4 エ 5 イ
〈解説〉同じような意味の単語や成句の使い分け，助詞の適切な用法が理解できているかを含め，語彙力が大きく問われる。正答以外の語句の意味や用法についても辞書で確認しておくこと。 1 英文は「ロンドン行きの飛行機はあと10分で離陸する」の意味。in ten minutes「10分で」。 2 英文は「2，3分時間をとっていただけますか」の意味。spare「(時間などを)割く」とsave「蓄える，節約する」の違いに注意すること。 3 英文は「Charlesは数学の課題の期限が来週の月曜だと知らなかった」の意味。「期限」を表すのはdueであり，validは「有効期間」の意味である。 4 英文は「沖縄の熱帯的な気候や素晴らしいホテル，それに浜辺は毎年何百万人という旅行者をひきつけている」の意味。yearly「毎年」。動詞が現在形である点に注意すること。5 英文は「Henry Wilsonの新作映画はこの前のものとは趣がちがう。実話に基づいているという点だ」の意味。in thatは「…という点で。…だから」の意味である。

【2】1 found the job more and more attractive 2 his arms folded at the window 3 who know little about it should hold 4 making every effort to increase the number of guests by cutting 5 is no doubt as to who caused this problem

〈解説〉1　完成した英文は「私はその仕事がますます魅力的だとわかった」という意味になる。　2　完成した英文は「私は上司が窓のところで両腕を組んで立っているのを見た」という意味になる。第5文型で，with以下は副詞句で分詞構文である。armsの後にbeingが省略されていると考えればよい。　3　完成した英文は「その件についてほとんど知らない者は口を出すべきでない」という意味になる。hold one's tongueで「黙っている」。　4　完成した英文は「今日では，世界中のホテルは，料金の値下げと特別サービスの提供で宿泊客数を増やすべくあらゆる経営努力をしている」という意味になる。　5　完成した英文は「誰がこの問題を引き起こしたかは明白だ」という意味になる。as to …「…に関して」。

【3】1　It is a country where more than half the population lives in poverty. 2　By making the wooden blocks magnetic.　3　Because they were super proud that the name of their capital city was going out on their product and representing what they were able to do.　4　(Because) They felt it was important to make toys using a natural resource in a way that is sustainable. / (Because) They wanted to make sure they took good care of the land(, too). 5　It can start with an appreciation for the life forms that are in your backyard.

〈解説〉ホンジュラスの天然資源を利用して企業活動を行い，持続可能なシステムを作り上げた企業の物語である。　1　質問は「ホンジュラスとはどのようなものか」。第2段落1文目のa country where以下が答えである。　2　質問の大意は「兄弟は伝統のおもちゃにどのような革新的手法を取り入れたか」。第4段落最後の1文に答えがある。

3　質問は「なぜTeguの従業員は会社名を承認したのか」。第5段落4文目がヒントである。会社名に首都の名前をつけたからである。

4　質問は「なぜWillとChrisはホンジュラスの人々を単に助けるだけでは不十分だと感じたのか」。第6段落に理由が2つあげられている。

5　「環境に配慮することの第一歩は何か」の意味である。第9段落1文

目のcaring for the environmentをitに変えて，あとはそのまま書けばよい。

【4】1　イ　　2　ウ　　3　ア　　4　ウ　　5　エ
〈解説〉1　第1段落1文目と4文目を考えれば，アは「見過ごされてきた」，ウは「半分になった」，エは「あまり変化していない」で誤りとわかる。　2　第3段落最後の文がヒントである。positive outcomesはsuccessfulと同義である。アはabout以下が，イはjust以下が，エはcreate以下が誤りである。　3　イはFamilyからroleまでが誤り。第4段落最後の文がヒントである。ウはparentsからcareersまでが誤り。第1段落1文目には逆の内容が書かれている。エはon averageからhouseまでが誤り。第1段落の最後に「71％の母親が外で働いているのに，子どもと過ごす時間は57％増えている」とある。　4　設問をよく読むこと。正しくないものを選択する。アは正しい。子どもと質のよい時間を過ごすための提案として第7段落冒頭に「音楽を一緒に聴く」とある。イは正しい。第9段落に「宿題を一緒にやる」とある。ウはit can以下が誤りである。第10段落4文目がヒントである。エは正しい。第11段落がヒントである。　5　文章全体のタイトルを選ぶ設問である。各段落の内容を考えればよい。アは「教育と家計収入」の意味で，第4段落のみの内容である。イは「子供たちに関する両親の主な影響」の意味だが，本文では影響を特定はしていない。ウは「両親が子供を育成する際に直面する諸問題」の意味で，第6段落以降の内容に反する。したがって，最も適切なのはエ「家族の時間を過ごす正しい方法」。

【5】1　(1)　イ　　(2)　ア　　(3)　ウ　　2　エ　　3　エ　　4　ア，オ(順不同)　　5　The books which were once owned and used by my grandfather are special to me. After his death, my father took some of them in order to remember him.

These books are more than 70 years old and we have kept them for 20 years. The books are academic ones he used when he was in medical school and reference books he used for his practice as a doctor. I once opened some of the books and found them obscure.

Though these books do not have material value, they are priceless to our family and remind us of the precious memory of our grandfather. (104 words)

〈解説〉他人からはガラクタと見えても，本人は価値があると思う，あるいは思い出の品について書かれた文章である。　１　(1)　イのsuch discoveriesがポイントである。第1段落の最後に「芸術家が私たちの感覚にショックを与え，見過ごしていたものを私たちに示してくれる」とある。　(2)　アのthese objectsがポイントである。第4段落3〜5文目にかけてのspools, oarlock for a gondola, one of the reedsがヒントになる。　(3)　ウのinstinctからcollectorまでがポイントである。第5段落2文目にinstinct「本能」について書かれている。　２　第7段落3文目のjustから4文目のlibraryまでがヒントである。「存在自体」と考えればよい。　３　第10段落5文目がヒントである。These masterpiecesという表現に注意。　４　イはduring his wife's travelsが誤り。第4段落1文目がヒントである。ウはwhen he was a childが誤り。第2段落2文目がヒントである。エはdifferentが誤り。第7段落3文目のjust felt以下と4行目，および第8段落4文目のjust looking以下がヒントである。　５　下線部は「金銭的には価値がないが，所有者本人にとっては明らかに特別な思い入れがあるもの」という意味である。この内容に沿って記述すればよい。以下に別解を示す。It is an airline ticket that is very precious for my life. When I was in my thirties, I flew to Australia first time. Those days I believe that I was very good at English grammar but was not so good at speaking communicative English. In Australia, I was very interested in how to speak English communicatively in daily lives. Since then, I have been interested in using English communicatively. Now the airline ticket always reminds me of the first day when I began to study communicative English, and since those days I have been good at using English practically. (100 words)

【6】 In order to develop students' abilities such as conveying information, ideas, etc., making presentations in English is an important language activity. I believe this activity will improve both the speaking and writing abilities of students.

First, in class students should be taught how to summarize what they have heard and read. Summarizing information, their ideas, etc. helps them develop their vocabulary and be aware of sentence construction. Second, students write outlines for their presentations in a style suitable for the audience and purpose. Next, students in pairs or groups are given a certain amount of time to practice so that the content and expressions they use will be more clearly understood by listeners. Finally, they make presentations not only individually but in pairs or groups. This process will reassure students who are less confident in giving presentations. Through learning presentation methods, and the expressions used in presentations, students will be able to apply them to real-life situations.　(157 words)

〈解説〉設問には「情報や考えなどを話したり書いたりできる能力」とある。高等学校学習指導要領(平成21年3月告示)　第2章　第8節　外国語には，英語に関する科目として7つが設定されている。そのうち，「話すこと」と「書くこと」の言語活動に重点を置くのは「英語表現Ⅰ」と「英語表現Ⅱ」である。したがって，これら2つの科目で求められる言語活動について記述すればよい。以下に別解を示す。To develop students' abilities to speak and write about information and thoughts, consideration should be given so that English teachers make good lessons through various language activities. When conducting language activities stated above, consideration should be given to the following instructional points. That is, A: Speaking with due attention to the characteristics of English sounds such as rhythm and intonation, speed, volume, etc. B: Writing due to attention to phrases and sentences indicating the main points, connecting phrases, etc. and reviewing one's own writing. Instruction on speaking and writing should be conducted more effectively through

integration with listening and reading activities. In the instruction of each
subject, teachers should devise teaching methods and styles, incorporating
pair work, group work, etc., as appropriate, utilizing suitable audio-visual
teaching materials, computers, communication networks, etc. Moreover,
team-teaching classes conducted in cooperation with native speakers, etc.
should be carried on in order to develop deepen their international
understanding.　(153 words)

【7】1　A　使用場面　　B　対話　　C　音読　　D　意見の交換
E　簡潔　　2　多様な特性を持つ生徒が在籍する高校で，全ての生徒
に確かな学力を身につけることができる。適切な目標を設定して日々
指導を工夫するとともに，生徒の実現状況を確実に把握し，その実現
状況に基づいて指導の工夫を行うには，生徒の実現状況を目標に照ら
して分析的に捉えることが必要である。それには目標に準拠した学習
評価により観点別学習評価を行うことが適している。また生徒一人一
人の進歩したところや他と比べて優れたところなどを把握することが
大切であり，それらを適宜生徒に伝えることで生徒の学習意欲を向上
させることにつながる。
〈解説〉1　「コミュニケーション英語Ⅰ」は英語を履修する場合，すべて
の生徒に履修させる科目であり，中学校の「外国語」における英語の
学習や，(履修させる場合)高等学校の「コミュニケーション英語基礎」
の学習を踏まえ，情報や考えなどを的確に理解したり適切に伝えたり
する基礎的な能力を養うために設定されたものである。
2　まずは，「目標に準拠した学習評価」と「観点別学習状況の評価」
について定義する必要がある。前者は，「学習指導要領に示す各教
科・科目の目標に基づき，学校が地域や生徒の実態に即して定めた当
該教科・科目の目標や内容に照らしてその実現状況を捉えるもの」で
ある。後者は，「各教科・科目の目標や内容に照らして，生徒の実現
状況がどのようなものであるかを，観点ごとに評価し，生徒の学習状
況を分析的に捉えるもの」である。これらを踏まえて，次の4点が考

えられる。①すべての生徒に確かな学力を身に付けさせる，②生徒の学習意欲を向上させる，③大学等が多様な資質能力を有する生徒を求めることに応え，生徒の様々な進路希望の実現となる，④高等学校卒業生についての高等学校側からの質の保証となる。以上の内容でまとめればよい。

●書籍内容の訂正等について

　弊社では教員採用試験対策シリーズ（参考書，過去問，全国まるごと過去問題集），公務員試験対策シリーズ，公立幼稚園・保育士試験対策シリーズ，会社別就職試験対策シリーズについて，正誤表をホームページ（https://www.kyodo-s.jp）に掲載いたします。内容に訂正等，疑問点がございましたら，まずホームページをご確認ください。もし，正誤表に掲載されていない訂正等，疑問点がございましたら，下記項目をご記入の上，以下の送付先までお送りいただくようお願いいたします。

> ① **書籍名，都道府県（学校）名，年度**
>   （例：教員採用試験過去問シリーズ　小学校教諭 過去問　2025年度版）
> ② **ページ数**（書籍に記載されているページ数をご記入ください。）
> ③ **訂正等，疑問点**（内容は具体的にご記入ください。）
>   （例：問題文では"ア〜オの中から選べ"とあるが，選択肢はエまでしかない）

〔ご注意〕
○ 電話での質問や相談等につきましては，受付けておりません。ご注意ください。
○ 正誤表の更新は適宜行います。
○ いただいた疑問点につきましては，当社編集制作部で検討の上，正誤表への反映を決定させていただきます（個別回答は，原則行いませんのであしからずご了承ください）。

●情報提供のお願い

　協同教育研究会では，これから教員採用試験を受験される方々に，より正確な問題を，より多くご提供できるよう情報の収集を行っております。つきましては，教員採用試験に関する次の項目の情報を，以下の送付先までお送りいただけますと幸いでございます。お送りいただきました方には謝礼を差し上げます。
（情報量があまりに少ない場合は，謝礼をご用意できかねる場合があります）。
◆あなたの受験された面接試験，論作文試験の実施方法や質問内容
◆教員採用試験の受験体験記

- -

| 送付先 | ○電子メール：edit@kyodo-s.jp
○FAX：03-3233-1233（協同出版株式会社　編集制作部 行）
○郵送：〒101-0054　東京都千代田区神田錦町2-5
　　　　　協同出版株式会社　編集制作部 行
○HP：https://kyodo-s.jp/provision（右記のQRコードからもアクセスできます） | |

※謝礼をお送りする関係から，いずれの方法でお送りいただく際にも，「お名前」「ご住所」は，必ず明記いただきますよう，よろしくお願い申し上げます。

教員採用試験「過去問」シリーズ

岩手県の
英語科 過去問

編　集	Ⓒ 協同教育研究会
発　行	令和6年1月10日
発行者	小貫　輝雄
発行所	協同出版株式会社
	〒101-0054　東京都千代田区神田錦町2‐5
	電話　03－3295－1341
	振替　東京00190－4－94061
印刷所	協同出版・POD工場

落丁・乱丁はお取り替えいたします。

2024年夏に向けて
ー教員を目指すあなたを全力サポート！ー

●通信講座

志望自治体別の教材とプロによる
丁寧な添削指導で合格をサポート

●公開講座 (＊1)

48のオンデマンド講座のなかから、
不得意分野のみピンポイントで学習できる！
受講料は6000円〜　＊一部対面講義もあり

●全国模試 (＊1)

業界最多の **年5回** 実施！
定期的に学習到達度を測って
レベルアップを目指そう！

●自治体別対策模試 (＊1)

的中問題がよく出る！
本試験の出題傾向・形式に合わせた
試験で実力を試そう！

　上記の講座及び試験は，すべて右記のQRコードからお申し込みできます。また，講座及び試験の情報は，随時，更新していきます。

＊1・・・ 2024年対策の公開講座、全国模試、自治体別対策模試の
　　　　情報は、2023年9月頃に公開予定です。

協同出版・協同教育研究会
https://kyodo-s.jp

お問い合わせは
通話料無料の
フリーダイヤル

0120 (13) 7300
（いいみ　なさんおうえん）
受付時間：平日（月〜金）9時〜18時　まで